WHAT WILDNESS IS THIS

SOUTHWESTERN WRITERS COLLECTION SERIES
Connie Todd, Editor

The Southwestern Writers Collection Series originates from the Southwestern Writers Collection, an archive and literary center established at Texas State University to celebrate the region's writers and literary heritage.

what wildness is this

WOMEN WRITE ABOUT THE SOUTHWEST

EDITED BY

Susan Wittig Albert

Susan Hanson

Jan Epton Seale

Paula Stallings Yost

FOREWORD BY

Kathleen Dean Moore

UNIVERSITY OF TEXAS PRESS

Austin

Requests for permission to reproduce material from this work
should be sent to:
  Permissions
  University of Texas Press
  P.O. Box 7819
  Austin, TX 78713-7819
  www.utexas.edu/utpress/about/bpermission.html

⊗ The paper used in this book meets the minimum requirements
of ANSI/NISO Z39.48-1992 (R1997) (Permanence of Paper).

LIBRARY OF CONGRESS CATALOGING-IN-PUBLICATION DATA

What wildness is this : women write about the Southwest / edited
by Susan Wittig Albert . . . [et al.]. — 1st ed.
    p.   cm. — (Southwestern writers collection series)
  A collection of women's writings (short stories, poems, and
essays) about their experiences of the natural world of the
Southwest.
    ISBN-13: 978-0-292-71630-8 (pbk. : alk. paper)
    ISBN-10: 0-292-71630-3 (alk. paper)
    1. American literature—Southwest, New.   2. American
literature—Women authors.   3. Southwest, New—Literary
collections. 4. Women—Southwest, New—Literary collections.
5. American literature—20th century.   6. American literature—
21st century.   I. Albert, Susan Wittig.
    PS566.W47   2007
    810.8'03272—dc22

                                              2006033057

Blue sky. Bless me. Wall of rock. Bless me. Animal friends: Red Ant, Blue Heron, Bighorn Sheep, Chuckwalla. Bless me. Plant friends: Desert Willow, Brittlebush, Snakeweed. Bless me. This is your home. I am merely a visitor. Bless me, be gentle with me. Let me pass through your beauty, unharmed.

DENISE CHÁVEZ, "A LITANY FOR SENTIENT BEINGS"

CONTENTS

HOME ADDRESS: THE NATURE OF URBAN LIFE

EARTH IS AN ISLAND: NATURE AT RISK

THE SUSTAINING LAND

THE KEY IS IN REMEMBERING: GROWING UP ON THE LAND

EAGLE INSIDE US

WHAT WE LEAVE BEHIND

FOREWORD

I first awoke to the Southwest in Death Valley. The coo of a dove I didn't know opened my eyes to a dawn such as I had never seen: behind a jagged black mass of mountains, orange flames licked across a pool of purple light, and yellow beams shot into the stars. Our son was sitting straight up in his sleeping bag, his small back silhouetted against the splendor. That day he would find the track of a snake inscribed across the trail like a river course and discover a chuckwalla so tightly wedged in a crack that he couldn't have pulled it out unless he'd deflated it with a pin, and he would pronounce this day the happiest day of his life. The sun charged up over hills and hit us full in the face, scattering the smell of creosote and all the sounds of the desert morning—cactus wrens clattering, quails moaning, the click and thud of people emerging from travel trailers with coffee in their hands.

I first awoke to women writing about the Southwest when I opened *A Breeze Swept Through* and found Luci Tapahonso's poem:

> The first born of dawn woman slid out amid
> crimson fluid streaked with stratus clouds
>   her body glistening August sunset pink
>   light steam rising from her like rain on warm
>   rocks.

I loved this poem so deeply that I found a place for it in the logic class I was teaching then, understanding that a poem can be a way of knowing more profound than any syllogism, a way of seeing more astonishing than flickers of light at the back of Plato's cave.

Eagerly, I pulled anthologies off my shelves, looking for more women, more deserts, more of these mornings. They were hard

to find. Most of the essays in my nature writing anthologies celebrated green valleys, frog-graced marshlands, or frozen white mountaintops, not the sere truth of the desert. Except in the most recent
anthologies (*Getting Over the Color Green,* for example) almost
all the writers were men, and of those, most were Euro-American. I
realized that much of the work of the women who write in the harsh
shadows of the Southwest remained scattered across sand and time
and distance—work overflowing the shelves in libraries, museum
shops, and used book stores, piled in stacks on the bedside tables of
friends, tucked into a letter, or mailed from a distant, sun-scorched
town.

So I celebrate this gathering of women's writing about the Southwest. I read with the greatest pleasure as women in all their wild diversity—in the cities, in the Sonoran Desert, in canyons and villages,
in wild bosques—raise their voices in the warmth of the new day.
By amplifying the sound of women's voices in the desert, the editors—Susan Albert, Susan Hanson, Jan Seale, and Paula Yost—have
brought the whole ecosystem alive, a desert entire again, a dawn
chorus of singing, stinging, lamenting, laughing voices.

ALL THE WRITERS in this anthology are women; all are writing
from or to the Southwest. Beyond this, their differences may be more
striking than their similarities, except for this one thing: the women
in this book write with a heady freedom from definition and expec-
tation, exploring the folds and shadows of the whole geography of
language and land, heart and mind.

Truth be told, one advantage women gain from being tradition-
ally denied membership in the nature-writing club is that they don't
have to follow the rules. Women can write broken-hearted; we can
write naked under blue water or the body of a man. We write trium-
phant at the top of the trail or trembling in fear; we write bewildered
or with sudden understanding; we write as lovers, scholars, mothers,
daughters, sisters, animals, ghosts or river guides, memories of the
earth.

As we exercise this creative freedom, women writers provide examples of new or newly rediscovered ways to break down the cultural constraints of centuries-old European ideals of "man and nature": "man" as separate from nature, its conqueror, its lover or rapist
(depending on whether you listen to St. Francis or Francis Bacon).

"Man" as individual, self-sufficient and competitive, distinguished by the presence of mind from all of nature, which is as lifeless as a millstone and without sense or spirit. "Nature" as other, separate from our neighborhoods, our inhalations, the locations of our lives.

In contrast, many of the writers in this book, especially Native American women, point down paths toward a literature of place that whispers of connection, of balance, of north-south-east-west, of ancestral memories, of love and sorrow. I think of Gloria Anzaldúa returning to "*los pueblitos* with chicken pens and goats picketed to mesquite shrubs," scanning the sky for rain, as her father looked to the sky for rain, and her brother still looks up. I think of Joy Harjo, fishing, the memory of "that old friend Louis" somewhere on the thin stream between the sacred and the profane. And Ellen Meloy, dear Ellen Meloy, comforting us in our sorrow at her recent death with the assurance that "there will always be cliffrose and two mules, and they will always be there." These are human beings who are woven from relationships—biological, cultural, and spiritual. And this is a nature that infuses our lives, in town or in the wilderness or the scrubby places in between.

Our freedom is to tell the truth about all our relations, and to think ourselves no less persons for all that we are connected by longing and regret to men, to children, to grandmothers, to desert rain and flesh and seeds, to old stories and cunning words, the past and the future, what Rachel Carson called "the stream of living things." It's a powerful metaphysics, this unity of body and mind and earth, with powerful moral consequences. If we are all deeply related to places, as we are to people, then we must care for our places as passionately as we care for our human kin. I don't believe it's an accident that so many of these women's voices cry out against the desecration and poisoning of the earth; rather, it is the bone-hard knowledge that what poisons the earth also plants death in our breasts. It is the wisdom of women who know that they, like their neighbors, are part of the Southwest, the way a thunderstorm is part of the place it was born and where it will expend its flashing strength.

I rejoice in the voices of the women in this book, almost a hundred, raising our voices in celebration or warning, the words echoing off the canyon walls and the border fences, whistling through ocotillo wands. This body of work expresses what so many people most deeply feel and most clearly believe: gratitude for the gift of this place; astonishment at what each moment presents—peach jelly on the table, rain on the wind, fear in a standing wave, ghosts in the soil; an abiding love for this sere and mysterious patch of earth; and the terrible understanding that we cannot wreck this place without destroying also ourselves.

WE HIKED THAT DAY in Death Valley, up a sand stream between hot, rocky walls streaked with desert varnish and a single strand of falling water. Our daughter reached to catch a lizard but caught only its tail and put it in her pocket, where it jumped and twitched for longer than you would think a tail could do. The lizard stood its ground, doing pushups, flashing armpits that were vivid blue. Beetles staggered over sand pocked with rabbit tracks. I don't know how far we walked; it seemed like miles. But when night fell, fast and final as a curtain, we were back in camp, frying onions. The smell of onions and creosote bushes, absolute darkness, the clink of dishes in the campsite next to ours, my husband flashing a light toward a scuffle in a packrat's nest, cool night air on sunburned skin: what I wouldn't give to be there now. Instead, I will open this book again and let the voices of women sing me to this beloved place.

Kathleen Dean Moore
CORVALLIS, OREGON

EDITOR'S NOTE

Susan Wittig Albert

he truest art I would strive for in any work would be to give the page the same qualities as earth: weather would land on it harshly, light would elucidate the most difficult truths; wind would sweep away obtuse padding. Finally, the lessons of impermanence taught me this: loss constitutes an odd kind of fullness; despair empties out into an unquenchable appetite for life.

GRETEL EHRLICH, *THE SOLACE OF OPEN SPACES*

This collection is a celebration both of the natural world and of personal story. It gathers together women's writing about their experiences in the natural world of the Southwest, from the Gulf coast of Texas to the Pacific coast of California, from the southern borderlands into the southern Great Plains and southern Rockies. Taken as a whole, these pieces demonstrate and illuminate not only the rich diversity of landscapes of the Southwest, but the extraordinary range of women's voices and women's experiences of the land as well.

As editors working with both unpublished submissions and already published work, we were looking for writers who have experienced the natural world, not as Nature, objectively, arti-factually "out there," but in a deeply personal, intimate, and self-revealing way, "in here": as forms of the interior life dis-covered in the wild, wonderful world of landforms and life forms around us. We set ourselves the task of finding pieces of writing—prose, poetry, creative nonfiction, and memoir—that witnessed both to the ever-changing, ever-mysterious life of the natural world and to the vivid, creative, evolving life of the writer herself. We were especially looking for writing that testi-fied in some significant way to the topography of place *and* of spirit, that explored the congruence of where we are and who we are. We hoped (although perhaps we weren't as confident as we pretended to be) to find writing that celebrated women's bodies, senses, memories, identities, and spiritual selves within the context of *place*: plains and mountains, deserts and canyons, farm fields and forests, empty wilderness and the wildness of urban nature. We were not looking for writing that was merely decorative (substance was more important to us than style), or stories with happy endings. We expected to find—and we did—stories of loss and rejection, of pain and despair, of anger at justice denied and rage at humankind's un-caring exploitation of the land. But we also hoped to find writing that suggested how imagination and spirit intersect with the experience of nature in transforming and redeeming ways, and what potential these experiences and transformations might hold for all of us.

We succeeded beyond our most optimistic imaginings. Our invita-tion (extended through mailings and e-mailings to women's writers' groups, programs, newsletters, and magazines, as well as through our Web site: http://www.storycircle.org/WomenWrite/) resulted in nearly three hundred submissions of unpublished work—some four hundred fifty individual pieces of writing. The authors did not have to be residents of southwestern states or members of the Story Circle Network, the organization that sponsored the book; the only re-quirement was that they tell a true and meaningful story based on their own personal experience of the land.

The editors lived hundreds of miles from one another—in East Texas, the northern Hill Country, the southern Hill Country, and the Rio Grande Valley—so it was impossible for us to meet regularly. Instead, we worked via e-mail and the Internet, reading the writings posted to an editorial Web site by our talented and dedicated as-sistant, Peggy Moody, without whom this kind of communication would not have been possible. For months, the four of us read, dis-cussed, and considered all the submissions, gradually narrowing the possibilities, until we felt we had chosen the best—some fifty pieces, nearly fifty thousand words (or the equivalent) of prose and poetry. As we worked, we tried to be attentive to the possible organizations that seemed to grow out of what we were reading. When we finished, we saw that the work seemed naturally to arrange itself into eight different sections: the way we live on the land; our journeys through the land; nature in cities; nature at risk; nature that sustains us; our memories of the land; our kinship with the animal world; and what we leave on the land when we are gone.

Then we tackled the other half of the job: selecting already published work to complement and extend the unpublished pieces that had been sent to us. Gathering up every bibliography we could find, we made lists of authors, books, and journals in which we might discover the sort of women's writing we were looking for: not just "nature writing," but writing through which the writer revealed essential parts of herself, describing the transformations brought about by her experience in the natural world. Eventually, we would choose an additional fifty-some published pieces. We played with these selections via e-mail, sorting through dozens of possible placements and organizations, until we came up with the arrangement in the Table of Contents.

This book has been a long journey, but never a lonely one. As editors, the four of us were separated by distance but as close as our computers. And we were never alone, for our journey has been accompanied by the voices of hundreds of women, singing their lives, singing their stories, singing the land. And then there has been the land itself, described in the hundreds of pieces we have read: the land of wide skies and high mountains and vast deserts and open plains.

Barry Lopez has said that, as a people, contemporary Americans have learned the potentially disastrous trick of ignoring our local geographies. We eat imported food, wear clothing constructed on the other side of the globe, fly across the continent without setting foot on the earth, and light up the night sky as if it were day. Not knowing the land itself—its geology, topography, climate, flora, and fauna— we find it only too easy to romanticize it, exploit its resources, and market it as a backdrop for entertaining adventures.

But when the land becomes known to us through our ability to observe, to taste and smell and touch and hear and feel, it becomes real to us, in all its complexities and contradictions. The women's writings contained in this book reassure us that it is still possible to know the land, deeply and intimately, if we make that our purpose: to experience the land in the same way that we experience our bodies, our minds, our spirits. These stories of transforming encounters with the natural environments of the Southwest suggest that we can still have a profound connection with the earth and that our engagement with it can change our lives. We can still find ourselves at home in the world.

WHAT WILDNESS IS THIS

a land full of stories

We sleep in the desert
on a land full of stories ·
and all night the wind reads the news.

We wake to a world without word,
only scent and beauty.
The Word is written
everywhere on the land.

LAURA GIRARDEAU, "EASTER, PICACHO PEAK"

EASTER, PICACHO PEAK

Laura Girardeau

We sleep in the desert
on a land full of stories,
and all night the wind reads the news.
We've left our attachments—
expectations and a newspaper—
on the picnic table for the night,
surrendering our documented selves
and reported names to sleep.

All night the wind sifts our dreams,
reading the truth.
We sleep deeply but aware,
like stones skipping water,
and hear the news
doing somersaults over the land.
Finally, it blows into a cactus,
sacrificed on a crown of thorns.

The moon encrypts new names
into our dreams, and near dawn,
coyotes sing the real headlines
in yips of happiness.

We wake to a world without word,
only scent and beauty.
The Word is written
everywhere on the land.

THIS LAND ON MY FACE

Cindy Bellinger

How this land embedded its face in my own, I'll never know. It crept up from behind. I wear creases the way arroyos cut across a mountain, the way rugged cliffs rim the skyline. Together, we've withstood storms no one should have lived through.

I've come of age here, in the enticing, high desert mountains of northern New Mexico. People often say, "I was just passing through and stayed," as if under a spell. They fall to the seduction of synchronicity and believe it was all meant to be. And it was, of course. But the spell can shatter, too. Not all the wrinkles that spread like dry delta plains from the corners of my eyes are from laughing. I have stayed, which means that I've consented to being roughed up a little. Something here doesn't like small talk. Like an old, practiced shaman, this arid land exposes secrets. Many caught unaware eventually limp back to the city. It's not easy being stripped to the bone.

I arrived in New Mexico twenty-five years ago, young, in love, married. Then, like rocks falling from a canyon wall, everything came loose. My marriage ended, and I tumbled, losing one house, two houses, friend after friend, job after job, my family, even all my money once or twice.

For years, I slipped and fell, became raw and exposed. People wondered why I stayed. Yet something called. Even from my own ruins, I could see shimmering sky and birds migrating. I began finding fossils, the crusts of others' stories, just as vulnerable as I but lasting. Solace finally rose from the sandstone ledges where the gnarled, stunted piñons grew, and I did leave in my own way. I went inward.

Alone, I moved into a little cabin in the heart of the forest. From the moment I first set foot among the ponderosas, I was snagged by something more than the spiderwebs dangling between the trees. It called, and I heard: *Come this way, just a little further, a little further.* I felt bewitched, irresistibly pulled.

I began cutting trails in the forest behind my house, always needing to go deeper and deeper into the trees. Today, paths angle for miles on the mountain behind my home, and I came to know what the land and I share.

The quiet passings of bobcats leave indentations in the snow. Big padded marks of bears appear in the spring mud. Coyotes sometimes leave scat near the imprints of my boot heels. These beasts and I travel the same territory. I have tasted the bark of cedar that porcupines peel for food. I've learned to navigate by the ridges. This is what the land has done: thrown me into the middle of the unknown, letting me find my way to the other side. In turn, my trails have furrowed passageways in the terrain. We've weathered together.

A voice rises from the land, though it is nothing you can hear. The day I feel ready for change, a branch breaks off before my eyes. The day I need laughter, a raven hops from treetop to treetop, taunting me on my way down the mountain. Think something, and it will happen. Need something, and it will appear. Always, the timing is perfect. Just what you need, if you have the eye to catch it. That is the enchantment, the magic. The air breathes it over everyone, whether they like it or not.

This land requires you to withstand—externally and internally—rockslides, searing heat, blizzards, and drenching rains. If you don't turn away, but turn toward the sun, the land finds a way in. It seeps under your skin, coursing through your veins like footsteps following old mountain trails. Before you know it, the land settles on your face. And you know you're home.

HE 2-104: A TRUE PLANETARY NEBULA IN THE MAKING

Gloria Vando

On the universal clock, Sagan tells us,
we are only moments old. And this
new crablike discovery in Centaurus,
though older by far, is but
an adolescent going through a vital
if brief stage in the evolution
of interacting stars. I see it
starting its sidereal trek
through midlife, glowingly complex—
"a pulsating red giant" with a "small
hot companion" in tow—and think
of you and me that night in August
speeding across Texas in your red
Mustang convertible, enveloped in dust
and fumes, aiming for a motel bed,
settling instead for the backseat of the car,
arms and legs flailing in all directions,
but mostly toward heaven—and now
this cool red dude winking at me
through the centuries as if to say
I know, I know, sidling in closer
to his sidekick, shedding his garments,
shaking off dust, encircling
her small girth with a high-density
lasso of himself, high-velocity
sparks shooting from her ringed
body like crazy legs and arms until
at last, he's got his hot companion
in a classic hold and slowly,
in ecstasy, they take wing and
blaze as one across the Southern skies—
     no longer crab but butterfly.

DWELLINGS

Linda Hogan

ot far from where I live is a hill that was cut into by the moving water of a creek. Eroded this way, all that's left of it is a broken wall of earth that contains old roots and pebbles woven together and exposed. Seen from a distance, it is only a rise of raw earth. But up close it is something wonderful, a small cliff dwelling that looks almost as intricate and well made as those the Anasazi left behind when they vanished mysteriously centuries ago. This hill is a place that could be the starry skies of night turned inward into the thousand round holes where solitary bees have lived and died. It is a hill of tunneling rooms. At the mouths of some of the excavations, half-circles of clay beetle out like awnings shading a doorway. It is earth that was turned to clay in the mouths of the bees and spit out as they mined deeper into their dwelling places.

This place where the bees reside is at an angle safe from rain. It faces the southern sun. It is a warm and intelligent architecture of memory, learned by whatever memory lives in the blood. Many of the holes still contain the gold husks of dead bees, their faces dry and gone, their flat eyes gazing out from death's land toward the other uninhabited half of the hill that is across the creek from these catacombs.

The first time I found the residence of the bees, it was dusty summer. The sun was hot, and land was the dry color of rust. Now and then a car rumbled along the dirt road and dust rose up behind it before settling back down on older dust. In the silence, the bees made a soft droning hum. They were alive then, and working the hill, going out and returning with pollen, in and out through the holes, back and forth between daylight and the cooler, darker regions of inner earth. They were flying an invisible map through air, a map charted by landmarks, the slant of light, and a circling story they told one another about the direction of food held inside the center of yellow flowers.

Sitting in the hot sun, watching the small bees fly in and out around the hill, hearing the summer birds, the light breeze, I felt right in the world. I belonged there. I thought of my own dwelling places, those real and those imagined. Once I lived in a town called Manitou, which means "Great Spirit," and where hot mineral springwater gurgled beneath the streets and rose up into open wells. I felt safe there. With the underground movement of water and heat a constant reminder of other life, of what lives beneath us, it seemed to be the center of the world.

A few years after that, I wanted silence. My daydreams were full of places I longed to be, shelters and solitudes. I wanted a room apart from others, a hidden cabin to rest in. I wanted to be in a redwood forest with trees so tall the owls called out in the daytime. I daydreamed of living in a vapor cave a few hours away from here. Underground, warm, and moist, I thought it would be the perfect world for staying out of cold winter, for escaping the noise of living.

And how often I've wanted to escape to a wilderness where a human hand has not been in everything. But those were only dreams of peace, of comfort, of a nest inside stone or woods, a sanctuary where a dream or life wouldn't be invaded.

One beautiful afternoon, cool and moist, with the kind of yellow light that falls on earth in these arid regions, I waited for barn swallows to return from their daily work of food gathering. Inside the tunnel where they live, hundreds of swallows had mixed their saliva with mud and clay, much like the solitary bees, and formed nests that were perfect as a potter's bowl. At five in the evening, they returned all at once, a dark, flying shadow. Despite their enormous numbers and the crowding together of nests, they didn't pause for even a moment before entering the nests, nor did they crowd one another. Instantly they vanished into the nests. The tunnel went silent. It held no outward signs of life.

But I knew they were there, filled with the fire of living. And what a marriage of elements was in those nests. Not only mud's earth and water, the fire of sun and dry air, but even the elements contained one another. The bodies of prophets and crazy men were broken down in that soil.

I've noticed often how when a house is abandoned, it begins to sag. Without a tenant, it has no need to go on. If it were a person, we'd say it is depressed or lonely. The roof settles in, the paint cracks, the walls and floorboards warp and slope downward in their own natural ways, telling us that life must stay in everything as the world whirls and tilts and moves through boundless space.

One summer day, cleaning up after long-eared owls where I work at a rehabilitation facility for birds of prey, I was raking the gravel floor of a flight cage. Down on the ground, something looked like it was moving. I bent over to look into the pile of bones and pellets I'd just raked together. There, close to the ground, were two fetal mice. They were new to the planet, pink and hairless. They were so tenderly young. Their faces had swollen blue-veined eyes. They were nestled in a mound of feathers, soft as velvet, each one curled up smaller than an infant's ear, listening to the first sounds of earth. But the ants were biting them. They turned in agony, unable to pull away, not yet having the arms or legs to move, but feeling, twisting away from, the pain of the bites. I was horrified to see them bitten out of life that way. I dipped them in water, as if to take away the sting, and let the ants fall in the bucket. Then I held the tiny mice in the palm of my hand. Some of the ants were drowning in the water. I was trading one life for another, exchanging the lives of ants for those of mice, but I hated their suffering, and hated even more that they had not yet grown to a life, and already they inhabited the miserable world of pain. Death and life feed each other. I know that.

Inside these rooms where birds are healed, there are other lives besides those of mice. There are fine gray globes the wasps have woven together, the white cocoons of spiders in a corner, the downward tunneling anthills. All these dwellings are inside one small walled space, but I think most about the mice. Sometimes the downy nests fall out of the walls where their mothers have placed them out of the way of their enemies. When one of the nests falls, they are so well made and soft, woven mostly from the chest feathers of birds. Sometimes the leg of a small quail holds the nest together like a slender corner-stone with dry, bent claws. The mice have adapted to life in the presence of their enemies, adapted to living in the thin wall between beak and beak, claw and claw. They move their nests often, as if a new rafter or wall will protect them from the inevitable fate of all our returns home to the deeper, wider nest of earth that houses us all.

One August at Zia Pueblo during the corn dance I noticed tourists picking up shards of all the old pottery that had been made and broken there. The residents of Zia know not to take the bowls and pots left behind by the older ones. They know that the fragments of those earlier lives need to be smoothed back to earth, but younger nations, travelers from continents across the world who have come to inhabit this land, have little of their own to grow on. The pieces of earth that were formed into bowls, even on their way home to dust, provide the new people a lifeline to an unknown land, help them remember that they live in the old nest of earth.

It was in early February, during the mating season of the great horned owls. It was dusk, and I hiked up the back of a mountain to where I'd heard the owls a year before. I wanted to hear them again, the voices so tender, so deep, like a memory of comfort. I was half-way up the trail when I found a soft, round nest. It had fallen from one of the bare-branched trees. It was a delicate nest, woven together of feathers, sage, and strands of wild grass. Holding it in my hand in the rosy twilight, I noticed that a blue thread was entwined with the other gatherings there. I pulled at the thread a little, and then I recognized it. It was a thread from one of my skirts. It was blue cotton. It was the unmistakable color and shape of a pattern I knew. I liked it, that a thread of my life was in an abandoned nest, one that had held eggs and new life. I took the nest home. At home, I held it to the light and looked more closely. There, to my surprise, nestled into the gray-green sage, was a gnarl of black hair. It was also unmistakable. It was my daughter's hair, cleaned from a brush and picked up out in the sun beneath the maple tree, or the pit cherry where birds eat from the overladen, fertile branches until only the seeds remain on the trees.

I didn't know what kind of nest it was, or who had lived there. It didn't matter. I thought of the remnants of our lives carried up the hill that way and turned into shelter. That night, resting inside the walls of our home, the world outside weighed so heavily against the thin wood of the house. The sloped roof was the only thing between us and the universe. Everything outside of our wooden boundaries seemed so large. Filled with night's citizens, it all came alive. The world opened in the thickets of the dark. The wild grapes would soon ripen on the vines. The burrowing ones were emerging. Horned owls sat in treetops. Mice scurried here and there. Skunks, fox, the slow and holy porcupine, all were passing by this way. The young of the solitary bees were feeding on pollen in the dark. The whole world was a nest on its humble tilt, in the maze of the universe, holding us.

SEASONS OF A HERMIT

Joanne Smith

aution, Primitive Road. Use At Your Own Risk.

When they see this sign, friends on their way to visit me will have just left the end of the pavement and turned onto a gravel road, westward toward Arizona high country.

"First house on the left," I always tell them, and those who know the region laugh. The road zigzags like an indecisive roadrunner from rolling prairies to an elevation of six thousand feet. It will be another twenty-two miles over one-lane bridges, fallen rocks, and kiss-your-ass curves before the adventurers reach my haven.

In daylight, guests are greeted by the sign, *Paddock Place Wildlife Sanctuary,* mounted on a pine-green picket fence. Arriving after dark, they see candles lighting the cabin windows, an invitation to the tranquility that reigns here. The glow also mirrors Paddock's rusticity, for I live beyond the wired grid, without electricity, telephone, or even a flush toilet.

And I live alone. My writer's idyllic retreat is hidden in the Prescott National Forest, five miles from the nearest neighbor, fifty from the nearest town. I didn't set out to become a hermit, but when I first stepped onto Paddock's soil, I fell in love with the landscape's wild splendor and primordial solitude.

Paddock's thirty-five acres of field and forest grace a valley hugged by hills of alligator juniper and ponderosa pine. Fences flounder and yearn to lie down. Once essential on a working ranch, now storage for relics of bygone years and dens for wild critters, decades-old buildings creak and sigh, treasures worthy of admiration.

We have much in common. A sexagenarian, I squirrel away decades of memories, host the ordinary varieties of bacteria, and (according to my dearest friend) am still "sweet of looks and charm." So I prop, nail, and paint, observe, journal, and jog, and Paddock and I each do our best to age with spunk and

style. Its mysterious alchemy alters my outer and inner landscape
and creates new worlds to explore.

I shed the dross of certain beliefs and boundaries, customs and
niceties, as well as the spell of "thingness." My needs are water, firewood, and nutritious food; my wants are books, Mozart, and occasionally the company of special friends. Each morning I wake and
know, like Isak Dinesen at her beloved farm in Africa, "Here I am,
where I ought to be."

COME APRIL, I sense that same knowing in the winged multi-
tudes arriving at Paddock, certain that this is where they're meant
to be. No sleeping late now, for the avian extravaganza begins in
pearl light and their concerted focus on melodies, mates, and ter-
ritories compels my devoted awareness. Abandoning the typewriter
for binoculars and bird books, I take to the woods for eyes-on
research.

Like the breath of the universe made visible, morning mist weaves
through branches of ponderosa pine. Participating in a study on
hawks, I hope for a response to my calls, for the sight of a white-
washed pecking perch, for the discovery of a nest. At mid-morning, a
prize appears. A hawk's looping flight shapes a huge four-leaf clover
in the sky. I gasp at this first sighting of a Krider's red-tail, angelic
in feathers the color of fresh country cream. Exhilarated, I return to
the cabin, sit down to a cup of tea, and look up to see spring at my
window. Gleaming ruby and white and green, a broad-tailed hummingbird officially announces the season's opening day.

Outside at the feeders, feathered bouquets color the air with brilliant blues and reds, pure whites and blacks. Steller's jays arrive for
breakfast and the juncos flutter in annoyance. An acorn woodpecker
dives, acting the bully, and the jays scatter. A shadow darkens the
ground and I am stunned to see a hawk torpedo through the area.

Setting work aside, I change clothes and head out for a run or,
rather, a fast walk. There's no sprinting now for these knees, but my
arms pump like a boxer's, vigorous, my feet move in tribal rhythms,
the ancient tread of Yuman and Yavapai. I focus on breath, cadence,
and, always, alertness; this is mountain lion country. One morning
a bull elk challenged my right to his path. I recovered my manners
and gladly stepped into the trees. It is his neighborhood. When I first
came to Paddock, friends questioned the wisdom of living alone in

such isolation. Cell phones won't function here, and mail arrives only three days a week, if the road is passable. I keep no weapons. Animals usually mean no harm if I leave them alone, which I customarily do—unless they reach out to me.

SUMMER'S ARRIVAL is heralded by a dreamlike dance in the meadow. From sun-warmed grasses, thousands of ladybugs rise on pale apricot wings and fill the air with golden smoke. Burly carpenter bees pollinate waist-high lupine, and the pale white blossoms gradually metamorphose into rivers of lavender. In June, snowy banks of yarrow displace the violet streams, the willows' kitten-soft gray buds mature into green leaves, and tiny yellow blossoms dot the gooseberry bushes.

After July's rains, colors flaunt a riotous vitality. Yellow shouts "Look at me" on buttercups, monkey flowers, and mullein stalks standing tall in the fields. The hot pink of wild sweet pea vies with globe mallow's ripe orange. Paddock also offers elegant salads: goosefoot, dandelion, salsify, sorrel. Treasures abound, until the pesky no-see-um emerges.

I spend much of summer in a cage, the garden—also my country store, since I rarely make the hundred-mile round trip to town. The twelve-by-twelve enclosure is protected with chicken wire around, atop, and four feet under. Sun and rain coax meals from soil enriched with aged, powdered manure. The cow pies are free for the picking in sections of the forest leased to ranchers for grazing. Aztec beans burst into brilliant red or royal purple blossoms. There are nine varieties of lettuce, and leafy declarations of radish and carrot.

To tempt the eye, and beneficial bugs, I plant golden calendula and blue cornflower, and the sweet alyssum whose aroma lures me into reverie. I'm partial to oxeye daisies, but my favorite flower wears a fluted gown the blue of the sky. The seeds of morning glory, considered a weed, are not sold in Arizona. The Forest Service sends me their proposed plans to eradicate these and other "noxious vegetation" with chemicals that seem, to many, equally noxious.

I can always find satisfaction in the ranch's daily round of chores, some of them not so routine. One week I escorted a cow off the property, mended the fence, rescued a half-drowned poorwill, and spent four nights with a forest ranger, hooting for Mexican spotted owls until the wee hours, gathering data for an environmental study.

Early one evening, I heard the deep timbre of a male great horned owl's call. I hooted my pitch somewhat higher, in imitation of a female. Unfriendly, sometimes even aggressive toward humans, the owl answered and came nearer. Perched twenty feet up in a pine tree, he resembled a large, fluffy cat. We conversed until it grew dark, but within minutes after I'd gone inside, I heard him call from so close by that I grabbed a flashlight and went back out. Only nine feet separated us as he hooted and bowed from the top of the outdoor shower.

My camaraderie with Lynx, as I dubbed the owl, continued for three years. He once brought his mate and two offspring to the trees in my yard. One October I was astonished to see him in bright morning light at the meadow's edge. On sunny days he would sit for hours on the same tree branch. Studying him over the next three weeks, I realized that he was dying. I sat in the field, keeping him company and meditating on wildness, joy, death, and grief. One morning he was gone. His final season had ended, while I was blessed with the autumn of mine.

AUTUMN CAN QUICKEN HERE in the drop of a leaf, the fold of a flower, the beat of a wing. Grasses wither and my footsteps trigger brittle sounds as I tread on drying ground. Many birds have gone to friendlier climes, and the windless dawn is filled with silence. Then, subtle communiqués of birds still lingering signal their busy preparations for winter. The cottonwoods' gold flutters to ground. A leaf falls and appears to lift back into the tree, the bright flight of a lesser goldfinch reluctant to leave its summer haven. A band of elk serenely grazes nearby, until I raise my binoculars. A sentry barks a warning, every head lifts, and the herd surges and dissolves into the willows like sea foam onto a sandy beach. We are all wary now. It is hunting season.

This small acreage of sweet water and food draws prey and predators. I know it's the way of things, the death of plants, the killing of game. I've posted Paddock as a sanctuary to encourage passersby to revere and grant safe refuge to the wildlife I consider my neighbors, hanging *No Hunting* signs on fences and a quarter mile into the woods. Fortunately, there have seldom been confrontations between encroaching hunters and "that lizard-loving, tree-hugging gal who patrols Paddock." Being prudent, I wear bright orange, but it was most imprudent to go storming after a hunter, as I did once. He'd shot at a buck fleeing into the woods. A discussion ensued, his manner apologetic and appeasing, my voice raised and righteous. Afterward I vowed not to lose my temper again. Still, it amused me to later learn that area scuttlebutt spoke of "the Witch of Paddock."

Magical events are commonplace at Paddock. A bull elk and I startled each other one day, only yards apart. Surprise turned to curiosity and finally, wonder. The handsome beast bowed its head, touching its antlers to the ground. I curtsied. We stared at each other until he turned and leisurely made for the woods. It's true that the lowering of an elk's rack can be a menacing gesture, and my attributing sociability to it implies anthropomorphism, but a bear confronting a threat may turn sideways, as did the one I met in my yard. Though a human might interpret this as coyness, it's more likely a display of size and power. Encounters with animals leave me with the belief that they experience more emotion than we might ever imagine. For three nights and four days, an elk in Middle Meadow called in vain for her calf. The third night her sounds changed; I woke to hear what could only be interpreted as grief. Days later I found the remains of her baby in the willows.

The harvest moon is waxing, and the Milky Way sparkles. It is thirty-six degrees outside, but I crack the window and sit at the kitchen table, writing. There's night music not to be missed. An elk in the southeast meadow tunes his bugle. A possible opponent declares its presence in the far west field. A noisy flapping of wings publicizes a poorwill's erratic flight. A resonant voice floats into my haven; considering it an invitation, I rush out the door. It is a great horned owl, possibly an offspring or close relative of Lynx, and we exchange greetings before he wings soundlessly away. It's a fine thing to be present at the table of the harvest.

WINTER'S GIFTS, like those of other seasons, contain challenges. Snow lessens the usual scant traffic to just one or two vehicles a week; it also draws a few mountain lion hunters and their hounds. Cozily working inside, I create more pages; nothing gets sent, because mail service may cease for weeks.

Winter in the mountains means never going to bed with the wood box empty. During the first year, an early blitz of temperatures in the low teens taught me that stocking the woodshed is a year-round project, and the pleasing scents of juniper, oak, and pine always permeate the woodshed and cabin. There is the heartening solace of bread fresh from the woodstove, and late garden veggies in the soup pot. Romaine and arugula on the window ledge are green against the snow outside. Herbal bouquets and strings of wild mushrooms hang from the ceiling.

Winter's research takes me out in early light to follow critter tracks and try to decode their stories. For food and even fellowship, animals may frequent an ecotone: the place where forest meets meadow, desert touches river. It's the frontier where communities of humankind and wild animals touch each other. It's that shaky space between who we are and who we appear to be, the gap between reality and mystery, the certain and the imagined.

IMAGININGS, IT SEEMS TO ME, can reveal many truths. Enigmatic, exciting, scary, too often ignored, callings urge us toward authenticity and joyfulness. I was called to live, work, and commune with the empty space on the map. At just the right time in my life, I listened. My celebratory renaissance echoes a passage from Clarissa Pinkola Estes' *Women Who Run with the Wolves:* I "wade into the forest as though it is a river and . . . swim in the green."

PALAPA

Jan Epton Seale

We are in what we call the Sunday evening hara-kiris. Except we say harrie-carries, the way we said it as children. My husband sulks over the week's lesson plans. Our son is made melancholy by the world situation reported in the Sunday paper. I am fuming about Monday's inevitable tasks. Then the phone rings: Will we come to the *palapa?*

Yes, of course. I finish the sandwiches I'm making and stash them in the fridge for Monday noon, grab the mosquito spray, and we three head north on the highway in November's early dusk.

The two little roadside communities play out, and we turn back west, passing flat farms and fields. We watch for a flag on a post and nose the Plymouth through an open gate, entering a world of tightly embraced cactus and mesquite.

This land has never been cleared. The island of natural brush in a sea of cultivated fields is a holdout for the owner, our friend Al who lives in town. Al's family has been in *La Frontera* north of the Rio Grande for eight generations. He bought the 16 acres, which he dubbed *"La Migaja,"* the crumb, to answer a need to reclaim his heritage. Its location is traceable to one of the huge Spanish land grants given to one of the families whom Al is undoubtedly descended from. Al is hoping a son and the son's son won't sell it to an orchard developer or a rancher.

It is dark in here, darker than a closet. Now the inkiness gives way to a little clearing and there is Al readying the fire. We thread our way along a short path to his newly renovated *palapa.*

Palapa. Palapa. The word tastes like exotic fruit, makes the tongue indolent and naughty. This *palapa* has been totally refurbished and it takes a while to admire. A circular shelter built of native materials, it's maybe 35 feet in diameter and sports a new Saltillo tile floor.

The center pole is an ebony trunk, as are the smaller support poles around the edge, each chosen for its sturdiness and correct height. Young willow trunks connect the outer rim with the apex at the center pole. Strapped crosswise on the willows, forming a circular pattern, is fresh bamboo, and woven onto the bamboo, to make the thick roof, are new cattail rushes.

The three who did the renovation have slipped back into Mexico. Nothing much changes in this structural form; it's cross-cultural, archetypal. We laugh that this one has been fitted with an electrical outlet.

Now Al's other guests arrive, among them a couple from Washington, D.C. Don has spent a lifetime of work in industrial health and safety. It isn't long before Don reminds us that if we insist on sitting leeward, someone's hair may catch fire from the sparks of the mesquite burning briskly now in the huge iron caldron. More to humor Don than to take care, we move our chairs back a little.

Now we look up through the branches to see the stars. Each is magnified by carats compared to its city backyard version. In the distance through the undergrowth, a cow bawls, a coyote howls.

When the food is ready, we repair to the *palapa*. Al plugs in the overhead light to help the glow from the citronella bucket flames and we settle in to—of all things—bowls of ceviche prepared by our visitors from the north. When the bowls are slurped clean, they are refilled with soupy black beans topped with dollops of rice.

Tortillas warmed near the open fire come around. Everyone spoons and sops until groans of satisfaction replace the silence of hungry folk eating outdoors.

At ten a tiny TV is brought from a van. Seems there's a local news story of particular interest to Al. Our circular seating tilts.

"Good thing this *palapa* is not a boat!"

"Isn't this ridiculous—watching TV in an old mesquite thicket?"

But the Sunday night movie is running overtime. So a cellular phone is produced and a call made to the station to see exactly how late the news feature will be.

We agree we'll have time to get home before it's broadcast. So why do we sit, linger on? No one is willing to break the spell. Then a peculiar sound emerges from the brush a few feet away.

"Listen!" someone says.

"What is that?"

"A pump."

"A car on the road."

"A motor of some kind."

Finally comes the definitive answer. "That's a rattlesnake."

No one moves. We listen to the ancient sizzle. The sound effervesces, is oddly steadying.

Then someone wants to see it. The flashlight illumines only a giant cactus—how old?—sitting like a stalagmite in the cave of the thicket.

The snake is finally quiet. We agree it was disturbed by something—surely not us—and has gone its way. Suddenly we laugh, are noisy on purpose. Everyone pitches in, and the *palapa* and clearing are clean in minutes. Still, we go more carefully along the path, and never without the light.

The fire is smothered and we climb into our cars and thread back to the road, back to town.

When we wake in the night, we know we have been dreaming of bigger stars. The pattern of the *palapa* roof wheels onstage. Our hair smells of mesquite smoke. From the mind's store comes the snake's song.

So much for harry-carry this week.

A SONG FOR THE DIRECTION OF NORTH

Luci Tapahonso

Tsaile, Arizona

The sky is a blanket of stars covering all of us.
The night is unfolding darkness girl.

Just after midnight, we walk in the cool mountain air.
The stars glisten so.
Their bright beauty makes us dizzy.
Laughing, we bump lightly against each other.
I hold my daughter's arm.
We walk slowly, still looking at the sky.
The night is folding darkness girl.

Those few stars in the north seem so close.
Maybe they are right above Buffalo Pass.
Underneath the stars, the Lukachukai Mountain
lies dark and quiet.
It breathes with the sacred wind.
Clearly, clearly the barking of dogs echoes from miles away.
Right there under the pine trees,
the shiny, smooth horses snort and breathe loudly.
The night is folding darkness girl.

The Milky Way stretches wide and careless across the
    dark night.
It is a bright sash belt with thin, soft edges.
The night is scattered thickly with glistening specks
and blinking orbs of light.
In some night spaces, there is no order.
"Coyote sure did a good job," Misty says.
We laugh, and I love my daughters so.
The night is folding darkness girl.

The house sits strong and round against the base of the
    mountain.
In the dark stillness, slants of moon and starlight
wait within the curved walls for white dawn girl.
Slants of light wait for white dawn boy.

Ahshénee 'wéé, t'áá kóó neiit'aash dooleełée.
My beloved baby, if only we could stay here.
There is no end to this clear, sweet air.
To the west, immense rocks lie red and stark in the
    empty desert.
Somewhere my daughters' smooth laughter
deepens the old memory of stars.

Each night, I become Folding Darkness Girl.
Each night, I become Folding Darkness Boy.
Each morning, White Bead Girl arrives.
Each morning, White Bead Boy arrives.

TSAILE APRIL NIGHTS

Luci Tapahonso

*e*arlier today, thin sheets of red dirt
folded into the dark mountain
blown up from the western desert floor.
   You know,
   the whole, empty Navajo spaces around
   Many Farms, Chinle, Round Rock.

Later, light rain slanted into the valley.
The female paused for an hour or so.
She sat and watched us awhile,
then clouds of mist waited until evening and left.
The male rain must have been somewhere over the mountain,
near Cove or Beclabito, chasing children and puppies indoors.
But here, the quiet snow will move in
   a newborn breathing
   those first new nights.

The lake is frozen,
a glazed white plate suspended in the dark.

I long to hear your voice.
   Hushed, deep murmurs in the cold quiet,
   and low laughter echoing in the still.

I like to sleep with piñon smoke.
The cold dry air chills my skin, my breath.
   Stories descend into the dark,
   warm, light circles.

THE LAND'S SONG

Judith Ann Isaacs

*N*early every day, morning and night, I sit under the sky in the hot tub, naked to the elements—wind, snow, rain, sun. Floating warm in a surrogate womb, I'm forced to let go, dreaming under the stars. I see their reflection in the water. To relax my monkey mind, I hold an image of my thoughts floating down the river like a leaf carried by the current. I'm up to my neck in hot water as planets, meteor showers, and constellations spin through the seasons. Once a month, under the full moon, I take a moon bath. Rolling like an otter in my tiny pool to get maximum skin exposure to the moonlight, I honor woman's cycle, even though fertility is long past.

In many cultures, water is a blessing, believed to have healing, restorative powers that signal rebirth and renewal. Here in New Mexico, water is sacred and prized above gold. *Agua es vida*. When water is diminished, not only the land curls up and dies, but the culture, the communities—human, animal, and plant—wither and are soon gone.

I live in the Cañon de San Diego, formed in ancient geologic time by a primeval river that broke through the rim of a miles-wide caldera and thundered down the mountains. The monumental flood carved this valley, deep and narrow at the top, wide and flat at its lower end. The Jemez River, today's rippling, meandering descendant of that huge ancestor, travels through four life zones on its way to the Rio Grande.

Julia Cameron wrote in *Vein of Gold* that by learning to hear the land's song, you will recognize your own life song and learn what creates harmony and dissonance for you.

Harmony is the name we have given to the small mesa where I live with my husband. Here, silence surrounds me, palpable, a presence. The song I hear is below consciousness, present but inaudible in the rocks and red dirt, in the variegated shapes of sandstone rising in layers of unfathomable age. Mesas loom to the east, the west, the north, studded with green clumps of piñon and juniper. To the south, the land broadens and flattens, supporting the modern incarnations of colonial Spanish villages and pre-Columbian pueblos.

At dawn and dusk, light on the cliffs speaks to me. In the morning, clear yellow radiance is comforting, crooning softly *get up, get ready, day is coming.* In the evening, intense orange illumination casts a deep glow that says, *slow down, rest, look at the beauty here.* In a valley, daybreak and day's end are seen in reverse. Early light tips the canyon rim and crawls down to the valley floor as the sun gets higher. The last rays of the setting sun fire the opposite rim in a final good-bye before nightfall.

I track the seasons like the ancients, marking sunrise and moonrise on bumps and dips along the top of Mesa de los Datiles. In summer, the sun ascends far to the northern end. As winter approaches, the brightening that marks the start of each day appears farther south. On the other side of the valley rise the Nacimiento Mountains, my winter storm predictor. When the top of Pajarito Peak blurs in a white haze, a storm will be on us soon. I hurry to fill the wood box.

From the table where we eat and work and talk, I watch the play of light and shadow on Guadalupe Mesa, the highest point nearby. On rare cloudy days, the spectacle is captivating. Ever-changing swatches of light and shadow play over the steep sides, a moment's parting of the curtain. Sometimes clouds spill through the gap between the Guadalupe and Virgin Mesas. I can see a half-mile up the canyon before it curves out of view, fading in the subtle shades of blue found only in the mountains. The longer I look, the more focused and present I am. I breathe as though I were holding an asana in yoga practice.

On top of Guadalupe Mesa, out of view from my window, lie the ruins of the Jemez people's refuge in their battles against the Conquistadors. In the final conflict, they fought to the last man, hurling stones down on armor-clad soldiers who advanced bearing muskets. I've roamed that mesa, an island of rock. I've looked at the outlines of stone walls, run my fingers over fragments of centuries-old pottery, and stood in reverence beside the remaining piles of stones near the rim. From there, I can gaze down on our land across the valley.

We live in a passive solar house, and every room has one wall of windows. Smaller windows frame sections of red cliff and impossibly blue sky—living landscape paintings. We always can see what is happening outside. Without central heat or air conditioning, we can feel it, too.

The best view of the bird-feeders is from our bedroom. A large juniper flourishes just beyond the window, sheltering birds that flit in and out of the thick branches. They vanish when they enter the shelter of the tree, and I never know how many are there. Birds are fewer this year, a sign of the continuing drought.

Here in the lower valley, the piñon and juniper are more like bushes than trees, widely spaced so that each has a chance at whatever moisture may fall. I drive a mere thirty minutes and am surrounded by thick ponderosa pine forest. A little higher, above eight thousand feet, stands of blue spruce color the forest's palette. I believe trees are sentient in some way. The Warrior, as defined by Angeles Arrien in *The Four-Fold Way,* is like a tree, honoring the past, present and future from season to season. Roots are the past, trunk the present, branches the future or goals, and blossoms goals attained. Vrksasana, the tree pose, is a yoga position of balance. Some days, I'm more balanced than others.

The largest of the cottonwoods lining the river is a hundred years old. From my house, I see the bosque change with the season. Effervescent green in the spring seems to swallow me as I drive down the highway that parallels the river. Autumn gold is sunlight captured in the canopy. Intricately woven branches in winter sketch a spare poem above rimes of ice that hug the river's edge.

In a canyon where time is visible in the walls rising on either side, I feel the transience of this existence. I can live in wonder without knowing why the world is wonderful. I am content to dwell in the midst of mystery, to turn myself over to the unknown of creation.

MEXICAN SUNFLOWERS

Donna Marie Miller

I've heard them called *Tithonias*
though I call them Mexican sunflowers.
They grow like weeds
along the levee banks.
When April comes their spiny heads
bloom into petals
the color of orange rust with yellow centers.
I watched her
as she carried a bouquet of them in her dirty hands
walking barefooted
across the road and wearing
only a thin blue dress
that fell a little off her shoulders.
I wanted to call to her then
like a child myself to say *"que bonita."*
My woman/mother-love overflowed
as I dreamed I picked her up in my arms
to hold her close.
The wind whipped her dark hair
around her face
as she skipped away for home,
a shack of cardboard and two-by-fours.
Some of the dogs in the yard
came out to greet her barking wildly
and licking her toes.
"Que bonita, que bonita,"
I heard them say.
How pretty she was. How pretty.

SPRING IN THE DESERT

Ann Woodin

*T*hen comes spring with its darting eyes, and we are caught up in the frenetic Priapic burst of activity. If during the two or three months after Christmas we have our expected rainfall, or a bit more, the lavishness, the profusion, the very miracle of spring will leave us breathless . . .

In the spring, say late February on into April, providing the preceding months have been rainy, the desert will be carpeted with wild flowers, the small, yellow, delicate bladderpod appearing first, followed by lupine, gold-poppies, desert marigold, paperflowers, and desert verbena. The cacti, however, don't reach their peak until late April or May. Then it is that the small, compact, perennial shrubs like the zinnia and the brittlebush are covered with white or yellow blossoms and that the palo verde seem dipped in sunshine, turning the foothills to billowing gold. The catclaw hides its thorns behind fuzzy caterpillar blooms, and the desertwillow is covered with fragile, pale-lavender trumpet flowers.

Often, on a spring afternoon, I lie under a mesquite tree and listen to the stream, which runs deep and clear. The banks are covered with grass and clover, and where I have matted it down, the hot sun draws out the moist sweet smell of things growing. Flowers are scattered everywhere. Close to the water monkeyflower grows, elsewhere lavender owl-clover and phacelia, clumps of poppies like Easter eggs, yellow mustard, and borage. Every insignificant weed is wearing some tiny blue, purple, yellow, or white jewel that reveals its beauty only on close inspection. Great mops of deer grass line the banks with drooping tips that sweep the ground whenever the wind blows. And in the water itself is a patch of pepperwort, a very primitive fern with leaves like a four-leaf clover that causes a pollen expert's eyes to light up.

I hear the chirp of a black phoebe and I watch it dart about. It is joined by its mate and together they sit in a tree, while below them an exceedingly fat robin investigates the bank and then hops down to the water for a drink. A group of noisy house finches fly by like a gang of giddy girls just let out of school. Very high in the clear air two ravens soar and tumble in ecstatic acrobatics, tracing on the sky an infinite variety of baroque curlicues. Spring has enchanted them, for never have I seen ravens fly so nimbly and with such grace . . .

On the other side of the stream a Gila woodpecker scolds the dog, who is sniffing at a rock squirrel hiding beneath his tree, and a pair of vermilion flycatchers are briskly chasing flies. It is easy to follow the brilliant red male, less easy to see his drab-brown mate. When a Cooper's hawk flies by, dipping in and out of the trees, everything is suddenly silenced. Nothing moves, nothing sings. Everything waits, as if some mysterious hand has pulled a switch and all life is instantly frozen. The hawk disappears upstream. Seconds go by and then a sparrow begins to sing, tentatively at first until others shake themselves and catch up the song. The shadow of danger is dissolved by splendid sound, and spring goes pulsing on more jubilantly than ever.

If I had my way, I would shoot that Cooper's hawk. I resent his filling his belly with our pretty songbirds. The stream appears to be a trap, luring small birds to it with the promise of food and water, and then loosening on them their mortal enemy. Should I mention my murderous intentions to my husband, he would only look at me with shock and chagrin, for obviously I have not grasped the fundamental law of nature, that one species has as much right to live and eat as another, and that the songbirds are as much the hawk's to eat as they are mine to listen to.

I watch a handsome black-and-orange swallowtail butterfly flit by, the sun shining through its wings; and close at hand with a Gulliver eye I watch a ladybug struggle up the stalk of a fiddle-neck, a spotless ladybug. On the next stem a gaudy blister beetle sets out for a dinner of leaves. This beautiful creature secretes an irritating fluid that discourages small boys, as well as those who might wish to make a meal of him, from picking him up. I think, as I lie there, that the real luxury of time is not merely to have enough of it in which to get done all the things that one wishes, but to have enough to squander idly, in clover.

In April the mesquite fling wide their branches and are covered with new downy leaves. They, along with the catclaw, are the last of the trees to succumb to the sweet disorder of spring—no elegant *quattrocento* spring as Botticelli painted it, but an urgent one, which knows its time is brief.

Everywhere birds are building nests, sitting on eggs, or feeding voracious young. The boys and I take a nest-viewing tour. First we stop to see the road-runner that sits determinedly on a large sprawling nest in the middle of a cholla. All that we can see of her is her long tail sticking up amidst the spines. She spaces her eggs as does any intelligent modern parent; the first-born, being the largest, receives the most food, which gives him an advantage and increases the possibility of at least one surviving. The road-runner is one of our favorite birds. No one can resist him, and he has rightly earned the nickname "the clown of the desert"—not surprising for a member of the cuckoo family. Once a road-runner found himself in the boys' play-yard and went running frantically around and around looking for a way out, forgetting that he was first and foremost a bird and could therefore easily fly over the fence.

In another cholla nearby a thrasher has laid three beautiful eggs, pale bluish with brown freckles, and next door a house finch is sitting on two clear-blue ones. This clump of cholla is a veritable bird maternity ward. Certainly, if one does not mind the spines oneself, the cholla provides excellent protection.

The mesquite thicket along the stream is another favorite nesting place. On one side of the path a canyon towhee has produced four white eggs splotched with purple in a neat nest of woven grass. On the other side a pair of Abert's towhees are already feeding their young. The tiny cuplike nest of a black chinned hummingbird clings to a branch of a small ash next to the water, and in the large sycamore baby hooded orioles swing in their suspended home.

The younger boys want to see what has happened to a quail nest holding twenty eggs, so we walk up the wash to where the nest is lying on the ground near a pack rat's home. The nest is empty except for a few broken shells. Hugh picks up the eggshells and says, "Oh, dear, that quail is a careless mother. She ought to build her nest in a cactus like the other birds."

Then Peter insists that we go to see the dove nest he discovered in the staghorn near the cattle guard. I am exhausted by the surrounding display of seething motherhood, and at the end of the day I am grateful that I am not a bird.

But sometimes I wish I were a twelve-year-old boy. In the sycamore close by our south fence we have built a tree house. It is large and sturdy, accommodating four boys in sleeping bags. The boys, mostly in the spring, take turns sleeping there with their friends. Up at the house, in my bed, I think of them enviously. I think of the primroses shining white in the moonlight, of the water over the rocks, of the round eye of the moon in a pool, of the call of an owl, of the warm breeze off the desert, which passes the house and me to bring to those sleeping boys the smell of honeysuckle. It must be good to be a boy in the spring in a tree house.

FIRST SNOWFALL

Ann Zwinger

In the mountains, I often sleep out on the deck at night. To-night isn't as cold as I expected for a mid-October night full of celestial quiet. I close my eyes to a waning moon and Jupiter, sliding across the sky.

The mallards awaken me at four o'clock, a disorienting sound in a milky-skied night. Deep *qua-aa-a-cks* from a single female duck echo off the pond's cold surface, repeated and repeated, answered by a higher thinner call from a drake. Sometimes the calls are separate, antiphonal; sometimes they overlap with urgency.

This single drake has remained on the pond weeks after other mallards have migrated through. In the past few weeks, groups of six or seven have come by, splashed down on the lake, fed for half an hour or so, then left, leaving the drake to ply the pond alone, back and forth, as if tethered to a track on the bottom, unable to join them. I know it cannot survive the winter—if not to a marauding coyote, it will succumb to a feral cat or a prowling weasel, or killing cold. There is no room for it in the winter world of the mountains.

The calls continue for what's left of the night. I never knew a duck's honk, such an ungainly, brusque, and awkward call, could carry such poignant overtones. I never knew a hoarsening quack could convey such deep disquiet, such "come-with-me," such "I-can't," such loneliness, such desperation, such winter, such omen, such death.

The sky curdles and clots over. The gibbous moon blurs, clouds blot the pinpoint reflections out on the lake. The night comes down. I slip into restless sleep with an image of winter new to me, chilling, complete with sound.

First light reaches me, even submerged as I am in the blackness of my sleeping bag. Daylight sits on my back, kicks me in the ribs, rides me awake. A Steller's jay clomps along the railing, noisy as a kid running a stick along a balustrade, making sure everyone hears. If I had a rock I would bean its cocky crest.

As I lie on the deck, chickadees hit the hanging bird-feeder, snag the sunflower seeds, pound them to get at the nut inside. The feeder sways with the impact of their assaults.

Wind facets the lake, shooting sparks of light like skyrockets in a dark sky. A trout rises, out of sight, and the ripples destroy the fine upside-down spires of a reflected hillside of pines. The sky is gray but the east glows pearly, non-colors turning bright, streaked with scarves of clouds like needle fish swimming north.

A white-breasted nuthatch minces down the wall, arrows to the tray, whirls away to a ponderosa. A chipmunk descends the edge of the wall by my sleeping bag. At six inches we are momentarily eyeball-to-eyeball. It leaps to the ground and, on the way, lands on my pillow with a surprisingly leaden thump—I expected a more feathery fall. Another patters across the deck, jumps into the tray filled with birdseed, its tail switching, looping, snapping back and forth. The heartbeat in its throat is too rapid to count, a metabolism that has to be stoked for winter.

The chickadees, marshmallow bodies with stuck-on beaks and legs, are flurried, spastic, quick, disheveled, as if they didn't take time to comb their feathers and brush their beaks before they went out foraging. Into their frenetic midst arrives a junco, sleek, suave, urbane, feeding quietly at the tray. The chickadees spray seed all over the place. The junco feeds neatly, fastidious and oblivious.

All day long the wind blows holes through the aspen grove. A late grasshopper clacks in that particular incessant way they have, threatening to wind down if you personally don't come and wind it up.

The moving colors gentle the heaps and hollows. I'm not fond of fall but there's something to be said for alizarin and salmon-rose leaves, butterscotch willows, and cadmium yellow aspen quivering against spruce shadows. More variation than spring, much as I hate to admit it, but then spring is not tainted with the emotional baggage of farewell.

An anxiety, an urgency, hangs in the air. The birds, sky, grasses, grasshoppers, and I all seem to share a pre-knowledge of snow that gives walking the meadows a poignancy. The lake meadow, despite the lack of animated light, is burnished-salmon gold, strawberry blond, coloring that surprises me at this receding time of year, when I mourn every broken grass stem, every fallen leaf. The image that comes to mind is that of Renoir in his last years, painting with his paintbrush strapped to his arthritic arm, and the lusty, fleshy, overblown colors on his palette. So much color fills the meadow that it is no longer "meadow," no longer the familiar greensward, but something else—burning with color even when the sky dampens and cools the rest of the landscape to stainless steel.

The rain begins in early afternoon, coming down in bits and pieces, stippling noisy circles on the pond. It grays everything, washing away color like a pitcherful of dirty water poured over a bright watercolor. But no snow. Just dingy wet aspen boles and dripping pine needles.

The day goes slowly, time fettered by the rain. In the early nightfall, it still drizzles. I read and grade papers and, at midnight, when I look out on the blackness of the deck, I think for a moment I won't have to sleep inside. Underneath the roofline the deck boards are dark, and beyond them the planks are lighter in color which says the rain has stopped, the deck has dried. I step out and find instead snow, a quiet snow that has whispered in, so different from the verbal rain.

All night it snows. In the morning the cow parsnips and yarrow and black-eyed Susans hold cones and pyramids of snow. The lake gleams black against its white banks. Snow delineates every grass head and stuffs the ponderosa needles into white porcupine balls. Stillness muffles the land. No wind, no breeze, no breathing. Tomorrow is blocked in, yesterday is expunged. No tracks show—the animals remain closeted away, leaving the world to snow.

This first snow has a character all its own, pristine, untrodden, self-contained. The first snow simply blankets summer, obliterates fall, irrevocably changes the color of the year. This snow has a lethal innocence later snows will not have. It will melt within a few days, even within the shadowed spots, but the world will never be the same again. This is the first snow and its coming is marked, measured, mourned, welcomed.

This is never so with the last snow—one never knows about the last snow, only in retrospect. Endings are blurred, frazzled with—is this *really* it? are there any more snows to come? is spring *really* on its way? Endings dribble time away, each superseding the last, until one late pasqueflowered day, there really isn't any more winter and spring slithers in on a green garter snake. Somewhere in spring or early summer, the mountain rains stay rain.

Not so the first snow. I peer at the year's first snowflake on my sleeve through a magnifying glass, as my mother showed me as a child. There is only one first snow and I stand in it, like a figure in an old-fashioned paperweight turned upside down, snowflakes catching on my sleeve, my eyelashes, my psyche. There is only one first snowfall.

geographies

JOURNEY NOTES

Where am I? What wildness is this? This is a different chaos; here there are no edges. Skin against skin, I can find no boundaries.

LINDA ELIZABETH PETERSON,
"INTO THE ESCALANTE"

GEOGRAPHIES

Sandra Lynn

Territory of lipstick, candlestick,
pines' dark gossip about collapsed
shacks, and red roads that wander
off into the trees like bloodlines
into their dotage. East Texas.
Where the South stains the edge
of the Southwest. As a child there,
I desired and feared tornadoes.
Black angels, they still stride
into my dreams. But I was taught
a general rule: seek cover.
In bare rooms, it is hard
to say anything but the truth.
Rooms are made safe
with polished silver and brass,
dried arrangements poised on pianos.
You must stop climbing to the tops
of the trees and put on blue organdy
and forsake bark and old roots
for the womanly graces. Burial,
my dear, is but another of the faces
of charm. What a pretty woman
these hills are, dressed fit to kill
in needle green. You'd never guess
iron beneath.

    And then I found
West Texas, the other end of the sky,
the planet's flesh revealed,
the unclothed globe sprawled
flank to the wind
as if cover were never conceived,

fiercely innocent.
Buttes, rimrock, talus arroyos,
bajadas, the hipbones, the groin:
this is my body
which is broken before you.
Scars of faulting
and erosion are flaunted
as if they were hammered silver.
Dust devils are seen across miles,
whirling into their harmless trances.
The clear downward stroke
at the end of a distant mesa
rings in the eye a summoning.
Minerals crawl to the surface.
In old, unroofed rooms
scattered unceremoniously among
rocks, nothing lives hidden.
All is skin.
Without knocking, night walks in.

THE ACT OF ATTENTION

Susan Hanson

She is doing tai chi in the middle of the path.

What is the proper etiquette for this? I wonder. Do I stand here, pretending to admire the bark of the nearest tree? Do I ignore her and simply walk right by, training my eyes on the ground ahead?

I am stumped, I'll admit—and more annoyed than I care to say.

Young and thin, the woman appears to be very much at home with herself. Like me, she has been at this South Texas retreat center for several days now. But unlike me, she wears a certain lightness, a grace that bespeaks a kind of inner calm.

I am wearing a backpack full of books.

Pausing on the sandy path that winds some two miles through the trees, I watch her for a moment, watch her standing with her arms raised in the air like wings. She has become a crane.

Not knowing how long she will pose there, readying herself for flight, I decide I have no choice but to slip discreetly by. Holding my camera close against my chest, and keeping my eyes on the path, I follow the wheel rut to the right. I am careful not to make a sound, not to let my clothing rustle, not to breathe more loudly than I should.

The woman simply stands there, motionless and mute.

What annoys me, I realize as I walk, is that this woman's practice isn't mine. Lissome as the saplings growing underneath the oaks, she has a grace I envy, a composure I imagine that I lack. Somehow, I suspect, her way of working toward the center of her life is far more enlightening than mine.

Rounding the corner, and passing by a deer trail through the brush, I watch for the sign that will mark a pathway to my left. For several mornings now, I have taken this detour to a pond beyond a motte of oaks and palms. And for several mornings,

I have waded through the young spring grass, set up my campstool just behind a screen of reeds, and waited for the birds.

On my first day here, I encountered several blue-winged teal, the male distinguished by the stripe of white between his bill and eyes. Gliding back and forth across the pond, the birds seemed oblivious not only to the turtle sunning on the muddy bank but also to the Wied's crested flycatcher, snatching insects as it tumbled through the air.

This morning, though, there are no ducks. I find a colony of cormorants instead.

"Five cormorants are swimming in the pond today," I note in the journal I hold balanced on my lap, "five cormorants like a haiku skimming the surface, grinning apostrophes on water."

While I am not looking, they all get out, flex their wings, and then run back into the water like children, splashing each other as they go. If it weren't anthropocentric to do so, I'd say these creatures were in love with the lives they lead.

Taking a closer look, I see that my count is wrong. "There are ten, not five," I write at the bottom of the page. "Cormorants on holiday, I guess."

A comical lot, these birds wear perpetual grins. With their up-turned bills and their snake-like necks, they ride low in the water like loons. It seems fitting, then, to read in my 1951 *Audubon Water Bird Guide* that when double-crested cormorants are first hatched, "the naked, coal-black young look like rubber toys." They are not much different now.

Perched on my stool, and out of their line of sight, I make a small confession in my book. "I feel a bit like a voyeur," I write as a final note, "sneaking up on a group of bathers skinny-dipping in the pond."

Leaving the birds to their play, I fold up my stool, place my journal in my pack, and head back down the trail the way I came. Best not to be too quiet, I think, padding silently on the sand. In the grass, at the edge of the path, a javelina stares at me, turns, and trots into the brush on stiff-legged tiptoe.

Within minutes, I am veering past a pile of deer dung on the trail. Instead of walking on, though, I stop to watch a pair of beetles struggling to carry a single pellet away. Ignoring the shadow of my boots, they roll it toward a clump of straggler daisies near the path.

And there, while I stoop to see exactly how they work, they bury the dung in the sand.

What is my practice? I wonder as I think back to the young woman on the path. *What is authentic life for me?* All too often I've imagined that the answer lay in reading the right book, finding the right program, emulating the right spiritual guide. But I've found it in none of these.

In a key episode in his novel *The Dharma Bums,* Jack Kerouac follows Ryder Japhy, Henry Morley, and narrator Ray Smith as they attempt to ascend a mountain in the Sierra Nevada. After a day of climbing has taken them to the foot of Matterhorn peak, the trio must decide whether to continue toward the summit or begin the descent toward camp. Smith and Japhy elect to go on.

Novice climber that he is, Smith has been duly impressed by the grace and agility with which Japhy leaps from rock to rock. Earlier, in fact, he had tried to copy his friend's technique, finally realizing that he would be more successful if he were simply to "pick [his] own boulders and make a ragged dance of [his] own."

It is only on the way down, however, that Smith actually gets it. Having clambered almost to the top of the Matterhorn, he makes his descent with joyful abandon, intuitively creating his route through the rocks as he goes. All of a sudden, Smith exclaims, "everything was just like jazz." No longer worried about how his performance compares to Japhy's, he is at last free to experience his life as his own. Like the jazz musician, Smith is finally letting the music come, naturally flowing from a center that is deep within himself.

What might my life be like were I to give in to the rhythms of my own ragged dance? Like this, I imagine, walking down the trail, past grapevines and winecups and huisache blooming in the sun. Just like this attentiveness, this pleasure, this being present to the world.

CONTEMPLATING QUANTUM MECHANICS ONE MORNING AT THE RIO GRANDE GORGE

Judith Strasser

Sun creeps down the western face,
picks out the structure of strata—
rubbled ledge perched on vertical
drop, chaotic gully of rockfall,
the V of the canyon where the river
takes a turn; sun slips with the swallows
toward rapids, flecks the lacy froth,
slides toward a still backwater
tracing a silver sheen.

Perched on solid basalt just at
the canyon's rim, eating breakfast
of toast and jam, some things seem
certain enough: the rising sun
will dry the arroyo trickling at my feet,
crack mud left by last night's rain,
warm my pack, melt the ice
in my water bottle. My black rock seat
will stick to this spot today.

But it's only a matter of time
for the rock, and as for the rest—
suppose the turkey vulture
playing the thermals overhead
deconstructs the classical world
with one glance of its sharp eye.
At once, the sun's rays sting like BBs.
Invisible quarks and leptons
buzz positions that used to sweep
toward the river in the guise of
massive walls. The Rio Grande
reflecting nothing, suddenly
disappears.

Where does such thinking lead?
I shake off the crumbs, pack up
my crusts and camera. On the hike
back to the car, I startle
a local jack rabbit. He bounds off
in no special direction,
slips through this rock-and-sand world,
melts into grama and sage.

YOM KIPPUR FAST IN TAOS

Judith Strasser

*P*erhaps, says the rabbi after Kol Nidre,
we fast to be more like angels. Perhaps,
I think just past noon the next day. Do angels
get headaches because they don't eat?
Do they shiver at their computers, chilled
near to death by two missed meals,
a weekend of clouds, the thinly veiled threat
of snow? Do visiting angels in foreign lands
shun Yom Kippur Torah service, not wanting
to daven familiar prayers set to peculiar tunes?

    I punch up the thermostat; still I can't
get warm. I dress for a walk outside.
No diaphanous gown; no wings. I pull on
woolen gloves, a sweatshirt over a turtleneck,
a lined nylon windbreaker jacket. In a few blocks,
blood starts to flow. The headache begins to diffuse.
A breeze herds clouds like sheep; they flock
against Taos Mountain. The sun breaks through.
I shed jacket and gloves. When angels take walks
it's like this: small birds sing from the power lines,
the orchards are gifted with apples, the spice of
a rain-soaked meadow sharpens the wood-smoke air.
Gold blessings drift from the cottonwoods.
Plastic flamingos strut in a cactus garden.
Patches of blue sky promise: tomorrow
the mountaintop will be revealed.

COMING OF AGE
IN THE GRAND CANYON

Susan Zwinger

*M*orning, 9:20, already a late start in Grand Canyon National Park. I sit in the dirt drawing *Oenothera caespitosa marginata,* an immense primrose that flings open gleaming petals shamelessly, gloriously. Drawing, my form of meditation, precludes worry. I've come here to study natural history pensively, slowly. Above me, the trail zigzags 450 feet straight up the sandstone cliff like a high-top bootlace. Soon I am climbing straight up it, out of breath, slowing people down. At the top, Michael, the trip's photographer, strides jauntily to the edge. I gaze at him in horror.

Last night, as cracked, brown fingers traced the route on a topography map, I realized that this hike would demand I do what every cell in my body told me not to do many times over. The longest hike of our nineteen days on the Colorado River, it would loop up one wild canyon, through Surprise Valley and down another, no turning back. I had serious doubts. Our trip had begun ten days earlier at Glen Canyon Dam with forty people, including much media, for the purpose of celebrating both the eightieth birthday of professional river runner and lifetime environmentalist Martin Litton, and his umpteenth time rowing the Colorado River through the Grand Canyon by oar and small wooden boat. Fortunately, a number of people had left us along the way, driving off at Lee's Ferry or hiking out of the canyon at various locations. The hard-core group remaining wanted not only to honor our elder, the Grand Old Man of the River, but also to explore, to research the return of the beaches after the spring 1996 deliberate flood to restore the river's wild condition, and simply to have a fantastic time . . .

Now the trail turns sharply up a narrowing canyon sixty feet above thundering Tapeats Creek. I concentrate on the river's roar below: golden and turquoise, brown and white water. Silk and foam; silk and foam and danger. The trail drops down and crosses the river. Forming a human chain, we each step three feet down into waist-deep current. My sandals disappear from sight; my feet creep by Braille over stones slippery with algae. In the deepest water, I pull Barton back, forgetting he is barefoot. The water roars higher and higher on my chest (his waist). A slip, a break in the human chain could mean being swept downstream and pummeled on large boulders.

As Barton climbs out, his foot is spurting blood. The snow-cold water from the 8,000-foot Arizona mountains has spared him pain until now. This country, which unfolds the most spectacular exposure of geologic beauty anywhere on the planet, is unforgiving . . .

Our conversation bubbles along like a mountain brook, while the Tapeats turns ominous. Only April 12, and heavy May-like volumes unleash from the mountains. The winter of 1997 has seen record levels of snowfall all over the West. The snowpack is at record highs; flooding is prevalent all over California, Oregon and Washington. Here, the snowpack in the Arizona and Utah mountains translates into amazing hydrology: streams gushing under pressure from holes in the rock, creeks swollen above their normal obstacles and banks, and magnificent botany. The entire desert canyon shimmers with vivid greens; cactus flowers explode in saturated color.

Upstream, Thunder River roars in from the northwest. The Tapeats accrues depth; rounded river cobble expands to hip-wide boulders. Plunging over table-size stones, snowmelt transforms its glassy-rilled surface into roaring tumults around white air sockets— a raw-thunder sound. I am watching it out of the corner of my eye with trepidation. I cannot believe that water four feet deep is good for a 5-foot, 4-inch woman.

We sail right past the crossing cairn in disbelief, and add another half-mile onto our trip by backtracking. Clasping hands, we again form the human chain; this time Barton wears his mountain boots. The first step down takes me up to my midriff with foam bulldozing my chest. Fear, which I usually put off until midstream, begins at once. This time, a fall would mean being swept downstream and possible broken bones or death. Barton yells at the top of his lungs at me to move ahead. I am pulling him back. It requires all my will to step one foot forward. At this speed, water multiplies its weight by thirty times against any obstacle.

A brilliant orange Indian paintbrush bobs on shore. It burns into my brain with a hot blade of irony. This is the last flower I will ever see.

The icy river numbs everything below midthigh, so I cannot feel where my feet should go; my body disappears in the water's rapidly sliding layers. Barton grabs hold of Factor, who stands like a pillar near the other bank. For several moments—an eternity—I am alone in the roaring river. It takes all of my courage to work over to Factor.

Thus far, I have kept up just fine, but stopping to put my socks back on, I fall to last place. Slowly, Factor talks me up the next 900-foot elevation gain, up a canyon wall near the vertical drop of Thunder River from Thunder Spring. Factor, ever wise and encouraging, plucks a geological detail from his voluminous knowledge and points out a hill of Shinumo sandstone protruding 300 feet up into the overlying shale. The Shinumo was an ancient island in a 1.2-billion-year-old sea—the time it required to lay down enough fine-grained shale to cover an island. In my mind, I bury my island home in Puget Sound with seventy-five million years of sediment, then wonder if I should send my backup disks to the mainland.

At each switchback, my body aches with the lack of oxygen and refuses to go on. At each switchback, I force against my anaerobic cells. Solo, I would have stopped to conquer my blood-sugar problem by now, but here I ignore the dizziness and nausea, gulping a granola bar on the way up.

Lili drops behind for a long video shoot across a quarter-mile of empty space to the brightly clad human specks stuck to the vertical, red limestone wall. I am no longer last—that horrific moral pressure is off. Two more switchbacks and I am on that red wall, its shelf trail hanging me in space. This time I revel.

I am right on the edge. I gaze straight down, then straight across space, the plummeting side gorge we will cross, to the spot where volumes of white water, Thunder River, shoot out of a solid wall of stone. From high above, the water bores down through limestone, through anastomotic tubes until it hits an impervious layer of Bright Angel shale and exits dramatically. When the Colorado River carved straight down through the bedrock, it exposed two round holes anywhere from six to fifty feet wide. To see an "unexplained" and

perfectly round exit high on the canyon wall with a waterfall pour-
ing out of it is uncanny.

What joy! My spirit shoots through that giant canyon wall of resistance and flies with the white water out into open space. It flies
across chasms toward the hanging rock garden and lush cottonwoods
nourished by the falls—our haven for lunch. At each switchback I
pause now, not from exertion, but from ecstasy.

There is such raw power in being balanced on this narrow trail.
The minuteness of my fellow humans crossing the deep canyon on a
red limestone wall hundreds of feet thick, the multiplicity of flower
and mesa and stone and tree, the surreal image of a river shooting
straight out from a wall of stone and falling a thousand feet—and
the knowledge that with one leap I would fall 700 feet, to blend with
the Indian paintbrush quivering in an up-canyon wind.

It begins raining again. The other eight hikers tuck back into deep
red monkey flowers, ferns, lichens, mosses, and lush cottonwood
trees, gathering around Factor for his stories. He once climbed down
and through these labyrinthine tunnels carved by the water. He
crawled and slithered until he could peer out from within the limestone cliff face just as the water does before it plunges.

I long to hear these stories; the stories Factor carries from twenty
years of breakneck explorations reverberate in my own abbreviated
experience like harmonics on adjacent strings.

Yet, I also want to perch out here alone on this windswept switchback to watch the virga and snow stream diagonally from their laden
clouds—clouds that tear like scrims across the mesas layered in the
distance, a preternatural distance broken by mile-high earth tables
that are striated Prussian blue, maroon, cobalt, deep eggplant. I
want not only to watch these storms, but also to smell and embrace
them. To be swept along by the ever-spinning music of Grand Canyon thermal systems.

Another 300 feet straight up red limestone and we climb out on
the cusp of Surprise Valley, a wide, gently sloping piece of the Tonto
Platform, a classic hanging valley. In a hotter month, this long, water-
less traverse is potentially dangerous. Today, a vigorous stroll takes
us through tall spikes of century plants and yuccas, through deep-
purple larkspur, past trombone-shaped purple blooms of Colorado
four o'clock, *Mirabilis multiflora,* odorous mint sage, and thorny-
fingered mesquites. The Tonto Platform seems impenetrable until a

rift suddenly opens up—as if the Earth had ripped. We drop into Deer Creek drainage.

And drop and drop and drop and drop. Stepping down three-foot rock shelves, scrambling down ten-foot chutes, or picking through talus the size of pickups loses its charm. I feel wretchedly guilty because I am slowing my companions way down. I find myself down-climbing first, in front of the last few people. Suddenly, I gaze out into empty space. The trail disappears.

I stop dead in my tracks. A good route finder from years of hiking cross country, I see no trail up. No trail down. Just a bone-gray talus cliff face with 570 feet of exposure. Below spreads a luxurious valley where Deer Creek sparkles like a strip of tinsel.

A slim pale-gray line—only ten to twelve inches wide in spots—dots the face of the cliff for 300 feet. Could this be a track on the otherwise near vertical face where I am supposed to stick like a fly? Once again, every cell in my body cries, "Absolutely not." I think of backtracking, of crossing Tapeats Creek twice by myself—in the dark.

I put Jen, the twenty-three-year-old cook who does not yet know she is mortal, in front of me. Head down, I stare at her heels. Never did two heels look so fascinating. My feet step out into space, following Jen like two dumbstruck puppies.

Two thirds of the way over, I gaze straight down. My spirit seizes like an unoiled engine. There, 570 feet below, some ridiculously cheerful grasses blow in the wind. No respect for my terror. Yet, something strange shifts within. The wind whirs past, whipping up the vast empty space into something tangible, terrible and delicious. Something immense is born from utter nothingness. My skin springs wide open and swallows the air, my hair whips around like schools of silver jacks flashing in the ocean; my feet sprout roots that pull up from the talus like Velcro, then reattach with every step.

I gape at space, I court space, I leap through space. Hahhhhh, I *am* space!

We drop off the slippery gray talus into the red limestone, rest below a waterfall jettisoned through anastomotic tubes straight out from the cliff. I pray that all such wild rivers—within me and without—remain free-flowing.

INTO THE ESCALANTE

Linda Elizabeth Peterson

The self forms at the edge of desire.

ANNE CARSON

I had moved to Salt Lake City from central Michigan in 1980, drawn by mountains, city life, ragweed-free air, and every myth about reinvention in the West that a Michigan farm kid could possibly have imagined for herself. But—no surprise—the reinventing business had proven to be hard work. So when my new friend, Dawn, proposed a trip into Southern Utah, I was more than ready.

"So what's there?" I asked.

She rattled off the names of national parks—Arches, Capitol Reef, Canyonlands—and some of those western place names that always quicken my pulse: Deadhorse Point, Grand Gulch, Waterpocket Fold, Wildcat Mesa. I had read my *Desert Solitaire*, written a paper about it, and even had Edward Abbey growl at me at a book signing. But what had I really grasped about Utah's geography? Not much. After all, I'd moved to Salt Lake City without understanding that it was a ski town.

Our trip was more than twenty years ago, but in memory I still stand at the top of Boulder Mountain, the pine-scented wind in my face. My eyes sweep across the Waterpocket Fold, framed by the Henry Mountains hovering in light clouds far off in the east, and then down into the Escalante River drainage at my feet to the south. Nothing, not the Rockies, not the Tetons, not even the Grand Canyon, has prepared me. I am suddenly at the edge of my known world.

What is this? Rock, all rock, naked and alive. Rolling and undulating, thrusting upward and falling away, twisting and tumbling, it shimmers in a hot, clear June sky. From this height, my gaze can only skim the white and reddish-orange tops of the ridges and domes and the canyons cutting randomly and feverishly through the stone, take in their chaos and mystery, utter wildness scoured and scored into the rock. My Midwesterner's mind, shaped by flatness and the square-mile grid, is undone: safe, comfortable categories release and fragment. My breathing, when it returns, is quick and shallow. My limbs loose, I lean into Dawn. If I say anything, it is "God." If I know anything, it is that I am surrendering to this edge, falling into this land, already filling my hands with it.

Dawn enjoys my disarray; chortling, she finally nudges me back into the car. We descend into Boulder, stop at the Anasazi State Park, catch the Burr Trail just south of Boulder, and soon find ourselves setting up camp about a mile or so up The Gulch, one of the dozens of washes that make up the Escalante River system. My mind needs this simple activity—the familiar battle with the tent and the backpacking stove, the long search for matches, the eating, the talk, the laughter. And the sudden chill when the sun leaves the canyon, the innumerable stars, the full moon, the coyotes' yipping in the distance, the soft buzzing of the cottonwoods, the stillness.

Late the next morning, we hike slowly along the wide, sandy bottom of The Gulch, skirting boulders, gnarled cottonwoods, and willow thickets, as the towering Wingate sandstone walls fold around us. We have no heavy packs, no camp to set up, and no destination. We are at play in an Anasazi world, those ancient lives flickering behind the thinnest of veils. When the tamarack-fringed mouth of a narrow side canyon beckons, I yield, leaving Dawn behind. I slip through the trees, scramble over a couple of boulders, and slide into cool, smooth earth. Swallowed by serpentine mystery, I ease my way through the canyon's twists and turns. With the curved sandstone walls arching out over me and then tilting back again, I move alternately in sun and shadow. The sky, when I can see it, is a mere ribbon of intense blue high, high above. Finally, the canyon narrows so that I can stretch out both arms and run my hands along its sides as I walk.

The wild, open chaos of yesterday playing at the fringes of my consciousness, I am intent now on this stark simplicity. The supple walls ripple and curve above me, spiraling toward the sky. Sometimes dry and smooth, sometimes seeping and slick, they shape themselves to my fingers. Up near the rim where the sun still strikes, the walls gleam in iridescent red; here below, in the filtered light, they envelope me in muted, soft garnet. Eventually, the canyon narrows so that I can no longer move forward. I stop. Arms wedged against sandstone, I am held fast. For a moment, the walls seem to pulse, to contract and relax in a dizzying play of color and light. The sandstone grazes my cheek. I turn, brush it with my lips, and, in the release of a hundred inhibitions, with my tongue. I have come here to taste this skin.

Where am I? What wildness is this? This is a different chaos; here there are no edges. Skin against skin, I can find no boundaries. Whose pulsing center is this? What is inside? Who is outside? Who am I now?

My body, awakened and eager, opens to this passion, receives this primal knowledge. Held fast, I let go.

ON THE LIP OF THE
RIO GRANDE GORGE

Patricia Wellingham-Jones

*e*ach step deliberate
on the skin of the earth, we pick our way
across a plateau strewn with wildflowers and bones.

We hang on the canyon's edge, toes crimp in our shoes.
Churning boulders boom far beneath our feet.
Snowmelt tumbles through the slash in the earth.

A hawk swoops past our faces
and down, spirals on an updraft with a scream,
flings himself out of rock wall into blue sky.

Head spinning, I sink to my haunches,
then stretch out on my belly, head over the rim,
feel the stream roar through my bones.

SONGS OF THE PLAINS

Linda Joy Myers

The landscape of my childhood—the grand sweeping prairies of Oklahoma with azure skies that go on forever and a muscular wind pushing at my body—is alive in me always, even though I have lived for years in California. When I write about Oklahoma, I sometimes wonder if the landscape of my heart is real. Does it really look so grand? Is it as huge as I remember? Does the wheat ripple as it once did, or has my long time away from the landscape polished it in my mind?

Last June was my fortieth high school reunion. I had decided months in advance to go, praying that I would be gifted, for the first time since leaving Oklahoma in 1965, with the sight of the wheat sweeping in golden waves of grain as it does in the lyrics of "America the Beautiful."

Ten years before, I had gone to Oklahoma. It was May, and I needed to see that wheat, to experience the landscape that once fed my soul. But the winter was long that year, and the wheat was short and green in May, nothing like the dream in my mind. I stood beside open wheat fields and grieved the loss of my childhood, the grandmother who raised me, and the mother who never claimed me to her heart. Most of all, I ached to see the wheat that used to sweep me into ecstasy as the full moon rose overhead. I wondered if I had made it all up, a landscape created by a child who needed to be comforted by something beautiful.

For my reunion trip, I use the Internet to find out if I will arrive at the right time, after the wheat has grown to maturity but before the harvest. I Google "wheat harvest in Oklahoma and Kansas" and find the last harvest dates and a prediction of the harvest dates for this year. I make alms and offer prayers, the passionate need to see this fleeting grace, this beauty, building in me.

I fly into Kansas City, intending to drive across Kansas on my way to Oklahoma. My route includes the roads and byways that my grandmother drove in her pink Nash Rambler on our way to see her mother in Iowa. Along the way, we'd stop for sodas and malted milks, and, for the sake of my education, visit the historical monuments on our route. Gram would tell me about the Great Plains, how the pioneers crossed in covered wagons, about the James Gang from Missouri, about the trains that changed everything. In Coffeyville, Kansas, where the Dalton Gang was captured, we stayed at a hotel where cowboys must have ambled up to the bar for a beer. It was easy to imagine the Wild West, for symbols of it were everywhere—the neon Big Chief sign creaking in the wind at a gas station, the Ponca Motel, the Cherokee Theatre, the Kiowa Inn. We unfolded from the car to read signs telling us about the Arkansas River, the Missouri, the Mississippi. And then, as the fifties came to a close, we were diverted from the two lane highways because of the construction of the freeway. Our kind of trip—one that took three days through small dusty towns, through a history of an America that still could be seen and touched—would be lost to travelers on this grand new highway.

In Kansas City, I pick up my rental car and turn back the clock to my childhood. Beethoven's Third Symphony is playing as I drive through Wichita, where I once lived with my grandmother. I wonder if I could find where we once lived, wonder if my memories of that house are accurate, but I am eager to see if the wheat is waiting for me and find Interstate 35 instead. On the Interstate, I could drive all the way to Enid, Oklahoma, where Gram and I moved when I was seven. I almost miss the Highway 81 exit, shown only by a small note on an interstate sign. At an old-fashioned diner, I stop for a chocolate milkshake and toast my grandmother. *For you, Gram. For you.*

I was twelve years old the last time I traveled Highway 81, but the images of Burma Shave signs and roads ending at a grain elevator on the horizon are as real to me as my own changing face. Before me lie small rolling hillocks covered with gold. I catch my breath. Is the wheat cut, or does it still sway in the wind? I can't tell yet. Then I see golden puffs of dust and come upon a combine cutting the wheat, the field half shorn. I can hardly see the wheat because it is so short.

I drive on until I find an unfenced, unharvested field. Stopping the car, I get out, step across the ditch and inhale the delicious scent of dry wheat. I fling myself into it, caressing it, tears in my eyes. But this wheat comes to my ankles, not my thighs. It waves in the wind, but I can see the ripple only by hunkering down, desperate to recreate my memory of the wheat enveloping me whole, the field becoming my world. The red dirt that I remember is a brilliant copper, sifting over my feet and legs. I rub it in greedily, savoring everything. The field seems to have brought me back to something essential within myself.

After such shameless behavior, I drive on, thinking how different I am from the girl who took trips down this road, how much the world has changed. It is too silent. There are no trucks, and almost no traffic. But as the land flattens out, everything I have come for appears before my eyes.

At the end of the road, where the shimmering highway meets the horizon, the white monolith of a grain elevator rises in the distance. Golden fields, still unshorn, surround me, swirling and swaying. Puffs of white clouds are perfect in an azure sky that matches my dreams; and the wind, the delicious wind that I have missed so much, pushes at my body as it always did, whispering to me that I am still its daughter, that I belong here even if everyone else is gone. This is my place and my home, this grand prairie, this gold and azure world.

VIEW FROM A HOT AIR BALLOON

Mary E. Young

I came kicking and screaming to Arizona, transferred by an employer to a place I envisioned as hot and desolate. There were rattlesnakes everywhere, I was sure, and I didn't ride a horse. But my employer needed me in Phoenix, and it was a good job, so off I went.

I arrived in May in an unair-conditioned car with only a few days to find a place to live in a city completely unfamiliar to me. I gagged the first night when I stepped outside my apartment at ten p.m. for a breath of cool air only to be smacked in the face by a temperature that seemed more like midday. Covering the steering wheel and looking for parking places that mitigated the unrelenting sun were skills I had yet to learn.

I had been in Phoenix for several years and had never left the confines of developed areas. I had seen the stories on the evening news of people who had gone to hunt rocks or walk in the desert and succumbed to the extremes of daytime heat or nighttime cold. I wasn't sure I even wanted to make the drive up the Interstate to Flagstaff lest my car break down and I end up like one of these.

But then I was introduced to hot air ballooning.

A friend invited me on a chase crew one Christmas weekend. We were to meet our balloon pilot and a few others a half-hour before dawn. Shapes of saguaros and palo verde melded with the darkness as we drove away from the lights of the sleeping city. We gathered in an open field far from any structures at what I would learn to call oh-dawn-thirty. Introductions were traded in the glare of truck headlights, and we were given our assignments to push, pull, hold, and drag things. It didn't make much sense to me, but I did as instructed. A ruffle of sunlight etching the horizon, our balloon and five others lifted gently into the air. We—the chase crew—climbed into the truck and bumped along the back roads, casting eyes to the sky to make sure we were never far from our balloon. An hour later, the balloon was back on the ground, and we pushed, pulled, and dragged some more until all the equipment was stowed on the trailer. The sun on our faces was warm, the air was peaceful, and the desert smelled sweet with the dampness of a light rain that had fallen during the night. We were rewarded for our work with a glass of champagne.

I was hooked. Each succeeding flight enhanced my enjoyment of the tranquility and beauty of the desert, a terrain that I had once viewed as hostile and impervious. In spring, lemony yellow and rich magenta blossoms erupted on prickly pear cactus and palo verde trees. Saguaros were crested with milky white blossoms and cactus wrens burrowed inside to build nests. The hum of traffic was barely audible and the landscape that once frightened me became a second home.

I would soon earn my commercial pilot's license, and over the next twenty-plus years I would own three balloons: Papillon, Quo Vadis, and Stardust. While I would enjoy beautiful flights over little ancient villages in France, lush meadows in England, and open plains in Australia, no experience ever compared to the gentle flights over the deserts of home or the pleasure of introducing others to this land I had come to love. Drifting lazily barely above the tops of the bushes—we call it contour flying, but it's really showing off—gave us a unique view of jackrabbits, lizards, coyotes, and even an occasional deer or javelina as they chased each other or foraged for breakfast.

Memorable events come to mind, like the five-year-old boy and his father with whom I flew low over the ground, hoping to show the boy some of the wildlife. As luck would have it, none appeared.

"I thought we were going to fly way high up in the sky," he pouted.

I gave a blast of heat to the balloon, and we climbed over a nearby hill.

"Look," I said. "We're taller than the mountain."

"Oh," he said. Then: "Dad, can I hold your hand?"

No one flying over the flatlands of Iowa ever had that experience.

And then there were the passengers from New Jersey who were visiting the Valley of the Sun for spring break with their kids. They showed up for their flight dressed in tennis whites, unaware of what the dust of the desert does to white or what scrub brush and cactus would do to their bare legs. They seemed to have as much interest in their flight as they would have in a cross-country bus ride. I pointed out wildlife, the downtown skyscrapers ten miles away, and the general aviation airport where students learned to fly. They were unmoved. They talked about what they would do when the flight was over.

Determined to give them an experience to remember, I began to climb. One thousand, two thousand, three thousand feet. They didn't notice. At four thousand feet above the desert floor, and on a day as clear as innocence, I could see the snow-capped San Francisco Peaks in Flagstaff, a hundred and fifty miles away. I pointed the mountains out to them, and they stopped babbling. New Jersey did not contain the dichotomy of desert and ski slope.

But far and away, the most spectacular, soul-stirring flying any-where in the world is in Monument Valley. Together with the Grand Canyon, its majestic terra cotta monoliths are the ultimate symbol of the unique beauty and grandeur of the American Southwest.

It's quite difficult to obtain permission from the Navajo who own Monument Valley to take balloons there, but over the years, my crew and I have occasionally been able to do so. With no lights on the floor of the valley, the drive down to the bottom is slow and tricky before dawn. So we have developed a ritual that not only protects us from wandering off the road into the soft sand, but also creates a nearly spiritual atmosphere for our morning's launch. A half-hour before sunrise, gathered at the top of the hill, we listen to a tape of sacred Indian flute songs as we watch the sun push back the dark sky. For a group of loquacious balloonists, these few moments are as silent as any we know. It is a silence that joins us to the morning, that blesses us on safe flights, and reminds us of the power and the beauty of the land we are about to enter.

Typically, the winds in Monument Valley are light, eddying around the rock formations and allowing a view that few have the privilege of seeing. At the Three Sisters, hawks and wrens build nests far away from earth-bound predators. Scrawny scrub brush clings to the side of The Mitten, seemingly with no soil in which to sink their roots but eking out an existence nonetheless. Atop the sacred Rain God Mesa the swirling rock looks as though it had been liquid once, spin-ning in a maelstrom before solidifying into formations. One year we sprinkled the cremated remains of a balloonist on the sacred mesa. Tempting as it is to land there for a photo op, we have been warned that doing so will get us permanently expelled.

As predictable as the weather is in Arizona, there are times when a low-pressure system brings surprises. A calm morning and easy launch have quickly turned into a forty-mile-an-hour flight and subsequent high-wind landing in which the balloon drags on its side until the pilot can get it deflated. There was the morning when fourteen of us launched under a thin layer of clouds that deteriorated into rain and hail mid-flight. Eggs Benedict and champagne in front of a roaring fire back home persuaded the crew to return for the next weekend's flight. Those rare circumstances imbued me with a healthy respect for nature's vagaries and whims.

I stopped flying a couple of years ago, changing life demands limiting the time available for it. But I still love the open desert, particularly in the early morning. I take a book and a sandwich out away from town, intending to find some peace and solitude. But the book often lies unopened as I breathe in the dry air, dusty now after years of drought. The blossoms and wildlife are sparse, nature's response to below-average rainfall for seven years. Still, the desert has its own beauty, its own peace that reaches to the soul in a way the roar of a waterfall or the shushing of snow skis never can.

SHE COULD

Liza Porter

*T*he sun sets so damned slow
in this desert, from the moment
it hides behind the horizon

all the way through the red
and orange, the deep gray
to the last light of day,

a woman might have just enough time
to change her whole life.
She could be smoking on the front porch

as the last hot rays paint her face
from beyond the hills. In the yellow
afterglow, she could crush the butt out

in the gravel and walk silently inside.
She could pack a bag or write a note.
Or not. And when the darkness drifts

like waves on the warm evening breeze
she could pick up her keys
from the kitchen table and see

a single planet shining
through the western window.
She could climb behind the wheel

in the black howl of night
and turn that engine wide over.
She could go. West or north—
any direction at all—
toward that pale, teasing light.

RIDING THE RIVER HOME

Susan J. Tweit

*W*hen the call came, it seemed like a good idea: Would I like to join a women's Colorado River trip, as the trip's naturalist and writer? Having proved myself as a field ecologist studying griz- zly bears and wildfires, working an all-expenses-paid river trip sounded like a vacation. Besides, I was homesick. After three years in the desert heat, I longed for the Colorado Plateau's cool nights, red rock cliffs, and pungent sagebrush.

When I got off the plane at Grand Junction, the light was clear and bright and the chatter of magpies was familiar. I rec- ognized the polka-dot patterns of the sparse desert vegetation and could name the shale layers striping the nearby cliffs: it felt like home. This is going to be a good trip, I said to myself.

In the small airport terminal, waiting for the trip van, I scrounged a candy bar and a bottle of juice from a vending machine and chatted with other trip participants. In the van humming west on the Interstate, the open windows made con- versation difficult, so I retreated into silence and watched the sagebrush desert roll past. I spotted a golden eagle soaring in lazy circles high overhead and pointed it out to my seatmates. A good sign, I thought.

That night, bedded down outside an old ranch house not far from the river put-in, I lay awake, immersed in familiar smells and sounds: the sour-milk odor of cottonwood sap and the tur- pentine fragrance of big sagebrush; the patter of mice suddenly stilled by an owl's low call; the almost inaudible chatter of bats navigating under a dazzling canopy of stars. I drifted off to sleep thinking of my home in Wyoming, floating back to it on my dreams.

We reached the river put-in at mid-morning. We bumped down a short gravel road, and there was the Colorado, sixty feet wide, moving fast, and muddy brown. I swallowed, and gulped water from my bottle to wet a suddenly dry throat.

We parked and unloaded our personal gear. As the guides began to pack the rafts, I gathered the trip participants in a slender wedge of shade under a cottonwood tree. The river flowed in front of us, its current sinuous and powerful. I launched into my talk, drawing a map in the air to trace the river's path from its headwaters in the snowy peaks of the Rockies, cutting through the layers of the Colorado Plateau, heading for the Gulf of California. As I spoke, the water hissed and gurgled. The stream named Colorado for the sediment that tints it (in Spanish, "red" or "colored") was not only visible but audible. I shivered, and segued into a discussion of the endemic fish that haunt its turbid waters: Colorado pike minnow growing to six feet on a diet of minuscule algae; razorback suckers, their blade-thin bodies designed to slice through the roiling current of spring flows. The women peppered me with questions. I felt good. I was on a roll.

Until I stepped into a raft and felt it sway gently underfoot as it rode the skin of the river like a water skater. Then I remembered why this trip couldn't be easy: I am no river girl. Whitewater terrifies me; drowning is the worst death I can imagine. What are you doing? I asked myself in a panic. Why did you agree to this trip? Because you were homesick, I reminded myself as our two rafts shoved away from solid ground. Now, buck up and at least pretend to belong.

I pointed out the upward slant in the orange sandstone cliffs. I talked about the geology of the plateau and the way the river has cut through the thick layers of rock to form the sweeping canyons we would navigate. As I spoke, I began to relax. Then we bumped across a riffle as we swept around a bend into the first canyon—not enough turbulence to call whitewater, but enough to unnerve me. I gripped the rope on the gunwale and my words trailed off.

We stopped for lunch on a small alluvial fan at the foot of a side canyon. I wolfed a sandwich and read to the group while they ate, my voice singing out above the gurgle and rush of the river, above the twittering of swifts and the trills of canyon wrens. I can do this, I thought. Then, as we loaded up for the afternoon's float, the leader announced that the duckies, the two inflatable solo kayaks, were ready. The participants clamored for chances, but I remained silent. The leader eyed me narrowly, but said nothing. I swung onto her raft and settled in, my hat pulled low over my eyes.

It was a lazy afternoon, the water calm as the river swung around wide curves between high canyon walls. As the temperature warmed, the women stripped down and began working on their river-girl tans—except for me. I'm allergic to the sun. Feeling conspicuous in my long-sleeved shirt and pants, I began talking. I pointed out mud-formed swallow condos plastered to the sandstone overhangs. I imitated magpies' chatter and discussed their intelligence and the way their brain functions are related to their omnivorous diet. I explained why swifts mate in mid-air and muskrats build their burrow entrance underwater. The river's leisurely tempo smoothed the singsong rhythm of my voice and I relaxed. This is not so bad, I thought.

That night's camp was in a wide stretch of canyon where the river flowed past a generous sandy bench. I retired to the shade of a beach umbrella to write notes for my evening talk. I didn't have to think hard to come up with a topic: ants. They trailed in purposeful lines across the soil, the grass stems, the tree trunks. They were harvester ants, I explained to the group; their mission was not, as it seemed, to harass us, but to gather the seeds produced by the wildflowers and grasses that had sprouted during an unusually wet spring. But knowing that their activities would enrich both the soil and the plant community did not make it any more comfortable to sleep on the ground they claimed. The next morning, tired and disheveled from ejecting ants from our sleeping bags, our food, and our camp toilet, we named the place "Ant Canyon." For the first time, I was happy to clamber aboard a raft and head out on the river.

It was another mellow day, drifting in the two rafts, sometimes so close that I could tell the whole group stories of red-spotted toads and desert trumpets, sometimes moving apart into private conversations about love and loss and landscape. I felt a part of the group, and forgot my fear. But that night, we pulled into a campsite on a stretch of rough water where the river dropped over a layer of black schist, rock rendered so hard by eons of heat and pressure that it resisted the sediment-laden water's erosive bite. The two solo paddlers miscalculated the approach to the beach. One flipped. The other overshot and was swept around the bend and out of sight. After a long moment, the first paddler surfaced and I let out the breath I hadn't known I was holding. She was hauled out and swathed in towels and hugs. The lead boatwoman slid into her kayak and set off after the vanished paddler. By the time she and her charge reached shore, I was helping to unload the rafts.

Once everyone was safe on land, I relaxed. After dinner, I read to the women while the sun set behind red cliffs and light drained from the sky. Then the leader took us up the arroyo to an expanse of the same black schist that surfaced in the river. But this outcrop was high and dry, polished by long-vanished floods into flat, silky slabs that retained the day's heat. Supine as lizards, we stretched out on the warm rocks while the stars brightened overhead. I pointed out Venus, brilliant in the west, and then began to identify the constellations and tell their stories. We lay there until it was almost too dark to make our way back to camp.

The next morning's float was a slow traverse between curving sandstone canyon walls. I talked about the cottonwoods and recited the names of the species they nurture. I pointed to the salt cedar thickets and told how this alien species competes with native plants, sucking up water and dropping a toxic rain of salty leaves that poisons the soil. As we swept into the final grand curve, we spotted the flood-planted cottonwood saplings poking through a thicket of salt cedar alongside of the river. The women cheered. I glowed: they understood.

Then we rounded the curve, and the channel narrowed to a slot bounded by slick, river-polished walls. The river's voice changed from a hiss and murmur to a splashing rumble. Just above the first rapids, we pulled out onto a small gray-sand beach. But when the group boarded the rafts after lunch, I hung back, quiet. No one noticed my hesitation except the trip leader. Chilled by her cool stare, I gripped the gunwale rope tightly as we bumped through the series of small drops. Then the boatwomen rowed through the churning tailwater to a knob protruding from the sheer canyon wall to tie up for a break. As I looped the rope over the rock to secure us, a swirling whirl of errant current slammed the second raft into the first, compressing both against the wall and nearly twisting us into the river. The river pulsed beneath the skin of our rafts, the milky brown water splashing and slurping like a live thing. After the rafts steadied, the trip leader pulled out a book of short stories and read to us about women afraid of nothing.

I slept uneasily that night, waking often to watch the stars' slow progress across the black sky. In the morning, I led the women in our usual yoga routine, followed by a prayer to greet the day. I ad-libbed the ending, adding my hope that I wouldn't disgrace myself in the run through the rapids. Everyone chuckled, but I wasn't kidding. We dawdled over breakfast and our final morning's chores, and headed downriver late.

My memories of that final run are fragmented: I recall the chaotic roar of water pounding rock and the sucking sound of a large whirl-pool, its diameter greater than the length of our raft. I remember the raft bucking under my feet as I struggled to bail faster than the river poured in, the lurch of my heart as we slid toward towering standing waves, the icy chill of the water on my skin, the metallic smell of the silt-laden spray.

Then it was over, and we floated out of the churning tail currents onto calmer waters. Just before the last bend in the canyon, our boat-women pulled onto a narrow beach. We climbed the cliffs for a group photo, arms wrapped around each other. I stand out among the smiling bronzed women: I am not the tallest, but I am the palest.

That photo makes it clear that I'll never be a river girl. What it doesn't reveal, however, is what I learned on that trip down the Colorado. As we rode the river into the quiet of the canyons, as I told story after story about that slickrock landscape, I remembered what it is to be at home in a place, to belong in a way that touches your very cells. The river's lessons were written in the dazzle of stars overhead, the hiss of water, the warmth of silky black schist, the trilling of canyon wrens, the curving shapes of red rock canyon walls, and the metallic taste of my unceasing dread. They reminded me of the connection between place and the human heart, of the necessity of belonging to the whole landscape, to the parts we love and the parts we fear. They reminded me that home is not an abstract concept, but a real and often problematic place.

I'll never be a river girl, and I no longer mind. I was afraid, and I rode the river. And I came away with a truer understanding of who I am, a renewed sense of where I belong. In a very real sense, I rode the river home.

FOUR MEDITATIONS ON THE COLORADO RIVER

Denise Chávez

CROSSING BITTER CREEK

Through the trip I am struck by the similarities between this river road and the road I have just left behind. The name "Bitter Creek" is an all-too-real reminder of the terrible harsh road from Flagstaff to Page, Arizona, in the heart of the Navajo Reservation. The road is full of *descansos,* Spanish for resting place. These death markers pinpoint the spot where people have died by the side of the road. Any number of metal crosses line what should be fine open stretches of land.

The river, too, can be violent. I feel surrounded by spirits, some happy, some sad. There is torment here, and bloodshed. Sometimes I feel entombed in rock. Sometimes I feel as free as the ravens, those ancestral messengers who seek me out. To the others in our group, ravens are merely scavengers, here to pick up the scraps we leave behind.

A LITANY FOR SENTIENT BEINGS

Blue sky. Bless me. Wall of rock. Bless me. Animal friends: Red Ant, Blue Heron, Bighorn Sheep, Chuckwalla. Bless me. Plant friends: Desert Willow, Brittlebush, Snakeweed. Bless me. This is your home. I am merely a visitor. Bless me, be gentle with me. Let me pass through your beauty, unharmed.

LA RAZA

I may be the only Mexican rafting the Colorado. Everyone else is at Disneyland or in Las Vegas. I ask Wade and Doug, another guide, how many ethnic people raft the canyon. Few, they both say. I wonder why? Is it the cost? It *is* prohibitive, but not for all. It's more than that.

We are a people who want comfort, manageable thrills, self-made happiness. Our blood runs too deeply down the muddy river. We were and are its slaves, its laborers, its workers, its drones. The memory of hardship is still too much to bear. Our ancestors tried to conquer this river, but they turned back too soon. On land the Spanish ruled, but in this hallowed place they met their match. Conquistador Row is impressive, its high walls a temple to the power of nature. Inside these sheer cliffs every man and woman is insignificant, how much more so those already trampled by the road. Better to go to Las Vegas where at least the odds are higher, where we can take a chance and be assured a spin.

MOUNTAIN. SOLID

There is a Buddhist meditation gatha that goes, "Mountain. Solid."

I watch the seemingly never-ending spectacle of rock pass. Striated earth pushed up, broken down. What is time? One day or a billion years?

Protect me, show me your wonder, instruct me in your ways that I may learn to better serve. Help me to release fear.

Mother, be gentle with me. I've gone over the edge.

I'm in the heart of the canyon, at last.

Legs crossed, I relax. I am beginning to understand the river's flow.

SUNRISE

Lianne Elizabeth Mercer

In this canyon
where prayers of centuries
rush like wind,
I greet the dawn.
In the wash,
water sings
its careful song
over old footsteps.

Cottonwood and Russian olive trees
exhale green light.
The sun begins its slow smile
down red canyon walls.
Broken trees raise arthritic limbs
in supplication.

From the canyon wall,
benevolent eyes remind me
I am loved by this earth—
my mother. Her breath
blesses me.

Robins cannot keep quiet.
Nor can I. In motions of
an old dance, my feet move
like silk across red sand,
my hands posture gratitude.
I bow to an orange and black beetle
who crawls my prayer
into the bones of the canyon.

WORKING ON THE TEQUESQUITE

Diane Ackerman

*D*riving west of Amarillo, I notice cattle grazing along the runway, and endless, flat, wheat-gold fields over which the blue sky pales away to white. In the background are machines, factories, twentieth-century artifacts, but in the foreground five or six horses munch sagebrush and mesquite, a windmill whirls swiftly in the breeze, and, everywhere, barbed wire fences stretch to the horizon. What with the scrub brush, the long trenchy culverts, and a glaring sun that seems to reduce things to their structural minimums (horses look like kindergarten drawings: a few rough dark lines), I feel as if I'm watching *The Cisco Kid,* or *The Westerners,* as if the Saturday mornings of my childhood, full of black-hatted desperadoes, sexless cowboys, and universal values free from any extenuating circumstance or compromise, have come back to haunt me. I pass a road sign announcing SPUR 48 by which they undoubtedly mean spur route, not an exhortation to a ranch hand, but I find it odd in this country where every other store and gas station seems to be named Hi-Plains Grocery or Panhandle Dry Cleaners, and recall how the Budget Rent-a-Car girl had shown up in a pair of snug jogging shorts, halter top, and Dr. Scholl sandals. The radio station she tapped rhythm to on the steering wheel played locally flavored rock songs like "Southern Nights" and "Marie from Amarillo" (obviously a favorite) between advertisements for fast-food chains and car franchises. Amarillo she had pronounced in a drawl as "Emerald."

The little settlements all look temporary, as if they have been thrown up carelessly in the night, and won't be needed long. Even the large ranch houses, all of which are one-story, seem to suggest a contractor who, going bankrupt, never quite got round to adding on the second floor. Already, the air is 95° F, but so dry that I'm comfortable in my longsleeved sweater whose rainbow stripes look like the rind of some exotic fruit.

Casting long, subdued shadows, the sun sparkles on aluminum siding or chrome bumpers, and makes the dark, freshly ploughed fields, crusted with buff tones, bake like an enormous mincemeat pie. Never have I seen so many long golden fields.

Between two mesas, I come upon a road sign that warns of DANGEROUS CROSSWINDS, and, with visions of being swept up in a funnel, I slow the car to a discreet 50 m.p.h. The clay soil is salmon colored, Martian, but the woolliness of the scrub brush and the weathered, wind-tormented trees remind me less of the *Viking* photos of Mars than of Israel. All along Highway 40, flat-topped mesas pour into one another, now like breaking waves, and now like a Sphinx inching forward on its stone haunches. Another road sign reads PLEASE HELP PREVENT GRASS FIRE. And right next to it: KEEP YOUR CURVES. EAT MORE TEXAS BEEF. Far away—perhaps five miles, or perhaps a hundred—I see a string of mesas. Up north I'd be looking at the sharp, interfolding Alleghenies; here the mountains look lopped off, planed flat for some as-yet-undisclosed masonry.

What a cruel, harsh country this must have been for the turn-of-the-century cowboy; it sprawls unbroken through inedible scrub, cracked dirt, and ever-whitening grass. The sunlight is so bright it makes objects dance in a carnival vapor, which is perhaps why police cars, every so often, lurk in the cool shade of the occasional tree. The blue sky is everywhere, and, for a moment, I feel as if I'm driving into the ocean. Tufted as it is with spiky cacti and yucca plants and low kelpy sagebrush, the open prairie looks for all the world like a sea bottom. There are no fish on this reef, and the air is so dry it peppers the throat, but the shape of landfall is oceanic.

By the time I reach the tiny settlement called Logan, I've had a long lush drink of the prairie. I stop in at one of the town's two bars to pick up a bottle of Jack Daniels for my hosts, the Mitchells. The woman bartender wipes a thick layer of dust from the shoulders of the bottle, and quips that I'm getting a little New Mexico real estate for free. Outside, things look stark in the white-hot early morning sun. Even the crows look blacker. The subtle blends of talcy color along the mesas are devastatingly beautiful, a pastel apparition. Like Impressionist paintings, subtle-hued and vapory, they line the valley, the turbulence of whose landscape is heart-revving. Here and there, in a dried-up riverbed, a sudden luminous pool of water lies like a piece of slate. *A piece of water* I recall from Clint Eastwood westerns. Once, in New York City's Museum of Modern Art, I saw an exhibition of American Romanticism, and was struck by the rougey transparencies of light, which I assumed were a stylistic quirk. Now I understand what captivated those painters, and how doggedly realistic their lightings were. On my left, a cherry-red mesa rises steeply. The landscape is so intense and dramatic, it seizes you from moment to moment, grabs you by the lapels, shakes you hard, and says, "Wake up! Live!" And, in that earthly seizure, land becomes as eternal and persuasive as any abstraction.

[DIANE SPENT SEVERAL SEASONS on the Tequesquite, participating in the life of the ranch. "Working on the Tequesquite," she wrote in the introduction to the 2002 edition of her book, *Twilight of the Tenderfoot,* "I felt freed from all the mortgages on my spirit, all the professional demands, all the expectations of me (particularly my own), and there were times when I thought maybe I could live such a life forever." But her stays at the ranch always came to an end too soon.—*Eds.*]

HOW CAN I BE LEAVING, I wonder . . . as I drive my low-bellied Ford slowly along the main road to Highway 39, taking care not to lose any of the car's delicate underside in a pothole so far from fixability. *Leaving* is unthinkable . . . I feel too much at home in this desert caravansary, where the air hangs windless, like wash on a line, and the mind empties of all excess paraphernalia. Civilization doesn't exactly disappear; it just seems beside the point. Which day is which I began to forget early in my stay, when the sun generalized everything from toad to dust pellet. Daytime was bright hot, and evening dark hot. So clearly it is daytime as I crawl along the dirt road in a state of shock. How can I leave this ranch family I've grown so fond of . . .

Like a runaway, I pause at the main gate to fix the scene: sprawling flatlands the color of chamois broken by outcroppings of windmills, cactus, and cattle, pastel mesas striped like Jovian planets, and, at the far edge of vision, a tiny clutch of buildings only a native could define by its combination of angles. In one of the buildings, a little girl will still be asleep, in another will be the watch I left accidentally, and in another Juanita will just be starting a low fire under the morning's bacon grease.

INDIAN HOT SPRINGS

Pat Ellis Taylor

I learned several years ago how to find my way to Indian Hot Springs from off the highway at Sierra Blanca and into the rolling desert through a maze of dirt roads, following a path marked by No Trespassing signs. Jewel Babb told me how to get there the first time, what forks in the roads to take, what cattle guards to count. There is only one small wooden sign marked Indian Hot Springs along the whole 31-mile route which twists up and down hills and arroyos, the deep parts of the road sometimes washed out with rocks and the high parts hanging off cliffs and winding up higher from hills into mountains just at the point where two ranges meet—the Eagles and Quitmans. Then in a crescendo of mad rock slides and fast looping dips and turns through what has become walls of boulders and when it seems like any brave vehicle I have ever taken is about to either burn out its brakes or its clutch or blow tires from sheer rubber soreness, there comes a curve and a last rock outcropping, and when I look down over the ledge to the south, a valley will be stretched out below me. The Rio Grande will be running through the middle of it like a brown snake unless it is late afternoon at which time it runs silver. And if it is a bright blue-skied day, as the desert days generally are, my eye will be dazzled by the sun shattering beams over a crystallized plain which lies like a pool on this side of the river, its surface sparkling from a mineral deposit crust—an eye in the desert, fringed with green trailing off from it north and south with trees and alfalfa fields and cows grazing in pastures. In the center of the white plain lies a white hotel surrounded by small white cabins, and then across the river nestled in trees are glimpses of the small houses of a Mexican village, Ojo Caliente, its outlying houses built up into hills which rise into the first of seven mountain ranges. The first one is close enough to see its arroyos and sliding strata wrinkling brown and black in their crevices, each range less distinct as the distance increases, the far-thest mountains appearing at sunset almost transparently blue-white like fine china as if the sun is shining through them on the other side. Then I proceed down the road and onto the hotel grounds, fenced off with white rock driveways winding over the white plain like a lawn, where the hot springs well up into little pools, some marked with white walls, others with small clusters of salt cedar.

The hotel and its cabins have always been deserted the times I have visited except for an occasional ranch hand who would come to check out who had driven in unannounced. But the spirit of the Lock on the Door had been so strong that I had never been able to stay for more than a couple of hours, slipping into one of the pools like a criminal, as if I had crawled through the bathroom win-dow of some rich man's house. And in fact a whole string of very wealthy people have owned the place, the best known of them being H. L. Hunt, claimed by many when he was alive to be the richest man in the world. Since Hunt died, I had heard of other owners including a Houston man named Joe Brown, whose asking price for the two-thousand-acre ranch the hot springs sit on was two million dollars. Prospective visitors to Indian Hot Springs first applied, then were screened, and if accepted the hotel put them up at thirty dollars a day—not unreasonable compared to the Sheraton Motor Inn—but out of the question for someone like me. But congressmen came, brigadier generals, movie stars. And then for the past several years engineers were supposed to be set up on the grounds, and it was somewhat mysterious what they were doing there, something to do with the river, but there were fences reported and heavy equipment and intensified signals to stay-the-hell-out.

So many times I dreamed about going to Indian Hot Springs! Liv-ing in Austin, languishing and dreaming while shelving books and hustling money, thinking about the mountains and the desert and its crystal eye. Business was hard and rents were high. Human rela-tionships were confusing. I myself was old fat slack and somewhat dazed trying to survive by running a marginal and/or terminal used bookstore while living in it . . .

Chuck had money, he was teaching freshman composition at the university, but his money was going to his own books and so what if there was no gas no good food which he didn't need any of, or bitchy me either, for that matter, living as he did in a part of the upstairs room blocked off for his study inside a cigar fog of bookish oblivion . . .

"Chuck I have to leave," I said. "I can't stay here anymore. If I stay here anymore everything you have ever associated with the actual me will be dead—there will be nothing that remains of the Pat you once enjoyed." I pinned my eyes to the back of my skull as I said this as an illustration.

"Well I wish you would stop talking about leaving and just leave," he said. "If you keep talking about leaving and not doing it you are going to make me very mad."

"Well I am going to leave this time," I said. I turned to the window.

"Just go," he said.

"I am going to go."

"Where are you going to go?"

And I said, "West Texas."

NATURAL BRIDGES

Laura Girardeau

*T*here comes a time when we
no longer walk the trail alone.
Slowly, imperceptibly,
there comes to live
in our hand another,
and suddenly it seems
it was always this way.

It is not always a hand,
but a found stone;
a feeling, finally
of blessed connection,
and things look just right
where they are:
a rock, a word, a touch,
just so.

And suddenly,
we are walking the trail together,
and there are no walls.
There is no holding back.
The call of the canyon wren
tumbles down slickrock
without hesitation.
The colors of afternoon rock
deepen to warm skin,
and the canyons marry us
to the world.

WRITING WEST

Nancy Mairs

*M*y crippled life began when I moved from Boston to Tucson. This pure coincidence split my history: there was once a whole youthful Nancy, who grew up in a gentle geography though a severe climate; then there was an aging Nancy, who limped and later stumbled and finally stopped walking altogether, in a milder climate but a formidable geography. Young, I ambled through New England's variegated terrain—bridle path, beach, brook—in all weathers with authentic, though largely sentimental, affection for the natural world, which seemed to me compassable and therefore hospitable. I have lived now for more than twenty years in a landscape too large for me, and getting larger as my physical condition deteriorates, the conventional West—land, lots of land, 'neath the starry skies above—and the conventional responses to it—exploration, exploitation—demanding a physical vigor I've never enjoyed here.

ABOVE ALL, the West is expansive: beneath an immense translucent hemisphere, sere plains stretching to snow-crowned ranges and beyond them the sweep of the earth's greatest ocean, a geography so overwhelmingly empty, even today, as to make one long to be everywhere at once. The terrain itself may account for the "rootlessness, mobility, and rugged individualism" that, in the common view, continue to characterize "western experience," a classic formulation I came across just in this week's reading. Although rootlessness and rugged individualism seem to possess less value for the women than the men writing today, everyone appears to agree upon mobility. A recent newspaper article has this: "Out here, you can still drive fast." The forerunner of driving fast was riding fast. Thus, the American condition: wandering. The urge to saddle your car and move quickly through time and space has resulted in that ancient national ritual, the road trip, and the sacred texts that have accompanied it. On your feet, on your horse, in your car, movement's the thing.

I am, as one particularly unfortunate (circum)locution would have it, mobility-impaired. I don't walk, I don't canter, I don't drive. I roll. Seated in a frame of black-painted aluminum with twelve-inch wheels in the back and eight-inch wheels in the front, steering with a joystick, under ideal conditions I can do 4.9 miles an hour around my neighborhood. If I want to go faster or farther, I roll onto a platform that, with the flip of a couple of switches, deposits me wheelchair and all in the back of my van, where whoever is driving ties me down before taking off. It's a good thing rugged individualism isn't high on my list of personal virtues, since I can't purchase even a can of soup or a pair of socks by myself.

Although I can move for short distances over grass or gravel, I'm pretty well confined to asphalt or cement. And let's face it, pavements are not an essentially western phenomenon. True, quite a few western writers (like the majority of western residents) live in cities, and some even write about the urban spectacle, but the West of our hearts remains untracked wilderness. Most of the West, therefore, lies beyond my range. I can travel into the countryside as far as a car will carry me, and after that I can only look. In some state and national parks, paved paths now wind from parking lots into gentle terrain, and this access is better than none at all. But the paths are, of necessity, short; I can't wander off if a blossom or an insect intrigues me (nor can plants or creatures be persuaded to come present themselves for scrutiny); and at the end I must always stop and look out into a landscape closed to me absolutely and forever. This is the quintessential western posture—gaze ever longing into the beyond—stripped of its attendant capacity to act out the eyes' desire.

There is much to be said for looking, and I've gotten good at it, maybe better than most people whose vigorous strides alter their perspective distractingly. But it is not adequate compensation. I know. Though never an athlete, I was once an enthusiastic walker, who could stop and look, as deeply as I liked, whenever I felt like it *and then move on*. I can no longer move on, and sometimes I think I will die of grief at the loss . . .

"Mobility" really was once a necessary element of life in the West. I could not have survived here as an Anasazi cliff dweller, a colonial settler at a mission or hacienda, a Mormon pioneer hauling my worldly goods to Utah in a handcart, a Bisbee miner's wife. I needed to wait for pavement, for cities—and not just any city, not Bisbee, for instance, or San Francisco or Seattle, but a city on a plain, in a valley, warm and dry, too, since my wheelchair doesn't sport an umbrella or snow tires. Such cities exist now, have existed for decades, among them my personal favorites, Tucson and Los Angeles. The high-rise concrete cliff dwellings of Century City are as authentically western as the stone cliff dwellings of Mesa Verde (in geographical terms, several hundred miles more so), only they have elevators instead of ladders, a difference that means the world to me.

So, I would argue, easy mobility, like rootlessness and rugged individualism, is no longer essential to the western experience. They are anachronisms that should be discarded from the way we imagine the West. But the danger is that in removing such strictures, I'll render "western" too indistinct to be meaningful, and I don't intend at all to suggest that the West contains nothing that peculiarly sets those of us who write in and about it apart from our scribbling cousins in Boston, Baltimore, and Baton Rouge. On the contrary, there is plenty peculiar about the place: more, in fact, than conventional critics deign to notice . . .

"NO, NOT *THAT* STORY," say a couple of editors who have asked me to write about how the West has shaped me when I send them these reflections on the difficulties I have encountered in claiming an identity as a chronicler of the West. "That's not at all what we have in mind." To clarify, they give me examples of what they do have in mind, pieces built around backwoodspersons and long reflective walks by the verges of isolated lakes, about the uses of firearms and childhood encounters with Indians; and I can tell that they want me to write a story essentially like other women's stories with the trifling but possibly intriguing difference that I happen to experience whatever befalls me at the height of those women's belt buckles.

But that's not the way disability works. It does not leave one precisely the same woman one would have been without it, only (in my case) shorter. It does not merely alter a few, or even a great many, details in a life story that otherwise conforms to basic narrative conventions: the adventure, the romance, the quest. Instead, it transforms the tale utterly, though often subtly, and these shifts in narrative tone and type arouse resistance in both the "author" and the "reader" of the outlandish plot.

These disparities have had their consequences, for me and for those who have shared my misshapen life, many of which were encapsulated several years ago when my husband, my daughter, and I made a pass through this overlarge landscape in what we recall, with no fondness whatsoever, as the Camper from Hell. Anne, just out of college, was soon to join the Peace Corps and spend a couple of years in Zaïre, and she wanted to travel in the Southwest before leaving it, perhaps for good. On expeditions in earlier years, we had wandered from campground to campground with an increasingly shabby but serviceable Eureka Space 10 tent, sleeping bags, and air mattresses; but although I was still able to walk short distances, and getting down on the ground was all too easy for me, getting me up again was a group production none of us looked forward to; and so we rented, as cheaply as possible, a camper with a kitchenette, beds, and a toilet.

In hindsight, "as cheaply as possible" turned out to be the falsest of economies. We didn't have any money—we've never had any money—but if we had it to do over again, George and I would probably take a second mortgage on the house rather than search out that dubious director of a rundown nursery school and rent his infernal camper for a week's tour of New Mexico. We should have been wary when the camper wasn't ready as promised; but, as Anne would no doubt be glad to attest, George and I have always been deficient in the wariness department.

We loaded hastily and left just a little behind schedule, which would turn out to be our condition throughout the trip, arriving at our first campground, in Alamogordo, well after dark. There we discovered that the water in the camper's tanks stank sulfurously and the mechanism for converting the dining benches into one of the beds was so broken that the bed could be created only with great wrenchings and swearings. These I could not participate in, but the least I could do was volunteer to sleep on the outcome, a mound of lumpen upholstery whose metal frame poked my back and hips no matter which way I twisted. Since I wasn't doing any driving, I didn't think George or Anne ought to spend their nights tossing about à la The Princess and the Pea.

At Carlsbad the next night, the pump for the sulfurous water, which had been working only sporadically, quit entirely. In the morning we found someone to replace the water pump, but we couldn't start out for Santa Fe until after lunch, too long a trip, it turned out, so that we had trouble locating our campground north of the city in the dark. In the mountains miles to the north of Taos the next night, George hit a tree in the dark and banged up the camper, though he resisted the urge to finish the damned thing off. In the morning it retaliated by refusing to start altogether, and George had to call the owner, who seemed eerily familiar with the problem and issued elaborate instructions involving many hands and feet and bits of paper.

All along, our primary object had been a return to a place Anne had loved ten years or more before, Chaco Canyon, which didn't look too far from Taos on the map. But of course maps don't show you ways of getting lost on the hills across which Los Alamos is scattered or roads so steep that the wheezing camper won't chug over ten miles an hour. The scenery was breathtaking, especially a huge empty green valley enclosed on every side by mountains up to ten thousand feet high . . . The trip provided endless exercises in problem-solving and sheer brute force: hunting for accessible parking spaces, toilets, walkways; hauling me and then the wheelchair out of the vehicle and later stowing us both again; and in between incessant pushing, tilting, swerving, pushing, pushing, pushing, pushing. No one could forget for more than an instant that I am a cripple. Of course, I could be parked and left, but then the leaver had to deal with feelings of guilt or loneliness or dread of returning to me and so was still not wholly free. Whatever we managed to do—and thanks to modifications of terrain or architecture, we often did a lot—was tinged with the kind of regret I had felt a few days earlier at Carlsbad Caverns, wishing we could have hiked in instead of plunging 750 feet straight down in an elevator. Still, most of the inside trail was wheelchair accessible, so I'd gotten to see a good bit . . .

We would reach Tucson, it turned out, in one piece and more or less speaking to each other. But first there were the miles and miles of washboard road into and then out of Chaco, over which the camper jittered and bucked, raising billows of choking dust, until we were dizzy and bruised. There was the primitive campground in Navajo, arrived at late of course, where George accidentally stuck the electrical cord into an unmarked 220 outlet (which shouldn't have been

there) and melted the plug, so that our final stop was suitably be-
nighted. We were limp with more than relief by the time we wound
through the Salt River Canyon, rounded the Catalinas, and dropped
into the Santa Cruz Valley we had left—could it have been?—only
seven days before.

At the time, I half wished that we had stayed there and seen to our
responsibilities rather than traipsing off to squander a lot of money
and our spirits as well. But I also knew that nothing is ever entirely
a waste. Visions of dunes carved against searing blue, of glassy cave
pools, of a mother pronghorn with her twins behind her, of the little earthen plaza at Tesuque Pueblo, of the gash in the earth's skin
carved by the Rio Grande outside Taos, of low mountains striated
with rose and lavender and sage, of a precipitous rock stairway
hacked a thousand years ago into a canyon wall: all would stay vivid
and cherishable forever. The camper we could hurriedly return to
its smarmy owner, pushing its memory back, down, behind these
lovelier images . . .

The tale of westward migration has always been premised on possibility: gold hidden in the next black hill, endlessly fertile soil for
wheat and grapes and artichokes, vast tracts of rangeland for sleek,
white-faced cattle, and eighteen holes of golf every day of the sun-
drenched year. I moved into a West of impossibility. The East would
be just as forbidding today, but that doesn't matter, since the East
I have in mind is the land of childhood and perfectly inaccessible
anyway. I moved into an adulthood that I, like other dreamers of
the conventional West, could never have conceived: the strangest of
lands. Nevertheless, though instead of loping on Old Paint across the
lone prairie, I may be heading my Quickie P100 on down the alley
and out to Bentley's for an iced cappuccino, it's an honest-to-God
western adventure I'm having here.

CLOSING

Mary Sojourner

I am in the throat of the Turtle Mountains Wilderness, crouched at the base of a basalt cliff, studying a delicate braid of tracks in the sand at the bottom of the narrow wash below. I will never make it into the heart of the Turtles. I am fifty-eight, a big woman, and one of my lumbar spinal discs is flatter than it should be—too many canyon switchbacks and too much midnight city concrete, too many rapids run, too much, and never enough, boulder hopping.

The truck is parked where the roads end. If I stand up, I'll see the windshield catch the last Mojave light. Lace agate glitters and glows on the pale earth, white chalcedony roses, puddles of mineral cream. To the east, just beyond a portal that opens like a deep breath in the black rock, lies the unisex bathroom of a gang of coyotes. At the edge of a tidy deposit of scat is one scarlet flower, blossoms like bells holding light. I imagine how the flower seems to burn, as I imagine what lies west, downstream, in a streambed through which water must pour—I see the pebble curves that tell me eddies have swirled here, twice a year, once, seen only by what lives here. I would love to see that—flash floods no wider than my arm, thunder chaos of brittlebush, chalcedony, and scat.

And I am grateful to see what lies around me. Now. Here. A half-mile from the truck, a half-mile that took me an hour to cross, down into little arroyos, picking my way between fire-rock boulders, stopping to pick up a shard of crystal, an agate rose. I knew better than to bend over, but I did it anyway. I'll pay for it later with pain in my back. How could I not touch this lover, this fierce Mojave earth softened by winter light? How could I not, as I once lay in the perfect arms of the perfect lover who perfectly would leave, breathe in the miracle of being here, being *here,* only *now?*

The Buddhists tell us that joy lies in limitation. We Americans are taught the opposite. *More is better. Go for it all.* I move away from the cliff and look up at the ragged cobalt mountains. I want to *go* up, into the high saddle, into what leads into mystery, up where I can look out and see forever. I want more. I want it all.

My back holds me here. Some roads are closed to me forever. I consider that I have become the person whom the road-greedy claim to fight for. *But what about the handicapped? What about the elderly?*

On my slow way to this cliff, this wash, where light seems to catch on every facet of twig and stone, and shadows pour like blue lava, I walked across roads that went back to earth beneath my boots. Road Closed. Road Closed. I touched the signs. I whispered, "Yes."

I leave nothing at the base of the cliff except gratitude and make my clumsy way back to the truck. My friend, my road-buddy who loves road and roadless equally, emerges from the shadows. He is grinning. I look at his face and know I look in a mirror.

"How was it?" he asks.

"Very, very good."

"Yeah."

We walk in silence. Later, he will tell me how he traversed rock he might more prudently have avoided, and how that led him, heart in his throat, to a hidden arch in a saddle and the sight of the southern Mojave rolling in waves of mountains and desert, sunset and blue mist to the far curve of the earth. I will tell him about coyote house-keeping and bells of light and how enough is enough, and never enough. But for now, our silence is sweet earth without roads.

We camp on an abandoned mining claim. There are the requisite rusting bedspring, coils of wire, shattered Colt-45 bottles glittering like fool's agate. My friend cooks linguine with olive oil, garlic, and capers. I spread out my sleeping bag and stretch. My back throbs. Fire shoots down one leg.

"Trying to sleep is going to be a challenge," I say.

He laughs. "Would you have it any other way?"

I turn on my back, pull my legs up to my chest. Nothing releases. I look up into moonless night, Orion striding eternally young and strong across the eastern sky.

"You mean?" I ask.

"Doing it the easy way. I don't know, maybe driving up to the arch. A road."

I twist left, right, slowly. I keep my eyes open. The mountaintops that I will never see up close lie like sumi brushstrokes against the stars. I don't answer my friend. I don't have to. The way into the answer is perfectly clear.

home address

THE NATURE OF URBAN LIFE

The earth is old. Nothing lasts. All life is kin. Different eyes perceive different worlds, and much remains hidden. Ours is an age of extinctions; ours are the hands of the destroyers. Grief and beauty are knotted together. Curiosity and imagination are fundamental human forces. So are fear and hatred, passion and compassion. None of this is surprising . . .

SUEELLEN CAMPBELL, "THE WORLD IS A NEST"

HOME ADDRESS

Naomi Shihab Nye

Yesterday we paid off the mortgage on our ninety-year-old white house on South Main Avenue. I drove from San Antonio to Austin with a cashier's check in my purse and a receipt marked HAND-DELIVERED for the mortgage company to sign. I wanted to see that stamp marked PAID IN FULL, to step back out the door into the sun and blink hard and take a full fine breath.

When I entered the marble lobby of the office building—cool and blank as any bank—beams of light were slanting through high windows onto the gleaming floor and the music playing over loudspeakers was the very same trumpet anthem I walked down the aisle to at our wedding fifteen years ago. I laughed out loud. It's been said our lives might be easier if we had appropriate background music, as characters do in movies. It felt wonderful climbing that staircase with trumpets to the second floor.

Later, back at home, I noticed all the cracks in the walls. They seemed more vivid. Now they were really entirely ours. We could fix them or not, depending.

My husband suggested we take a walk before dark. He and our son put on their baseball caps. I locked all the doors. We passed our neighbors' yards, thirsty after fifty-seven days of no rain. We passed our ex-cat Maui, who divorced us and moved five houses down to live with the Martinos.

An elderly couple dressed in white was crossing the bridge by the river, leaning on one another for support. My husband said, "Is that us in the future?" For some reason I jumped to say, "No!"—maybe because our son just started first grade this week after getting his first short haircut and losing his first tooth and the passage of time feels tender and nearly unbearable right now—but when we got closer to the couple, I figured we'd be lucky to be them.

They looked gentle, intelligent, and still in love with one another. He helped her into a white car and closed the door. Then he looked at us. He had a fine grin and a white mustache. "Nice river you got," he said. "You live around here?" When we said yes, he pointed to the River Authority building and said, "Well, I grew up on this very spot in a lovely brick house with a full basement, all erased by now, but you can bet I do have some memories."

Naturally I wanted to embrace him on the spot and urge him to tell, tell, tell. "The house had marble pillars," he went on dreamily. "And was full of music. We kept the windows wide open, so the music floated outside into the air . . ."

The music man said this river was a lovely place to grow up. He said some days his head was still full of "the scent of pecan leaves piling up in the autumn, right here, right along these banks. Look! These are some of the same old trees." He seemed reluctant to leave us, but his wife was getting edgy in the front seat alone. I would have liked to tell him about our mortgage or invite him to dinner. Where did he live now?

But they drove off and we crossed the river . . . [noticing] a neighbor's house for sale that hadn't been for sale yesterday. This always feels disturbing and melancholy to me. We found two frogs hopping around in the monkey grass by the sidewalk. Their rough little bellies puffed in and out. Our son said the frogs were husband and wife. They seemed to live under a raised cracked place in the sidewalk.

I could feel an ache rising up from the ground, a desperate deep thirst from the roots of trees and vines. In a few yards, quiet sprinklers swished in the darkness. "How much longer till it rains, do you think?" and we all placed our bets, then came round to our own block again and the iron gate that never fit the fence, even on the first day, and has to be held shut with a shoestring.

Our porch swing was quietly hanging, waiting for us. The swing has a quilt top in its seat now, which used to be a curtain till I washed it and the oldest fabrics came out shredded. The banana palms and giant red hibiscus bush were breathing their slumbered breath, and the black mailbox on a pole stood at attention even in the dark. Its flag was down. Now and then, each detail stands out like a landmark.

We sat for a while before going in and I thought of the lady who lived in this house for fifty years before us. She raised one son in this house too. She outlived two husbands in this house. Each time we invited her back for tea, she said, "Well honey, I just don't think I can make it," though the service station attendant around the block said he saw her drive by all the time.

I thought of Norman Bodet, who lived in this house before her, whose family built it and started the travel agency I frequent downtown. Bodet Steamship and Travel still uses old-fashioned blue envelopes with little steamships floating across them. Mr. Bodet's portrait stares gravely at me each time I buy a plane ticket, which is often. He seems to say, "Can't you settle down?"

The day after we paid off the mortgage I was sweeping the back deck, moving flower pots around and humming. I don't think I'd swept it all summer. I dug my hands into the big purple plant that flourishes with no attention. I plucked off its dry leaves. I pulled out twigs and the stick of a popsicle, tucked in by some lazy someone, and startled backward when something cool slithered past my fingers. Leaves rattled and shook. I glanced fearfully behind the pot to see a long snake gliding smoothly down between the boards of the deck. Since I only saw his middle section, I can't tell anyone how long he was. I must have waked him up inside his cool jungle hideaway.

He looked—mottled. Grayish or greenish or brownish. I've never seen a snake in this yard in fifteen years and now, the minute it's all ours, surprise.

He lives here too.

MOWING

Judith E. Bowen

It is time again. Two weeks and a dash of rain have given both grass and weeds vigor and height. I have learned to start in the morning, before the heat of mid-day spills into the yard. I suit up. Jeans to protect my legs, a tee shirt, my blue sweatband, and my beat-up black plastic shoes. The hat will come later. I drink a full cold glass of water to fill up the sweat reservoirs and set to my task. Amber, the middle-aged Golden, and the mostly Border collie mix, Sweetie, dance around me with excitement. They know the ritual. I tell them they cannot join me in the front yard because there is no fence. They watch through the window.

How familiar this routine has become, a task not usually mine in earlier years. I reflect on how much of my life has been given to the raising of children and nurturing of family—more than half. But now all are grown and gone.

I push the mower out the gate into the driveway and gas up. I am proud that I have mastered this process. My husband, away, working, had always handled this job, and I had to learn about mixing oil with gas for a two-stroke engine, had to buy a red plastic container, and had to fill it at the gas station. I carefully put in a half-gallon, then the oil, then the second half-gallon, because that is what the directions said. As with all new things, the process was not automatic in the beginning.

I also had to work out a relationship with the machine. I had to learn its mood, its chemistry, the fine-tuning of the choke. The very first time I mowed, I had finished half the front yard when the machine puttered to a stop. I had just had it serviced, so I was annoyed. After all, I had just paid to get it working, and now it wasn't. My neighbor Rubén took my mower and me back to the shop in his truck. The mechanic unloaded the machine, filled it up with gas, started it, and its smooth hum filled the shop. I stood there feeling silly, and trying not to notice the look that passed between them. But they kept their faces polite and friendly and simply shrugged their shoulders. Since then I have learned the thirsty sound and the purring-at-prime-time sound, and my mower and I get along much better.

We start the pattern: one half hour to do the front lawn. I timed it one day, up and down the side strip, then up and down the large middle section, then up and down the other side strip. The grackles join me as I have come to know they will. They follow my path, gobbling up bugs my machine stirs up. They are quite bold and settle only one giant step away, take what they need, circle, and then come back. And there on a branch of the big tree is a Kiskadee flycatcher, only six feet away, watching my work. I am given the gift of a bright flash of golden yellow underside when it suddenly flies to a higher branch.

I continue with the ritual, up and down, the grass smoothing into a neat, clean carpet. There is calmness in this work even though I feel the exertion. I enjoy the breeze and the maypole dance under the huge oleander at the end of the lawn. It is heavy with white blossoms and I duck around and through the low branches to mow underneath.

I let the dogs out before I start the back yard. The Golden and the Mix excitedly bound after the grackles. Amber is good for one exuberant dash in the heat and then she finds the shade. Sweetie stays alert. It's her job to herd the grackles, and as I mow, they begin their game. The birds swoop down, delighted with the small insects stirred up by my passing, and she is delighted with the chase. Their patterns of play flow around me until she is finally too hot and has to find shade.

The strong breeze helps, but the heat is beginning to build. It takes an hour to do the back yard. Back and forth I go, neat row after neat row, bringing a calm order to the patchwork of good grass and weeds that makes the back yard green. Butterflies and bugs circle and a large grasshopper lands on my shoulder and rides with me for a while. I wonder if it wants me to stop disturbing its world. I hear the thirsty sound and the machine slows and then stops. I am glad.

After a brief respite in the dark coolness of the house, it is time for my hat. I clamp it on my head, feed the thirsty machine, and start again. But I am delayed for a moment by the hibiscus bloom. I brought the plant with me when I came to the Rio Grande Valley and it has flourished here, as I have. Its blooms are brilliant magenta.

There is something about these flowers that speaks to my soul, my spirit. They are the perfection which humans cannot create. I bend to let the petals caress my cheek. They feel soft against my hot skin.

It is time now to finish. The sun is climbing higher and even though the brisk breeze continues, I am feeling the heat. As I continue one neat row after another, I begin to think as my Depression Era mother taught me. The going rate for lawn mowing is twenty-five dollars. I paid a dollar nineteen plus tax for the two-stroke oil and a dollar sixty-five for the gallon of gas, so I have saved twenty-two dollars and sixteen cents by mowing my own lawn. The righteousness of that thought keeps me going until the whole yard is done. The sudden silence comes as a blessing. I look at my work and feel good.

On the way back across the lawn, dragging the mower, I see a patch of tall grass against the fence. As I cut it, something catches my eye. I look again. There on the weathered wood of the fence is a huge moth of a kind I have never seen before. It is beautiful and dramatic, its wings pointed like holly leaves. It is the color of the wood and streaked with black. It sits, still and unmoving and noble. Again, I am in awe of perfection. I let it be. It is sacred.

I am ready to put the mower and myself to rest. It was good work but now I am hot and tired. The dogs are ready, too, for the coolness of the house. I see my face, red in the mirror, and know that I have overdone. But as I reflect on work well done, on its satisfactions, its unexpected gifts, I understand that in this most simple task I have met myself, and I am pleased.

MADRUGADORA/EARLY RISER

Sandra S. Smith

Yo soy madrugadora.
If not could I have seen four coyotes today?
Does acacia smell so sweet at noon?
When else is it so humanly quiet and filled with the noise
    of dove?
To feel the sun before it's hot.
To smell the creosote after last evening's rain.

Yo soy madrugadora.
Before the trash trucks.
Before the workers leave for offices downtown.
Before the builders bang today's first nail.
The quail are scratching.
The owl is hooting his last hoot.

Yo soy madrugadora.
Before the hungry ones cry.
Before the missing button is discovered.
Before the list is written.
First I will listen to the waking desert and celebrate its
    surprises.
Later I will feed the flock and accept requests.

Yo soy madrugadora.
    Yo soy.

THE WORLD IS A NEST

SueEllen Campbell

*i*t's been almost six years since I lay in the winter sun on the Pajarito Plateau and listened to a long filament of cranes moving north into spring. Sometimes I ask myself what in all this time I've learned—from so much reading, from moving around the land in search of something I could barely name, all that solitary brooding. Have I realized anything new and important? Or have I seen only what I should always have known?

The earth is old. Nothing lasts. All life is kin. Different eyes perceive different worlds, and much remains hidden. Ours is an age of extinctions; ours are the hands of the destroyers. Grief and beauty are knotted together. Curiosity and imagination are fundamental human forces. So are fear and hatred, passion and compassion. None of this is surprising . . .

I remember one evening during that spring of sadness. I'd been sagging in front of the television, overwhelmed by the usual bad news. "You need to get out of the house," John said, clicking off the set midword. "Let's take the pupsters into town for a walk along the river."

Twenty minutes later we'd set off along the Cache La Poudre River, switching from the paved bike path to the dirt track alongside at the will of the dogs, who pulled us everywhere with sniffing excitement, heads down and tails up. Clumps of weeds, a grasshopper, a buffet of varied and evidently fine manures, a passing cyclist—it all fascinated them. My knee was hurting, though, so I sent John and the dogs ahead and found a chair-sized rock to sit on.

I looked around me. The river was muddy, its banks a mess of rough-barked cottonwoods, mashed grasses and weeds, flood debris, churned-up mud. To the north, the raw desolation of a gravel quarry. To the south, sagging barbed wire, weedy brown pasture. It was an unprepossessing scene, familiar and banal.

The late sun was nice, though, warm and golden, with a bit

of color in the sky over the mountains. And John had left with me our new pair of binoculars—nothing fancy, but a step up for us. So I started my usual inefficient routine: find something to look at, take my glasses off, bring the binocs to my eyes, point in what I hope is the right direction, fiddle with the focus. A rusty, twisted barb on the fence, sharp against a field of tan fuzz. Cottonwood bark transformed into a landscape of shadowed canyons. Sharp-edged spikes of needle-and-thread grass catching some stray glints of light. A flock of swallows zipping across my field of vision, not quite in focus.

Just above the path to the west hovered a vague cloud of bugs, made visible by the sun behind them. I aimed towards the sun, shifted my angle until the glare disappeared, and brought the swarm into focus.

It was the most amazing vision. They looked like small moths, and I suppose there might have been a couple hundred of them. Some hovered in place as hummingbirds hover at feeders, moving in quick jerks, each one a clear circular blur of beating wings. But it was the others that surprised me so much. They looked like long, twisted ribbons, like sparkling streamers on New Year's Eve, each one a spinning helix of energy made visible. They floated up and down and sideways; they caught and held the light of the setting sun as if it were their own.

For a few minutes I forgot everything else and simply stared in astonishment. Then I concentrated on memorizing what I was seeing, knowing already that soon enough I might doubt my memory. Was it a quirk of perspective, of focus, something about the angle of the sun or the optics of my new binoculars, some kind of trick? In the intense elation of the moment, I didn't care.

Finally a waft of air moved the cloud of bugs out of my sight.

At home I tried to duplicate the helix shape, cutting strips of paper and scrounging for ribbon scraps, then twisting and twirling them. Yes, those were the forms I'd seen, but the magic was missing. I tried to draw them, too, but failed. Nothing I could make at my kitchen table could be more than the crudest approximation.

Still, I haven't forgotten the marvel of this moment—how in that most ordinary time and place, in the absurd and improbable form of bugs swarming over an asphalt path, I felt for an instant that I was *seeing*.

But what was I seeing? If I were more mystical, I'd probably call it the fire of life itself. Or maybe it was a reminder that joy and beauty can materialize suddenly out of what seems to be empty space. Maybe in this fleeting moment, my self and my place matched perfectly, and so I could see what was truly there, the swirl of energy all around me. Or maybe it was a glimpse beyond concept into fact: nothing more and nothing less than insects spinning and floating above the ground.

Now I wonder this: What if these were some of the invisible spirits of the air, simply revealed to me by a certain slant of light? Invisible because I don't usually see them, not because they have no presence in the material world; spirits because they hold their own place in the creation, cherish their own share of life. And I think about all the other things I've learned to remember are present even when I can't see them. It's such a long list! Radioactive particles and rays, the buried bones and fossils of the past, the motion of the continents. Marmots in hibernation, ptarmigans asleep under the snow. A white wolf in all the unwitnessed hours of its life. I envision Doris out on her snowmobile in the dark of November—but it is not so dark after all, for the moon is full and the aurora flames across the sky.

A year ago, a day or two before Christmas, I was alone in the house and feeling a little sad. So I turned on the colored lights and lit a bit of juniper incense. I found a loop of yarn and practiced making a fishing net. Then I sat on my couch and began to imagine the people I have loved who now are gone, sitting one at a time in the faded blue velvet chair across from me for a short visit. First, because the chair was hers, my father's mother in one of her trademark royal blue suits, broad-brimmed blue felt hats, thick-heeled lace-up shoes. Next was my mother's mother, eager as she always was to tell me what she'd been doing. Then Carol Ann appeared, and my great-grandmothers, cousins and uncles and aunts, lost friends. They sat across from me with the clarity and solidity that once had been theirs, and each one brought a measure of grace. With each visitor, I felt less sad. The room filled up with spirits.

This winter I'll throw a bigger party. I'll summon every spirit I can imagine with any concreteness at all, not only humans but all living creatures, not only the recent dead but the long vanished and we who are still alive. Maybe I'll invite them all to join me on a boat—we'll all fit, since spirits like these don't need much space—and then we'll set out to float for a while on the waters that mirror the sky.

ONE SCARLET PENSTEMON

Connie Spittler

I slipped into the heat, like a lizard basking on warm rocks. A move from the Midwest to Arizona let the sunshine warm my winter bones while I explored life on this other planet, the high Sonoran Desert. I hiked meandering foothills trails, walked gullies, and educated myself about the tough foliage that clung so desperately to life, even sprouting through rocky crevices. Around the house, tenacious plants and spiny cactus pads thrived on blast furnace temperatures. Once accustomed to the caliche rock bed around my house, I decided to extend the sculptural tableau of prickly pear, jumping cholla, ocotillo, and one red fairy duster that landscaped the front yard.

Along a hiking trail, I'd seen the crimson spark of a wild-flower that attracted hummingbirds. I learned its name, then purchased and planted a scarlet penstemon near the fairy duster, choosing a shade of intense red to satisfy the hummers. It wasn't long before the flitting birds double-dipped between the two plantings, sipping first from the bell-shaped blossoms, then from the fuzzy fairy balls.

I slipped into hummingbird summer, the shape of it, the mood of it, the flash of wings that moved through it. The cold snap came, but the memory of summer ran deep. The next spring, I waited for the penstemon to reappear. Every morning I peered down into the trimmed remains of last year's plant, looking for an infinitesimal trace of green. I watched the spot like an overbearing parent, but nothing happened. The fairy duster was ready to burst into red puffballs. Palo verde trees bloomed yellow. Aloe plants spouted orange. Tahoka daisy shimmered purple. Still, the penstemon failed to respond to the annual call to life.

With springtime waltzing by, I sensed it was time to replace the reluctant plant. I drove off to the nursery and was surprised to find no scarlet penstemons there, only pink. I wanted red to match the fairy duster. I needed scarlet for the hummingbirds. I drove down the road to another nursery, only to receive the same response: "Sorry, only pink, no red."

The next day I headed off in a different direction. I was amazed when two more nurseries, with row upon row of multicolored flowers, displayed not one scarlet penstemon. The third day, the story was the same. With no more nurseries within reasonable striking distance, I accepted the inevitable. I would not have my red plant this year. Nature was teaching me patience. "Maybe next year, one scarlet penstemon," I thought and headed home.

As I turned into the driveway, a sliver of red caught my eye. I got out of the car and walked toward the faint bit of color. There, under a mesquite tree, far from the fairy duster, I found one small scarlet penstemon, just beginning to unfold. Last year's plant had gone to seed. Holding a new thought, I examined our front desert for more seedlings. I began to count little green plants scattered here and there, springing up from the arid land. In wonder and appreciation, I discovered I had been given not one, but forty-three scarlet penstemons. With so many crimson trumpets to come, ruby-throated hummingbirds could not be far behind. The desert was not just teaching patience, after all, but demonstrating abundance, as well. And survival.

"Thank you," I whispered to the desert breeze that washed over the dry terrain. "For fragile red petals, for wings."

VOCES DEL JARDÍN

Pat Mora

*J*ANUARY

I look out at the covered porch that borders the garden, that shades us when we sit in the wide, rawhide and wood chairs, *equipales.* On warm days, sparrows wade in the fountain whose quiet splash, *ps-slp-plop, ps-slp-plop,* lures us all into these adobe walls. In Nigeria, Morocco, Spain, Syria, fellow humans also find comfort from such mud-rounded protection. Rumors of my unending questions alter the pitch and rhythms of speech within these walls I know. All know: I'm after stories, brewed in the bone. It's the older voices and bodies who have the patience to talk and remember . . .

This is a "world that we can call our own," this family space through which generations move, each bringing its gifts, handing down languages and stories, recipes for living, gathering around the kitchen table to serve one another; in the walled garden, engaging in the slow conversation of families sitting to pass the time. Voices mingle with the voice of the fountain, parrot, broom, wind, *voces del jardín.*

The walled garden, a design indigenous to Mexico and also Iranian, then Islamic, brought to the Americas by the Spanish, is a tradition Moorish and Mexican. A garden can be enchanted, bewitched, bewitching. To enjoy the lush beauty throughout the year, Persians in the sixth century even created garden carpets patterned after the courtyard foliage and blooms. And gardens flourished on this continent. When the Spaniards entered Mexico in 1519, they found *chinampas,* which *los españoles* mistook for floating gardens, plots covered with dahlias, amaranth, chiles, corn, willows. Moctezuma, who had established an aqueduct to bring springwater from Chapultepec to the island city of Tenochtitlán, is credited with the construction of splendid, verdant spaces tended by experienced horticulturists.

In the desert, a garden demands as love does everywhere, care, intentionality. Ignore the soil, food, light, and water needs of caladiums or cannas, and they will soon shrivel from neglect, vanish from this space both private and communal; a space of labor and frustration, also of meditation, solace, hope, and sensory delights.

Plants, humans' first medicines, through ritual and religion intertwine with our lives, become sources of food, shelter, warmth, weapons, clothing, dyes, cosmetics, wine. The world's flora nourish, inspire, intoxicate. Rich sources of mystery, magic and mythology; they flavor our dishes, beautify our rooms, soothe our aches, scent our beds, decorate our bodies and altars, perfume our paths and poems; these green lifeforms that rise from the dark tangle of underground life, like our subconscious, fertile and full of promise.

FEBRUARY

I walk out to the garden enjoying the pleasure of a warm afternoon after last week's cold, unpredictable February, *febrero loco*. I walk by my maternal grandparents, Papande reading a law book, Mamande praying a novena.

"Watch out for the crocuses, Lalo," Aunt Carmen calls worried about her husband's rake. "Did you see them, Pat? Come and look. Yellow and purple crocus. And over there see the daffodils and the iris? And look at the color of these pansies, the little velvet faces. But honey, I'm so maaaad. All this warm weather is going to ruin my fruit trees. Come on out back and see how they're covered, covered with buds. But it's too early, honey."

I look at the trees with my aunt, think of the origin of the word "pansy," *pensée*, French for thought, the flowers once believed to make your love think of you, petal power, gardens of multicolored, velvet musings. I wander back to the central garden, go find the old book on the gardener's year I was reading last night that says a gardener, "is a creature who digs himself into the earth." We probably dig some of ourselves into all that we pursue, but there's something eerie or maybe appealing—all that Catholic dust-to-dust stuff—about digging ourselves into earth, loosening the soil and burying some of our essence, our breath, as we turn the earth, even while we're alive becoming part of the compost.

The February evening arrives on the desert mesas; clouds blush pink, then peach. At night, I sleep with the full Snow Moon. Sparrows and robins wake me early enough the next morning to see mauve clouds and to watch the alabaster moon set to the west as the sun rises over the mountains in the east, the white globes that light our world silently greeting one another.

MAY

San Isidro Labrador, a May saint, the patron of farmers, was so devout that God sent an angel down to plow Isidro's fields while he prayed, his statue venerated all over New Mexico, carried into the fields for the blessing of the earth.

> San Isidro, barbas de oro,
> Ruega a Dios
> Que llueva a chorros.

When I ask my father if he's heard of San Isidro, he barely shakes his head no, so drowsy is he in the spring air, but he chuckles at the humorous prayer for rain.

I sit next to him enjoying both the sound of a mockingbird playing with sounds and the thought of its accurate Latin name, *mimus polyglottos,* many-tongued mimic. I read about how to attract hummingbirds and butterflies to the garden, wondering if we should try penstemons, maybe the bluish purple and the scarlet bugler. Who wouldn't want a bugler with its scarlet sound? Accompanied by trumpet vine, yes, its orange blarings, symphonies of color. We'll buy a mix of scents and colors to lure the wings: wild hyssop, beebalm, purple coneflower, columbine, gaillardia, cosmos, zinnias, and Mexican sunflowers, *mirasoles,* and their craning necks.

They'll come, the whirring black-chinned hummingbirds, *chuparrosas,* rainbowed reflections of light. Again, I'll watch my son when he's a young boy; green net in hand, chasing the monarchs, painted ladies, black swallowtails and great spangled fritillaries, luring him to dart under wisteria's lavender clusters, to leap over alyssum, irises, Indian hawthorn.

JULY

"*Mala hierba nunca muere,*" says Mamá Cleta glancing at the stubborn milkweed I've pulled. In the cicadas' drone, Aunt Carmen and I pull out petunias wilted by summer heat. I'm hot, tired, and welcome sitting in the shade of the *portal* to watch clouds swell over the desert, blue-purple clouds that threatened a downpour for days finally release themselves and the fat drops pelt the desert, the river, the fruit trees, *acequia,* and garden. After weeks of waiting for such drenching rain, we all come out to the covered porch to watch and listen . . .

The sky broods gray and purple. Thunder booms, lightning zigzags . . . Watching the adobe and colors of the hills and mountain darken, and feeling our own parched selves renewed by the blessing of rain, we say little in the presence of the celestial drama. When the rain stops, we listen to the streams pour down from the *canales,* watch drops slide from leaves and petals. Aunt Carmen goes in to make coffee and the chatting begins.

"*Las flores contentan pero no alimentan,*" says Mamá Cleta also heading for the kitchen to fix a platter of cookies, *orejas* and *corazones.*

My children and I walk through the garden with its wet, fallen petals, like damp confetti, and walk out back as the sunlight strikes puddles turning them gold, *ojitos de agua.* Grackles congregate their feathered racket in the cottonwoods, shoot gleaming ebony whistles through the air. The children talk about the kingfishers they'd see where there are lots of carp down the canal and reminisce about tadpoles, filling jars with them after a good rain. We take deep breaths as we listen to the irrigation canal tumble with new life, then walk through the fruit trees down to the fast, flowing river, mesmerized by its slidings and swirlings, looking for minnows or sunfish near the bank. We smell the desert, creosote on its breeze, hear the chatter of sparrows telling their water tales as they settle in the cottonwoods, the *moras,* and the Chinaberry tree for the night. Seeing the first night star, we say,

> Star light, star bright, first star I see tonight.
> I wish I may, I wish I might, have the wish I wish tonight.

Since my children were born, all such wishes are for them.

Cissy gently touches the trio of saints carved out of an old tree trunk, their eyes closed, arms stretched high in joy.

"Maybe this was carved after a rain like this," Bill says.

"Or maybe at dawn," Libby says.

"Or maybe at sunset," says Cissy again touching the saints.

"Look!" Bill, our observant naturalist, points to a great blue heron in the river, the large bird that always surprises me in the desert. It opens its wings wide and soundlessly lifts its body from the murky water, like a ballet dancer lifts self and doubt, resists gravity, and flies.

SPINNING WATER INTO GOLD

Lisa Shirah-Hiers

In a triple-digit August drought, the city of Austin waits for rain. The brown grass crunches underfoot. Burn marks speckle the medians where tossed cigarettes have scorched expanses that in spring flourished with bluebonnets, evening primroses, and Indian paintbrush. The Texas Hill Country is brown and beige and dull. "Leaves don't change color here," we tell the folks back home. "They just wilt and wither and die."

I am waiting for hurricane season, when storms push pregnant clouds north from the Gulf coast. With a fierce, dark joy at the sight of overcast skies, I will relish the sound of rain on the patio roof, the smell of wet pavement, the splash of cars through flooded streets. In the gray Midwestern Januaries of my childhood, I yearned as deeply for sunshine and warm air. Now it is the enveloping quiet of low clouds that I miss, and the tingle of a sharp wind.

Transplanted Yankee, I have learned to drawl and say "y'all" for the second person plural. My vowels stretch out so that *down* has two syllables and lasts twice as long. I'm convinced the weather causes this. You can't move or talk too fast without passing out from heat exhaustion. I've learned to reuse the water in my dehumidifier to quench my thirsty garden. I plant lettuce in January, when the evenings are still cool, and seedlings in early March so they have time to develop roots before the land begins to bake. I mark the calendar with the summer watering schedule—addresses ending in two on the fifth, tenth, and fifteenth. But every five days isn't often enough for the roses. So I wait and wait and wait for water to trickle from the rain barrel into the watering can.

In August, I do errands before noon and cover my daughter's car seat with a towel to prevent it from searing her bottom. When I'm tired of picking at my brown scab of a garden and we've run out of indoor games, we escape to the Central Market Pond.

On the footpath, gravel crunches. Cicadas whir and grind. Turtle buttons polka-dot the water's surface. A mammoth hourglass oak guards its mirror, the elongated hourglass of the pond, belted across its middle by a wooden bridge. My daughter's feet slip-slap across the bridge, and pebbles plunk where she casts them over the rail. Fooled by her limestone offerings, wood ducks glide toward us, the arrows of their passage pointing the way for stragglers. A lone goose complains.

At the foot of a little waterfall, a blue heron plants himself, smashing a crawdad on the rocks and swallowing its broken body whole. The sticky, sauna-hot air clings to my arms and pastes strands of hair to my neck, cheeks, and forehead. But listening to the sound of the waterfall, I can forget for a moment how sweaty I am. I can appreciate the twice-blooming Silverado sage, the yellow and pink lantana, the flash of a mockingbird's wings, and even the raucous, iridescent beauty of starlings.

The Central Market Pond is a human creation, designed to filter runoff from the parking lot of the strip mall. I, too, have constructed retention ponds and aeration systems to filter the mind pollution of city life: road rage, noise, homeless and hopeless people scrounging hand-outs, the odd crowded loneliness of too many folks too close together physically and too far apart psychically. As the duck pond sustains fish, turtles, birds, insects, cattails and water lilies, the waterways of my mind breed thoughts, stories, resolutions, and prayers.

August in the Hill Country teaches you patience and resourcefulness. You learn to use and reuse experience, to waste nothing, to be grateful for everything. You learn to conserve your strength, drink plenty of water and rest in the heat of the day, skirt puddles in a flash flood. In this land of extremes, you wear layers and carry an umbrella. You practice flexibility.

There's a grit to Texans that I admire. It's different from the methodical sturdiness of Midwestern Germans, Norwegians, and Danes. It's the wiry grit of bamboo that bends so it won't break, the stubborn tenaciousness of live oaks that endure where haughtier Yankee trees would topple. In the Lone Star State, you grow diminutive like Texas deer, stern and prickly like cacti.

We never meant to stay so long. Two years, we thought, just until I finished my master's program at the University of Texas. Then we'd move back to Wisconsin. But my hydrologist husband found a job here, protecting the very waterways we now cherish. In the beginning, I complained like the goose, angry at the stony crumbs tossed my way. Finally, I adapted. I dug channels, breaking open the hard soil to find water where I could. I irrigated, mulched, and composted until the earthworms came to help aerate the stubborn clay. My roots went deep and discovered the aquifer. My garden flourished. Here, far from our native Great Lakes, my husband's water work supports us. Water is the straw we've spun into gold.

I am grateful for this duck pond that is both an oasis and a meal ticket. I am grateful for what the dry land has taught me about patience and adaptability. If we find our way back to the Midwest, I will never again take water for granted. Yes, I'd be overjoyed to see cornfields and dairy cows and lakes that stretch to the horizon. But I would miss these feisty hills and the scraggy cedars that cling to the cliff sides, proclaiming: *Home is wherever you are planted. Water is there for those who are patient, who let their roots go deep.*

For the Challenger Seven

SUNSET ON THE BAYOU

Sybil Pittman Estess

Now dusk is on Houston: flat and breastless.
Not on Seattle, red-hilled Greensboro,
nor Concord, Kona, old Jerusalem—
those subtle or volcano slopes they could have climbed.

It's the last of January, virginal
until last Tuesday. It's 5:30,
six weeks past winter solstice.
Soft southern deadness, broomstrawed and brown.

Sun, setting we say, is red placenta, edging
the child's promised sky not yet night . . .
Walking one block from my house,
I'm by the concreted, graffiti-marked bayou, circling this city,

churning rain debris, turtles, trash, tires,
unfound trapped bones—a woman's who drove off
in last year's rainstorm catastrophe.
Stars, boats, babies, all that goes forth here
will travel again—down, down such dark canals.

THE PEOPLE AND THE LAND
ARE INSEPARABLE

Leslie Marmon Silko

I did not really learn about my relationship with the land or know where "home" was until I left Laguna for Tucson. The old folks and the old stories say that the animals and other living beings have a great deal to teach us if we will only pay attention. Because I was unfamiliar with the land around Tucson, I began to pay special attention. The Tucson Mountains are the remains of a huge volcano that exploded long ago; all the rock is shattered and the soil is pale like ash. The fiery clouds of ash and rock melted exotic conglomerates of stone that dazzle the foothills like confetti. I was happy to find such lovely, unusual rocks around my house. I sat on the ground looking at all the wonderful colorful and odd pebbles, and I felt quite at home.

Before I moved to Tucson, I had made one visit, during which my friend Larry Evers took me to an Easter Deer Dance performed at the New Pasqua Yaqui village, located west of Tucson. New Pasqua village was the result of an act of Congress passed in 1973 that recognized the Arizona Yaquis as "American Indians." Until that time, the Yaquis who lived in Arizona were not considered to be Indians, but Mexicans who had fled north to the United States to escape the Mexican Army's genocidal war on Yaquis. Anticipating Hitler's Third Reich by many years, the Mexican Army, under orders, attempted to eradicate the Yaquis. Hundreds of women and children were herded into dry washes or into trenches they were forced to dig at gunpoint, and were shot to death. But long before the appearance of the Europeans, the Yaquis had ranged as far north as Tucson, and it was on this aboriginal use that the United States government based its decision to proclaim Arizona Yaquis American Indians.

After I moved to Tucson, I learned there were two older Yaqui villages within the Tucson metropolitan area, as well as a farming community of Yaquis at Marana, north of Tucson. One Yaqui settlement is located off Twenty-ninth Street and Interstate 10. I don't know its name. The other is located off Grant Road and Interstate 10 and is called Old Pasqua. Although the city of Tucson has sprawled all around these Yaqui settlements, still one can tell immediately where Tucson ends and the Yaqui villages begin. At Old Pasqua, the Tucson street names suddenly change. Fairview Avenue becomes Calle Central, and the houses become smaller and closer together. The center of the village is a plaza surrounded by a community center, across from a little Catholic church. The little yards are neatly swept, and used building materials, car parts, and firewood are neatly stacked amid fruit trees and little gardens. Corn, beans, melons, roses, zinnias, and sunflowers all grow together; there are no lawns. I was not used to seeing a pueblo within a city. In New Mexico, all but the outlying pueblos were burned, so that Albuquerque, Santa Fe, Los Lunas, and Socorro have no pueblos within their boundaries.

I thought it must be very difficult to exist as a Yaqui village within the city limits of Tucson. These were my thoughts because I had just moved to Tucson from Laguna, and I was thinking about what it means to be separated from one's homeland.

The post office station for my area is located on the edge of Old Pasqua village, so after I had settled in Tucson, I used to find myself driving past Old Pasqua at least once a week. At first I didn't notice anything in particular except the hollyhocks and morning glories or lilacs in bloom. On warm winter days I would see old folks sitting outside with their chairs against the east wall of the house, just as the old folks used to sun themselves at Laguna. After this time, whenever I drove through Old Pasqua I could sense a transition from the city of Tucson to the Yaqui village, where things looked and felt different—more quiet and serene than the apartments and trailer parks just a few blocks away by the post office. In Old Pasqua, no one was in a hurry to go anywhere. People liked to sit or stand outside and talk to their neighbors while the children played leisurely games of catch or rode their bicycles up and down the street. The longer I lived and drove around Tucson, the more I began to appreciate the sharp contrast between the Yaqui village and the rest of the city. The presence of the Yaqui people and their Yaqui universe with all the spirit beings have consecrated this place; amid all the clamor and pollution of Tucson, this is home.

The Santa Cruz River across Interstate 10 from Old Pasqua flows north out of Mexico past Tucson, to empty into the Gila River, which then flows south. The Santa Cruz flows out of the mountains in Mexico where the Yaqui people still live. Thus the Santa Cruz River makes Old Pasqua home and not exile. I came to realize it was the wishful thinking of Tucson's founding white fathers that had located the Yaquis exclusively in northern Sonora.

One afternoon, after I had been to the post office, I felt like a drive through Old Pasqua. It was about two o'clock, and as I approached the village I didn't see anyone. Even the school grounds at the elementary school were empty. I was thinking to myself how quiet villages are sometimes, how they can seem almost deserted, when suddenly the most amazing scene unfolded before me. At almost the same instant, as if on cue, the doors of nearly all the houses began to open and people of all ages came out. I could hardly believe what I was seeing. I felt a chill, and hair on the back of my neck stood up. A moment before, there had been no one, and now suddenly people of all ages were streaming outside all at once from every house. They were not talking to one another and they did not seem excited or disturbed, but they all were headed in the same direction. When I looked, I saw a white hearse parked in the driveway of one of the houses, and I realized that someone in the village had just passed on. The people were going to comfort their relatives and to pay their respects. What I found amazing then, and what I still marvel at, is the moment all the front doors opened at once. Even if every household had a telephone, and most do not, it would have been quite a feat to orchestrate—to have all the doors open at once and the people step outside.

I understood then that this is what it means to be a people and to be a Yaqui village and not just another Tucson neighborhood. To be a people, to be part of a village, is the dimension of human identity that anthropology understands least, because this sense of home, of the people one comes from, is an intangible quality, not easily understood by American-born Europeans.

The Yaquis may have had to leave behind their Sonoran mountain strongholds, but they did not leave behind their consciousness of their identity as Yaquis, as a people, as a community. This is where their power as a culture lies: with this shared consciousness of being part of a living community that continues on and on, beyond the death of one or even of many, that continues on the riverbanks of the Santa Cruz after the mountains have been left behind.

A FULL LIFE IN A SMALL PLACE

Janice Emily Bowers

A soft buzz at my elbow announces the arrival of a leaf-cutter bee. Slightly smaller than a honeybee, she is banded with white and black her entire length. She lands on the edge of a lilac leaf, then scissors out a circlet of tissue, clinging to the cut portion as she works, a lumberjack standing on the wrong end of a limb. With the last snip she saws off the limb and drops into thin air, then zips away, holding the circlet, now rolled into a tube, beneath her.

At that moment, a western kingbird—a flash of yellow belly and black tail—somersaults off the telephone wires overhead. I'm afraid he'll catch my bee, but he loops after a sputtering cicada instead, snaps it out of the sky and returns to his perch. There he bangs the bug against the wire, flips it in the air a few times and finally gulps it down.

As I start to record the bee and the bird in my garden journal, a pair of black-chinned hummingbirds grabs my attention. The female hangs in mid-air like a crescent moon as the male spirals high above her, then plummets, wind bleating in his tail feathers, and sweeps upward again. For a moment he hangs invisible against the sun, then he dives back into visibility, a metallic green bomber, a hurtling, ounce-sized package of feathers and lust.

Nearby, two giant swallowtails are putting on a similar performance. The female, a large, yellow and black butterfly missing one of her commalike tails, feeds nonchalantly at one zinnia blossom after another. She coils and uncoils her capillary tongue in and out of the tiny florets as though she had nothing else in the world to do. Meanwhile, the male hovers frantically behind, beside and sometimes before her, never stopping to rest or feed. His body is nearly vertical, and his rapidly beating wings are spread wide like a duck about to land on water. Suddenly, losing all patience, he rushes at her, and they spurt upwards, beating against one another. I can hear their wings brush together. Then they float over the hedge and out of sight.

As I pick up my journal, I glimpse the cat crouched among the herbs, lashing her tail. Hurrying over, I see her bat cautiously at a newly emerged butterfly, an orange fritillary with silver-spangled wings. Its chrysalis, a tattered husk as frail as a dried leaf, hangs empty on a nearby twig. The butterfly huddles, wings folded, in the protection of the rosemary bush. I grab the cat and we watch together. Has she already damaged it? No. The fritillary opens and closes its wings a few times, then laboriously crawls up the leafy staircase to the topmost stem, where it opens its wings one more time, then glides like a paper airplane to the flower patch six feet away.

I toss my journal aside. Obviously, this is a day for living, not recording life. How amazing that first flight is. One second the butterfly is completely new and untried, then with a single downbeat it becomes airborne, floating on tissue paper wings with instant expertise. As Erica Jong says, it is no less a miracle for being ordinary . . .

Merely in planting a few vegetables and flowers, I have set in motion an entire ecosystem. Bumblebees, carpenter bees, honeybees, leaf-cutter bees, as many kinds of wasps, gulf fritillaries, pipevine swallowtails, giant swallowtails, mockingbirds, kingbirds, hummingbirds, and on and on—all these enliven the garden and even depend on it for sustenance. Their abundance shows what a cornucopia the city is during these early summer months when the desert is empty-handed. While cabbage whites, giant swallowtails, painted ladies, and pipevine swallowtails jostle one another in urban gardens, there's not a butterfly to be seen beyond the city limits.

Over the few years of my garden's existence, I've kept an informal tally of organisms seen there. Every time a new bird or butterfly makes even the briefest appearance, I rush outside with field guide and binoculars. So far, I've counted twenty-three species of butterflies, thirty-four of birds and three of lizards, not to mention hundreds of insects that will, unfortunately, remain forever anonymous since I can't do much more than categorize them by order, suborder and, sometimes, family: beetles, true bugs, leafhoppers, grasshoppers, flies, aphids, wasps, bees, ants, damselflies, dragonflies, moths, and so forth. Some I know to genus by their activities: the bee that cuts my lilac leaves is, perforce, a leaf-cutter bee and belongs to the genus *Megachile;* same with the leaf-cutting ants—genus

Acromyrmex—that collect leaves and flower petals from all over the yard. A few are so distinctive I can call them by name: the green fig beetle that piles up in windrows after summer rains, the obnoxious black cactus beetle that gnaws the pads of my prickly pear, the rather terrifying staghorn beetle, a cross between a lobster and a rhinoceros, that comes to lights in the summertime. But most are simply Grasshopper or Katydid or Damselfly, as though my garden were some children's book come to life.

If I were willing to kill my insect visitors and residents and submit them to identification by a proper entomologist, I'd have an extremely large figure to report, no doubt. Many years ago, an entomologist who lived in the suburbs of New York City did just this and found over fourteen hundred species of insects in his yard. Four hundred sixty-seven of these were butterflies and moths (mostly moths). Flies and beetles ran neck-and-neck at two hundred fifty-eight and two hundred fifty-nine species apiece. He collected seventy-five species of Homoptera, mostly aphids of one sort or another.

But I prefer not to employ a killing jar in what is, after all, a pesticide-free zone. If I capture and poison each solitary insect as I see it—the orange dragonfly that perches over the fish pond on hot summer afternoons, the lone mountain emperor butterfly that nectars at fallen dates—what will be left of my garden's diversity? The arch predator in my garden—Katie, my tortoiseshell cat—has already made considerable inroads in the numbers and diversity of the lizard population, and the mouse she brought for my inspection was the only one I've ever seen in my yard. I'd say one top carnivore per garden is enough. More interesting and less destructive is speculation about why this small space should be home to such a variety of living creatures.

One reason is that, even in the middle of the city, the desert around us makes itself known. City and desert are not, after all, mutually incompatible entities like the positive poles of two different magnets. Instead of repelling one another, they interact in unpredictable and interesting ways. The perimeter of the city is also a zone of contact with the desert, the coarsest in a series of screens that becomes successively finer towards the center. An enormous variety of creatures can pass through the outermost screen, and people who live on the city's edge coexist with animals that I'll never see in my garden: javelinas (wild pigs that root for bulbs and roots); jackrabbits, perennially thirsty and apt to nibble any green, growing shoot left unprotected by a wall or fence; coyotes, quick to learn which households are a soft touch for water and food scraps; rodents of many sorts and a variety of snakes to prey upon them; and the richest possible array of birds, from vermilion flycatchers in low-lying mesquite forests to whispering flocks of black-throated sparrows on higher, more arid ground.

Few, if any, of these creatures pass through the series of screens to the city center where confirmed urbanites like pigeons and English sparrows scrounge a living on sidewalks and parking lots. But between the outermost ring and the central core is a wide zone of ordinary neighborhoods, a mosaic of houses, little parks, shopping centers, gardens, ravines, trees, lawns, and vacant lots where a number of desert animals find habitat that suits their needs. These are, for the most part, not the wildest, rarest creatures; they are, rather, the ones that can coexist with human ways, like horned lizards or mockingbirds, or that can live on such a small scale they generally escape detection, like pillbugs or ants. My garden supports many such.

City gardeners unintentionally entice certain animals into town by cultivating small deserts in their own front yards. Even a lone paloverde or a single saguaro can be an island of desert. Multiply this by hundreds of yards across the city, and you have an archipelago of wild and half-wild places. On almost every island in the archipelago, no matter how small, you can find some creature that belongs to the desert—in the spring, giant mesquite bugs, vividly painted like African masks, cling to new pods and fresh green growth of mesquite trees, and all year long, Gila woodpeckers, raucous birds with houndstooth backs and red caps, treat saguaros as oversized birdhouses. In this way, the desert imprints itself on the city, another reminder of who we are and where we live.

Once in a while, when I find myself thinking that any other place would be better than this, when I feel intolerably constricted and hemmed in by my life, it's enough to step out into the garden. Instantly, I am in touch with larger spheres. My citrus trees and melons originated in the Middle East, my gerbera daisies in South Africa. My tomatoes came from South America by way of Mexico, a beneficent legacy of Cortez's otherwise brutal conquest. The Gila woodpecker squawking among the palm fronds reminds me of the encircling desert. The rufous hummingbird darting at the feeder connects me to points as distant as Alaska and Vera Cruz. My garden becomes the world at my doorstep.

That's when I realize that the natural paradise I seek is not in Hawaii or in the Sierra Nevada or anywhere else: it is right here in my own backyard where a verdin twitches on the telephone wire, ants make wobbly exclamation points as they march under pyracantha leaves held aloft, the dog next door rattles his dish, and wind chimes talk from yard to yard. This world may be objectively small, but I could spend a lifetime learning all about it. Its limits are as broad and deep as my understanding.

I pick up my journal again. A white-winged dove calls from the telephone wire, its voice throaty and muffled. He sounds as though his head is buried beneath a pillow. The watermelon vines silently plot to take over the backyard. Tiny blue butterflies spark from the zucchini plants. The scutter of an invisible bug under fallen leaves brings the cat to attention. If these ordinary miracles aren't enough, that's too bad, because this garden—this here and now—is all I've got. It's more than enough for a full life in a small place.

INTO THE WOODS

Jan Jarboe Russell

"What's this?" said my fifteen-year-old son, Tyler, as he pointed to a crawdad squirming on the edge of Double Lake, one of my favorite childhood haunts near my hometown of Cleveland, in East Texas. "It's gross."

My grandfather Dock Jarboe had once brought me to this very spot in the Big Thicket. Surrounded by the great stands of pine trees and hardwoods, he had entertained me with stories about how old-timers had hunted in this forest for bears, panthers, and wolves. Now here was my only male child standing on the edge of the lake on a July afternoon, unable to identify a simple crawdad.

Tyler planted his size 12 Nikes in the boggy soil—first the left shoe, then the right. His feet made a sucking sound on the wet earth. "Hear that, Mom?" he said. "The land sounds like it's farting."

We walked on without speaking, watching fishermen cast their lines into the lake and listening to the absurd sound of Tyler's nervous march. Then he asked if he could borrow my cell phone. I explained that he would get no reception here. The woods are too dense.

"That's okay. I just want to take a picture," he said as he aimed my cell phone's camera toward the spot where he'd seen the crawdad. "I just want to try and get a shot of this attack fish." He not only got the shot but also entered it as the new wallpaper on my cell phone. Thus my two worlds—the old, rural Texas of my childhood and the new, urban Texas of my present—collided in a single image.

Tyler and I had gone back to Cleveland so that I could show him the kinds of things I used to do in the summer when I was his age. Swim in Double Lake. Climb the Liberty Hill fire tower. Run a mile around the track at the high school. Have a piece of cherry icebox pie at the Liberty Cafe. Shell peas. Make deviled eggs. Hike through the forest.

The Cleveland I remember was a timber town, poor and isolated, slow moving and inward. I haven't lived there since 1969, when I gladly struck out on Highway 59 for the University of Texas, thinking I would leave behind the xenophobia simply by leaving the woods. Over the years, I returned for holidays and to mark certain milestones. I used to come back in the spring when the dogwoods first bloomed. When my children were young, we made regular visits to my parents.

After my mother died, in the fall of 1993, I discovered that some of the same feelings I felt for her I also felt for Cleveland: a strong sense of belonging, a disabling dependence, and deeply buried anguish. I decided to cut all ties to Cleveland, to stop thinking of it as home. By then I had lived more years of my life in my adopted home of San Antonio—where there are no pine trees and I have a clear, liberating view of the horizon—than in Cleveland. Cleveland felt finished for me, the curtain of the forest closed.

It's my children who regularly remind me that no matter where I am, some part of me mentally inhabits Cleveland. My daughter, Maury, who is nineteen, says that my worldview is warped by Cleveland's smallness and limited options. Once, when we were at a San Antonio Spurs game, for example, I remarked that there were three times as many people in the SBC Center as in my entire hometown. "Poor you," Maury said dryly. Last season, when the Spurs faced the Los Angeles Lakers in the playoffs, Tyler told me that several boys at Alamo Heights High School wore Lakers T-shirts to class. I couldn't believe it, because I have a small-town, be-true-to-your-team mindset. "It's a big world, Mom," Tyler said. "Room for both the Spurs and the Lakers."

My parents and I were separated by a generation gap, divided by conflicting ideas about race, politics, and religion. The Cleveland of my childhood was segregated, conservative, and dominated by fundamentalist Christianity. It was a deeply Southern place where generations came and went yet nothing seemed to change. I defined myself by a determination to change. I embraced civil rights. I left fundamentalism behind. I moved to a city that is, in every way, Cleveland's opposite: predominantly Mexican American and Catholic and, for the most part, free of Southern obsessions.

And now, all these years later, my children and I have a geographic gap, separated by more quotidian matters, like food. When I was growing up, we almost never ate in a restaurant, except on Sundays after church. I associate mealtime with eating at home—at a table, with all family members present. My kitchen, like my inner compass, spins between two places. Most days I operate a San Antonio kitchen. There is homemade salsa in the refrigerator and a pot of beans on the stove. However, Maury and Tyler can tell when my mood has turned dark and sad, toward Cleveland. They come home to find black-eyed peas, cornbread, and mustard greens on the table, served with a main dish of overcooked roast beef. Inevitably, one or the other child moans: "Oh, no, not mustard greens. Mom's on Planet Cleveland again."

Then the ritual begins. They make fun of my East Texas twang (sometimes I forget and that word spills out of my mouth as "forgit"). They can't believe that my family had one telephone and shared a party line with our neighbors. They ridicule the fact that my view of the world is fundamentally agrarian while theirs is fundamentally technological. I live in real time on real landscapes. They live in virtual time and space. But it's not all bad: At least they know how to work the DVD player.

On the morning we left for Cleveland, Tyler packed our Suburban with a small TV and a suitcase full of video games, and I made sure that we both had plenty of insect repellent. It had been raining for days in East Texas. I knew the mosquitoes would be big and hungry, not as easily vanquished as the virtual enemies in Tyler's games.

On the long drive, I tried to tell Tyler about the remembered world of my childhood: the old men in khakis smoking on the front porches of wood-frame churches and the women harvesting watermelons from the red dirt, and how I would explore the forests around Cleveland, places of fantastic diversity where cacti grow alongside camellias.

"Are there snakes?" Tyler asked.

"Not only snakes," I replied, "but quicksand too."

Tyler shuddered and turned the conversation to Britney Spears and Paris Hilton. He told me his favorite song is one called "Hot Mama." I chose not to brood on the relationship between quicksand and a fifteen-year-old boy's preoccupation with dangerous women.

These days, Cleveland has lost its sense of place. When I lived there, the population was about five thousand and the distance to Houston seemed vast. Now Cleveland's population has swelled to more than seven thousand, and Houston has sprawled out on Highway 59 to meet its edge. The suburbanization has been in progress for decades, but when Tyler and I were there in July, the transformation seemed complete. The town where I grew up no longer exists.

As we drove around, I called out the changes.

We would not be having cherry icebox pie at the Liberty Cafe. It isn't there anymore. I drove by all the schools—Southside Elementary, where my mother taught for years, my old junior high, the high school. All of them had vanished, replaced by newer versions. Years ago, the Twin Ranch Drive-Inn, which was owned by my best friend Margaret's parents, shut down. The Drive-Inn had been the center of my social life. Margaret and I spent hours there, telling each other stories, stargazing, dreaming of true love, planning our escape from Cleveland. A boy named Butch gave me my first kiss at the Drive-Inn when I was fifteen, just Tyler's age. "Yuck," said Tyler when we passed what was left of the Drive-Inn. "There's nothing here." He was right—nothing but memories.

We proceeded to Circle Drive, and I pointed out the house where I used to live. Tyler had his own memories of the house. He was four when my mother died and had last seen her there. "She hugged me hard on the back porch," he said "It was nice."

After Mom died, my father sold the house and moved to nearby Coldspring, a smaller town that has held on to its sense of place. We drove to Dad's new home, where Tyler hooked up his video games and spent the evening on familiar terrain. It was raining again. I sat outside under the carport, listening to a choir of frogs sing their full-throated song, suddenly aware of how removed from nature I am in San Antonio.

The next morning, I told Tyler that he was in for a treat. I was taking him to my secret place, a place I had visited often both as a child and as an adult. We drove out FM 2025 toward Cleveland, then made our way to the Big Creek Scenic Area. The narrow, red-dirt road was lined on either side by tall pines. As we drove deeper and deeper into the forest, I traveled back in time. I was in my native habitat, a cloistered, sacred universe. Tyler woke me from the trance. "Mom," he said, "do you know the way out of here?"

We continued on for several miles, then pulled over to a four-mile hiking trail. I wanted Tyler to get an eyeful of what's left of the Big Thicket, what little has been spared from logging. I have hiked this trail hundreds of times, usually by myself. It's where I've made the big decisions of my life, where I came to celebrate after both of my children were born, where I grieved when Mom died. Tyler and I slathered insect repellent on our arms and necks, and he grabbed a giant stick. Snakes and quicksand weighed heavy on his mind.

We walked along in silence for a while. The trees made cracking noises as limbs fell from on high. Water dripped from the leaves of the giant hardwoods, making a percussive sound that emptied my head of all thoughts. We crossed several creeks and heard animals stirring. "What's that?" Tyler asked with every noise. "Natural sounds," I said. The vegetation was lush and the air thick with humidity.

Near the end of the hike, Tyler began to settle into the rhythm of walking in the woods. His breathing became more relaxed. The nervous chatter stopped. On that sylvan path, sheltered by pines, we walked where my grandfather and I had walked. I felt serene, more at home and less self-conscious than I had in years. I showed him the things I love   old stumps from felled trees, toadstools with fat caps living in the humus of those stumps, lacy spiderwebs.

For a moment, I thought Tyler felt at home too. But when we were back in the car, he said, "That was creepy, Mom. Can we go home now?"

"Sure," I said, turning the Suburban westward—away from Cleveland, toward San Antonio.

earth is an island

NATURE AT RISK

Liquid cold ripples, falls
in frozen fingers on the moss.
Canyon walls thread thin sky and stream
to strands of azurite and silver.
But where are the condors?

NANCY ELLIS TAYLOR,
"CONDOR COUNTRY/NEW YEAR'S EVE"

ISLANDS

Ceiridwen Terrill

*A*sh Meadows National Wildlife Refuge is located seventy-odd miles northwest of the clink and jangle of Las Vegas and adjacent to eastern California's Death Valley. Thirty spring-fed pools and marshlands bubble with warm subterranean waters, isolated from each other, creating islands of water in a sea of land. Biologists have a name for these inside-out islands. They call them reverse islands—one of the most isolated habitats on earth.

Ash Meadows is a place where resource managers moved quickly to preserve an endangered fish, on their own time and without pay. To better understand the history of Ash Meadows and what island managers did to keep a rare desert fish alive, my colleague and friend, Crystal Atamian, drives with me south, down Highway 95. I invited her for intellectual companionship—we share a fascination with the natural world—and for safety. Even in the wildest places of America, neither of us feels safe traveling alone.

The land of western Nevada stretches like the tanned hide of a deer, its surfaces a uniform russet devoid of any shade trees or even a jumble of boulders. It's a strange place for two women to travel looking for an endangered fish no bigger than a pen cap. The only water for hundreds of miles is what bubbles up from the ground after circulating through earth's veins for more than eight thousand years. Like the forbidding Martian atmosphere, reverse islands intrigue scientists, but we still know very little about these watery caverns, into which divers have gone and never returned. Scientists want to understand more about Ash Meadows springs because the concept of endemism, of a plant or animal belonging to only one place on the planet, has its clearest meaning here. Ash Meadows contains at least twenty-four endemic species, the highest concentration of any place in the United States and second highest in North America.

And yet, despite the uncertainty that comes from a highly specialized existence, an ancient fish flourishes in these watery islands. Called pupfish for their playful, puppy-like behavior, these fish have survived environmental change for thousands of years. They spawned when the wolf and saber-toothed tiger stalked mastodon and camel here, and they outlived them. So why, after surviving the climatic changes of the last ice age, when what is now southern Nevada transformed from a cool, wet climate to the present hot and arid one we know today, have these fish declined to the brink of extinction in the last 150 years?

The water in Ash Meadows gushes upward as an artifact from the belly of the earth, cleaner than any water I've ever seen. Life in the springs depends on healthy aquifers to heave fossil water from under the surface. In Nevada and California, pupfish varieties, some no larger than a paper clip, live in the spa-like waters of Ash Meadows, where waters run to one hundred degrees Fahrenheit. Other pupfish thrive in the cool streams and rivers of Death Valley, neighbor to the west, where waters may be as chilly as thirty-two degrees.

When Crystal and I arrive in Ash Meadows, we sit silently at the edge of a spring-fed pool until streaks of blue iridescence wiggle into view. We peer at pupfish as they pilot through sedges, nip at each other's tails, and bolt. I notice a male Ash Meadows Amargosa pupfish. I train the binoculars on him, but the breeze picks up, ruffling the surface water. When it dies down, I see him grazing the limestone ledge slick with algae, the pup's staple food. He catches sight of a silver and olive-green female and courts her by shadowing her movements. When they come to a patch of algae, they stop and feed together. Then the male swims in place beside the female, coaxing her to release the eggs she carries by nosing her flank. She swims away to an area of sand and silt. The male follows and settles beside her. If she releases her eggs, he'll fertilize them on the spot.

A family approaches the spring with small children in tow. A small girl, about two or three years old, squats next to me. Occasionally a careless parent allows his little lamb to lob rocks into the springs, but most children I see at this spring love the pupfish. The girl's diaper swishes as she bends over the pool, and the skin of her knees pudges. She wags her index finger in the water, and an inquisitive Amargosa pupfish swims toward it. The girl shrieks and yanks her hands to her chest, stamping her feet and giggling. "Fiss," she says to me, and I smile at her. Her quick movements and high voice are the bow that shoots the slender shaft of the pupfish into hiding. But he'll be back.

Butterflies flit over gumweed (*Grindelia fraxino-pratensis*), a threatened plant. One butterfly hovers over the gluey yellow flower heads, and another alights on the yellow-green stalk of grass stiff as a picket. We guess from the color of its wings—a mixture of lemon peel and dark orange, each veined wing framed by a thin black line— that it is a Salt Grass Skipper. It appears to wink with its wings. They quiver and pinch closed, as on a hinge, the way an impatient child knocks her knees together at the dinner table.

What draws people to this bone-brittle place, largely unbroken by shade trees or rockshelters? What is it about pupfish that people like? They aren't furred like black bear or deer. They don't exhibit the human-like intelligence of dolphin or humpback whale. And yet, fifty thousand people come here each year to peer into the springs and watch pupfish play. Pupfish, despite their near extinction, persist— but not without help.

I PICTURE FISHERY BIOLOGIST Edwin "Phil" Pister, who, in August 1969, clutched two white buckets containing the last individuals of the Owens pupfish, a fingerling-size resident of Fish Slough in Owens Valley, eastern California. That was the day Phil had to hurry. He had to hurry, but he had to be careful, too. Already some of his pupfish had turned belly-up to the sun.

In 1948 the Owens pupfish was believed extinct. The waters it relied on had been diverted for agriculture, pumped out, exported, or dammed. It was a lucky day in 1964 when someone discovered a small, surviving population in Fish Slough. But just four years later, in August 1969, Phil learned that Fish Slough was becoming a puddle. He wasn't about to allow the Owens pupfish to go extinct twice. He and a colleague used nets and buckets to remove about four hundred of the pups from the shrinking waters and relocate them to another spring. In Phil's own words: "I distinctly remember being scared to death. I had walked perhaps fifty yards when I realized that I literally held in my hands the existence of an entire vertebrate species. If I had tripped over a piece of barbed wire or stepped into a rodent burrow, the Owens pupfish would now be extinct." For Phil, pupfish are no more and no less deserving of life on earth than human beings. Often asked what good they are, Phil responds, "Well, what good are you?" He cites Aldo Leopold: "To keep every cog and wheel is the first precaution of intelligent tinkering."

CRYSTAL CALLS OUT TO ME from the opposite side of the spring. "See that crawfish?" She points to the bottom of the spring, but as if the crawfish feels the weight of our stares, it scuds across the sand to hide beneath the limestone shelf. This Louisiana or red swamp crawfish (*Procambarus clarkii*) is a new tenant who may have moved in sometime during the nineteen sixties and started terrorizing the neighborhood. It is a voracious eater, pruning aquatic plants and eating pupfish eggs with abandon. Louisianans call it the mudbug. It digs like a lonesome backyard dog, burrowing into spring walls, which then weaken and collapse. When introduced to habitable waters, this crevice dweller becomes the top carnivore in the community and the keystone species: an animal that determines the evolutionary direction of an ecosystem. It would take thousands of years for pupfish to develop defenses against the crawfish—if they ever could.

How did the Louisiana crawfish get to the Nevada desert? It certainly didn't crawl all the way from Atchafalaya Bayou. Perhaps somebody viewed Ash Meadows—prior to its designation as a wildlife refuge—as a place to raise crawfish. Crawfish cuisine never quite took off in the western United States, but the crawfish population did. A single trap can catch more than a hundred crawfish in a few hours.

As Crystal and I wander around the pools, where water runs just under the boiling point, burnt umber-colored crawfish scuttle along the bottom, just undercooked. Sometimes I see only their shadows as I kneel at the water's edge, wiggling my fingertips in the spring to see whether one of them detects the movement. Before I have time to reconsider the stunt, a pincer scissors my thumb. I jerk my hand out of the water and the crawfish with it. The mudbug won't shake loose, so I whack it against the ground until it relinquishes its hold. Blood pulses to the tip of my thumb, and a red line wells up from a split in the nail.

It's my own fault. I stare at the crustacean in the dirt and imagine it swimming in creamy bisque. I could eat it, and there would be one less mudbug to prey on pupfish. Or I could step on it. I leave it baking in the sun.

That evening, somewhere off State Line Road, Crystal and I crawl into our sleeping bags and sleep in the open bed of the pickup truck. When we wake the next morning, sunlight spills over the Grapevine Mountains. We layer sweaters against the morning chill and cross into California's Death Valley National Park, on our way to Salt Creek to see the pupfish of the same name. We pass Devil's Golf Course and the Funeral Mountains, and enter Titus Canyon. Tires climb over humps of gray stone swelling out of the dust as we turn one corner and then another. Desert rock nettle with its pale cream flowers grows straight out of the sheer walls. We get out to take a closer look, and the hairy nettle leaves stick like Velcro to our pants. We notice desert primrose and Mojave aster growing beside the single track as rain trickles down the canyon walls. All we can see from inside this steep, narrow slit is a thin ribbon of gray sky stretched ahead of us. I wonder if pupfish ever look up and see slender wrinkles of sky.

When we exit Titus Canyon, we reenter the park. Crystal and I sprawl belly-down on the wooden boardwalk along Salt Creek, which is some two hundred feet below sea level. Enthralled, we stare at the frenzied dashing of Salt Creek pupfish along the streambed. They don't face immediate threat, but an introduced predator, the western mosquitofish, is just six miles south of here, swimming in the irrigation ditches around Furnace Creek.

Salt Creek waters also feed several small pools along the stream's length. They're mud holes, really. One of these has formed alongside the boardwalk, and Crystal and I, chins in our hands, peer at the puddle's contents. Several inch-long pupfish wiggle in the splash of water, where seasonal evaporation creates water-filled depressions away from the main artery of Salt Creek. These pupfish may die in the shallows. But occasionally, a stray rivulet runs between the puddle and the stream, and a fish escapes across the watery bridge.

The wind picks up, a northeast wind out of Daylight Pass. Grains of sand swirl along the edge of the boardwalk and catch in our teeth. I think of men moving buckets of fish from this spring to that slough. The image replays in my mind as I watch one pupfish and then another catch a wave back to Salt Creek. Some of them won't make it, trapped in a shriveling, temporary reverse island. Earth itself is an island and we are all islanders.

The people who introduced the mosquitofish and the Louisiana crawfish to the remote and watery islands of this desert were cheating evolution, tipping the scales against the pupfish. The managers with their buckets couldn't reach all the threatened plants and animals, and many went extinct. I think of Phil Pister with his buckets and something he'd said to me. "The most selfish thing humans can do in the long run is to show concern for other species because ultimately it comes down to preserving the habitat we both occupy and depend on."

I also think of women like Crystal and me venturing alone into wild places. Leaning over the boardwalk, I dip my palm in the vanishing aquatic island and ladle a pupfish back into the creek.

MY MOTHER RETURNS TO CALABOZ

Margo Tamez

_The Lower Rio Grande, known as the Seno Mexicano
(the Mexican Hollow or Recess), was a refuge for
rebellious Indians from the Spanish presidios, who
preferred outlawry to life under Spanish rule._

AMERICO PAREDES, _WITH HIS PISTOL IN HIS HAND_

The fragmented jawbones
and comblike teeth of seagulls
sometimes wash up from the Gulf
to the levee of the river
and gather striated along the berms
where my grandfather irrigated sugarcane.

My mother, returned after forty years away,
walks there often,
hassled by INS agents
when she jogs by the river.
They think she runs away from them,
that she is an illegal,
trespassing from Mexico.
Used to the invasion,
she asks them how they assume,
how _exactly_ do they know
if she came from here, or there?
_I am an indigenous woman,
born in El Calaboz, you understand?_
she says loudly in Spanish,
and they tear out,
the truck wheels spinning furiously,
sand sprayed into the humid air.

When I was a girl walking on the levee,
I thought I saw gull teeth
chomping at the soil wall.
The air was dank steam,
the scent of sand, roots,
and something alive beneath the soil,
deeper and older than memory.
When I immersed my hand inside
the cloudy water,
it became a fluid form,
soft, something becoming,
something ancient.

The air is still heavy with heat and damp,
but smells like diesel and herbicides.
The scent reminds me of failed gestations.
My reproduction, the plants', and the water's,
each struggling in the same web of survival.

When I was a girl, my grandfather taught me
to put a small clump of soil in my mouth,
and to swallow it. I watched him.
Then I did.
I used to watch the gliding and swerves
of uprooted reeds in the river's unhurried flow
to the Gulf.
I reached with all my body,
stomach on the bank of the levee,
hands and arms stretched out like an acrobat
to touch and grasp their slender stems.
Once, my feet pressed into the soupy bog,
and stepping up was the sound of gurgles,
like seaweed breathing.

Now, I think I'd like to be running with my mother
when she tells of *la migra.**
Listen to the bubbling duet of water and plant life,

listen to their sound,
closely.
Again and again.

*U.S. Border Patrol. *Migratorio* and *migratoria* are adjectives that mean "migratory." Perhaps *migra* is a derivative of one of those words.

CONDOR COUNTRY/NEW YEAR'S EVE

Nancy Ellis Taylor

Liquid cold ripples, falls
in frozen fingers on the moss.
Canyon walls thread thin sky and stream
to strands of azurite and silver.
But where are the condors?
Only water moves.

We toast the wind-bright night
from tin cups. The butane-blue
of the stove flame is weak
magic against the chill.

Cocooned in down, we count
our futures in the constellations.
The Swan, the Bear, the Dog.
Which one is the Condor?

New Year's Day.
We carry our histories to be purified
by ice-blade wind and frost-knife water.
Cut free of our care-worn/car-worn lives,
once again we can dream.
Of condors.

A hawk inscribing enchanted patterns
on the stone-blue sky revives faint hopes.
Is our purification complete?
But condors live in condor canyons
    far away from human hives,
    living out their private lives
    out of the sight of urban eyes.

We must ease the transition.
No visions to share,
we return to our cars
and turn to the news.
Football is once again momentous.
In the cheers of the crowds,
the freeways rumble.
And one by one,
    we forget how to fly.

COYOTE MOUNTAIN

Julia Gibson

*i*n some places, winter is a barren eternity. Winter in Los Angeles burgeons with green and blossom. Sprinklers coax parts of the city into perpetual verdancy. Where mountains split the vast cement smear, chaparral and oak groves cover the slopes, and the stilted houses have distance between them. When the rains come in late fall, the foothills sprout. The sages bloom and the scarlet toyon berries, for which Hollywood is named, ripen.

I lived for a time in what was once a silent-movie icon's weekend hunting lodge, a ramshackle faux castle cracking at the seams. The roof leaked relentlessly in winter, each year in a different part of the house. Vines found fissures in the walls and insinuated their way inside. Raccoons came in the cat door and made off with cantaloupe. Possums lived in the eaves, skunks in the crawl space. From the yard, we could hear traffic on the Sunset Strip as well as woodpeckers tapping out their livings.

A short walk away was Coyote Mountain, as my little boy called it. We took our dog Yhonnie there, walking up a twisty street and a wide dirt driveway to a hill once gouged away for a building site. There had been some sort of zoning difficulty, or problems connecting to the city sewer system, or an otherworldly threat—a poltergeist, perhaps, or the restless spirit of a murdered starlet. Possibly to appease such presences, someone had gathered hundreds of pebbles and laid them on the flat ground in a medicine wheel the size of a garage. A hard rain would move the rocks around, and we'd have to mend the spirals and spokes of the design. We didn't mind.

It may have been the wheel that brought coyotes to that place. On bright nights, surely they danced around its perimeter, singing.

The coyotes were often with us. Coming around the final bend, we would see three or four of them sitting in a row up on the ridge, waiting for Yhonnie to run up the hill and chase them. He always came back breathless and grinning, tail exuberantly high. Had he not been an assertive German shepherd, they might have tried to eat him. Sometimes when Yhonnie was on a leash, the coyotes would stay put and watch us from their lookout, seemingly amused. It was always a thrill to spot them, a highlight of our day. And after dark, we opened windows, hoping to hear coyote yips and howls. Most evenings, we could hear them signaling each other, telling their news.

Coyotes are not popular with everyone. In certain neighborhoods, they are blamed for every cat that disappears. Their tastes are eclectic—shoes, fruit, rodents, greasy burger wrappers, caterpillars, frogs, whatever comes their way. The species has survived full-bore eradication campaigns and spread from its native deserts and plains to every corner of the country. When the whites first came west, coyotes were used to native people, who tolerated their presence and even respected them as equals in the overall scheme. Adaptable, curious, and clever, coyotes got hip quickly to the new world order. They became wary.

Surely, it served our neighborhood coyotes best to check us out while remaining cautious. I expect they tracked us to our home and sniffed around under cover of night, witnessing our passions and anguish and soon concluding that our appreciation of them didn't extend to putting out food. Still, they may have found things of interest. A dropped raisin, our music, a ball left outside.

While living in that house, I typically worked at least sixty hours a week. At home, I had a teenage daughter who drank much too much and a small child whose nanny was as much of a mother as I was able to be. Coyote Mountain was my source for a moment of renewal. But one day a padlocked gate bearing a NO TRESPASSING sign blocked the previously deserted dirt driveway. We had to find a new place for Yhonnie to run off-leash, and soon found ourselves driving to a crowded dog park.

Presidents' Day weekend arrived, and I had three days off. Sleep-starved, I fell into bed on Friday night, happy to know that I didn't have to be up at any particular time. Yet I woke up Saturday about dawn. It had rained in the night, and through the window, I could see an overcast sky. If the rain continued, we could toast speared bread in the fireplace for breakfast and keep the fire going all day. I had nowhere I needed to go, no phone calls to make, no memos to write, and my son wouldn't be up for a long while. I could sleep another hour, maybe more. My man didn't have to work that weekend either, so I nestled closer to him. It was warm beneath the quilt.

But I was wide awake, and the day called to me. The air would be clean. The eucalyptus leaves would be shiny and pungent. I left the bed, tossed a sofa throw over my nightgown, and padded barefoot out the front door, down the steps, and into my yard overlooking the tree-lined street. *Yes, the rain will start again soon. Yes, the smell of wet earth. I'm glad to be on this bit of ground this day. Yes.*

There it was, as if placed where I would see. I knew it was no dog. *He's been hit by a car,* I thought, *and tossed from the street onto my driveway.* I could see, though, that the body wasn't sprawled or mangled. The animal was lying on its side, legs straight out, the same way Yhonnie often slept. Maybe he was asleep. "Hey, coyote," I said. "That's not a good place for you." It wasn't all that bad, really. He could have picked a worse place to die.

The coyote seemed to have simply found somewhere to breathe his last. There was no distortion of the limbs, no grimace in the face, no blood; but something was protruding from his mouth. A stick? A slice of snake? Do coyotes have black tongues? Swollen and stiff, the object had the texture of a tongue and was the general shape of one. Poison. It had to be.

I've never felt so strange. I have to lie down just for a little while, he must have thought.

I had to think of the creature as a male. Coyotes mate in winter, so a female might have had pups growing inside her. The possibility of that, even slightly absorbed, might make me crumble. Then I would fall down on the job for which I'd been chosen, and that would be unforgivable.

It was almost light. Already a few cars were creeping up and down the hill. One driver slowed, peering out the window, wondering if I needed help. I waved him away. It was clear what must be done, and I needed someone to do it with me. Not my lover. He might try to talk me into a different plan of action. And if he came outside, my son would wake up alone in the house. There was one, and only one, right thing. It wasn't up to me to tamper with what had been ordained.

Though I hardly knew Sam, the woman next door, I had the feeling she would get it. Long gray hair loose over her shoulders, Sam came to the door. "Is everything all right?" she asked, touching me on the arm and looking into my eyes.

"I'm okay. There's a dead coyote in my driveway," I said.

Sam came outside wearing a tattered yellow slicker over her pajamas and crouched over the coyote, admiring his tawny sheen and graceful neck. "He's beautiful," she said.

"I figure Animal Control is closed today," I said. "Holiday weekend."

"If they came out, they'd throw him in the back of a truck. It wouldn't be right."

"He has to be buried" I said. "I've got a shovel. I just don't think I can move him by myself."

Sam rose. "I'll get a sheet. We probably shouldn't touch him." We agreed that the coyote had been poisoned.

I surveyed the yard, trying to remember the locations of the various graves already there—Oblonsky the cat, Twinky the rat, a roadkill squirrel and the stillborn kitten. I didn't want to encounter their remains. Sam came back with the sheet. We maneuvered the coyote onto it and lifted. He wasn't all that heavy, and the damp soil was easy to dig. Sam offered a little invocation for him. I wished I could find something to say. When he was covered, we dragged over big stones from the crumbling retaining wall so dogs or other coyotes wouldn't dig him up.

Sam went home, and I went inside. Nobody was up. My feet were freezing and I built a fire.

On Monday, two days later, I woke early again. Again, the morning seemed to want me in it. I stood shivering on the porch a moment, watching the misty drizzle. Turning to go back inside, I spotted something in the driveway. No. It couldn't be. It wasn't. Was I to contend with coyote corpses every morning before tea?

I walked over to the dead animal. This one was smaller, more delicate in the limbs and face. The other one may have been her mate, her brother, her friend. She lay on her side as the first one had, but her head was thrown back. Her mouth was open, as if gasping for air. She had the same dark, distended tongue. I was ashamed of my bad grace. Whatever mystery had assigned me this mandate, I was bound to honor it.

I went in the house to find a sheet. It was raining harder when I came back outside, and she was heavier than I expected. But I dug a hole and put her in it. The soaked sheet was like a caul. Finished, I stood in the mud of my own personal boneyard and trembled with cold, anger, exertion, and fear.

This time, I wept.

IN PARIDA CAVE

Carol Coffee Reposa

I view the paintings
Through a chain link fence, a wall
Of perfect interlocking diamonds,
Barbed wire looped across the top
In stiff festoons. Beyond
Are other walls and diamonds,
Geometric prayers brushed over limestone
Centuries ago,
Growing slowly
Through the storms
And blue-white afternoons
Along the Pecos.

Dwellers must have rested here
Before and after every hunt,
Watching through the night
Around flames high enough
To blacken even these damp walls
Heavy with their clumps of maidenhair
And wild tobacco, strawberry cactus
Sprouting just above. They might have seen
The spirals swept by hundreds of blue herons
Circling the rookery, giant turtles
Swimming through their centuries
of stone. They would have heard
The wind rise when the northers came.

Today the cave is mute, a darkened
Palimpsest of points and fire rocks,
Bones and ancient blood, its topmost layer
Covered with new leavings:
Beer cans, bottle tops and cigarettes

Settling slowly in the midden
With the other relics, paint gangs
From abandoned railroads leaving names
In block print three feet high,
Later logos from the Blades and Crips.

Further down the river
Lightning strikes a shaman's arm,
Burning it into the rock.
His hand bursts
Above the water line
Contours stretched with light.
    My fingers tighten on the wire.

DROUGHT

Hallie Crawford Stillwell

*D*ry weather had been creeping up on the country for several months; however, we ranch people took it as a usual matter . . . Our children were happy in school and I kept more than busy with everyday chores. In the early spring of 1930, as I attended the interscholastic meet being held in the Marathon school, in which my three children participated, my attention was suddenly attracted to the mountains and in a northward direction. I saw a huge dark cloud of brownish red rolling over the tops of the mountains, and it appeared to be crawling, covering the entire world as it crept toward us.

"Look!" I shouted at the school superintendent. "What's that creeping over the mountains?"

He replied, "It looks like a cloud and it's coming this way."

I did not like the looks of that cloud. I had never seen anything like that crawling blanket. I felt that we would soon be covered. I asked permission to take my children out of the contests, gathered them up, loaded my car, locked up the house, and headed for the security of Roy and the ranch. I hoped to outrun the rolling cloud, which I soon realized was a dust cloud, but it overtook me just as I arrived at the ranch house. I was relieved of my panic when Roy helped us into the house and closed all the doors and windows to protect us from that red-brown dust rolling over the countryside. We might as well have left the house wide open, though—nothing, absolutely nothing, kept that dust out of our house. Darkness was upon us even though the sun was still high in the sky. The chickens went to roost, the milch cow bawled for her calf, and the saddle horses came early for their feed. The scenario was strange and unknown to me.

Roy said that we could not risk building a fire in the wood cookstove to cook supper for fear that the wind would catch a spark and set the dry parched area on fire. We could not go outside, so it would be impossible to do the evening chores. All we could do at this point would be to just go to bed and cover our heads, and that we did. The wind howled all that day but finally died down in the night. When I awoke the next morning, I noticed that I could see where my head had been on the pillow, as dust had settled all over our bed and everything else in the house. Outside the dust storm had left its "calling card." Skies were gray and our dear mountains were dim and looked far away . . .

Each day brought a different challenge as we scanned the skies for hopes of rain, rain that would not come. Our cows became poor and weak and could not take care of their baby calves. Even though we lifted many of the cows to their feet when they were too weak to get up and tried to teach them to eat, they would often just give up and die . . .

The government came up with the plan of killing the cattle. They would pay twelve dollars per head for grown cattle and six dollars for calves. As a last resort and with tears in our eyes, we gathered the cows that were too weak to live and accepted the government offer; we shot our cattle. We herded them up against a bluff in the Maravillas Creek and let the government men mow them down with thirty-thirty rifles. They called it a mercy killing.

Our family could not eat supper that night following the shooting.

I went to my rock on the sand pile, and Roy joined me on my rock for his first and only time. We sat in silence as we watched the sun go down in a red glaze. Roy finally remarked, "See that red sunset? That means another wind and dust storm tomorrow. We'll have to work hard to save the few cows we have left."

I knew what tomorrow would bring, and there were many more such days as the red sunsets continued. Our neighbor, Joe Graham, who ranched in the Rosillos Mountains, had brought in sheep to stock his ranch. Graham was a well-known, prominent West Texas ranchman. He had put together a large spread just before the drought set in. His sheep had been doing well in his good ranch country. However, the hot dry days and months that followed without rain soon had his sheep scattering out for food and water. Some of his flock ranged over our way and settled in the Stillwell Mountains. Here they became wild and fattened on desert shrubs in the high rocky cliffs. The only way one could get one was to use a thirty-thirty rifle. Roy told Joe Graham about his sheep being on our mountain and

Joe said, "Roy, do whatever you can with them. I have sheep scattered all over the country. There's no way for me to save them."

Roy replied, "They're fat and will make good eating." Joe quickly responded, "Then they're yours to eat."

Roy wasted no time in killing one and cooking it in a hole in the ground. We feasted for several days. In the following months we ate most of those sheep. Then I sheared the hides and sent the wool to the Eldorado Wool Mill and had blankets made to keep us warm at night. They made those blankets in return for half of the wool we sent them.

We had a good milch cow and chickens that produced plenty of eggs . . . We often shared with our neighbors and they with us. We all grew mighty close in those lean times. One day my neighbor, Grace Lochhausen, came to me and said, "I have nothing to eat in our house. Otto will be home tonight after being in camp for three months with our goats. I know he's going to be hungry." I gave Grace three dozen eggs that Roy had brought in from the ranch. Grace later told me that they ate all of the eggs that night for supper . . .

SURVIVING:
WHAT THE DESERT TEACHES ME

Nancy Linnon

Survivability. The docent repeats the word several times. She says, "Let me tell you about survivability." She says, "Let's talk about the mechanisms of survivability." A small group of us trail close behind her, crouching as she instructs us to feel the microscopic filaments on the brittlebush leaf that helps the desert-hardy plant reflect the sun and protect itself. We look like schoolchildren, the way we stand precisely when she does and cluster close together every time she speaks. The only difference: we take copious notes and attend to each word as if it holds the answer to life's most perplexing questions. Kids are never that naive.

In fact, we're simply gathering information about the desert, a landscape at least three of us have lived in for more than a decade but still aren't sure we understand. We've come to the Arizona-Sonora Desert Museum for our instruction. Part zoo, part natural history museum, part botanical garden, the Desert Museum spreads over twenty-one acres of stunning desert a dozen miles west of Tucson. I've visited before, several times, my three-year-old son leading me animatedly through the reptile exhibit and hummingbird aviary. But this visit is different, both because I'm here with adult friends and because I'm sick—desperately so—a depression ravaging my brain so profoundly that despair has taken over my life: I can't work, I can't care for my son, I can't even pray.

I shuffle along with the group, hoping that getting out of the house will ease something inside of me. I already like Marilyn, our docent. She's in her late fifties, a retired biology teacher. She says she moved to Tucson from Wisconsin four years ago and immediately began the hundred-plus hours of training required to become a docent at the Desert Museum. She also immediately joined the Audubon Society, Arizona National Plant Society, Sierra Club, Friends of the Sonoran Desert, The Sonoran Institute, and the Center for Biological Diversity. I'm not much of an environmentalist myself. I don't even particularly care for the desert—I complain constantly about its unrelenting summers and monochromatic palette—but something about her enthusiasm and deep understanding of this harsh, thorny landscape feels comforting.

She says it again, waving her arm across the natural expanse: "Everything you see here had to figure out how to adapt. It's all about survivability." I want her to say the same about me: that I can adapt, that I'm a survivor—skills that too often feel just beyond the tips of my fingers. Were we in the dark green Pennsylvania forests of my youth, survivability might not be the recurrent theme of Marilyn's botany talk. Had I been born into another family or made different choices or possessed more resilient genes, maybe it wouldn't be the central issue of my life. But here we are together, Marilyn and I, in a landscape suffering a five-year drought and the invasion of African grasses. At first glance, these straw-colored grasses appear a natural, harmless part of the desert setting, but they're not.

"Buffle grass has taken over entire parts of the desert floor," Marilyn explains, "and the thick thatches crowd out native plants." She turns toward the Tucson Mountain range to our east, and I can see the fear in her eyes, even under her white broad-brimmed docent's hat, as she imagines the invaders choking out the saguaros, the creosote, the bursage, the brittlebush that she has talked about so lovingly. Brought here as forage for cattle, which ultimately rejected it, buffle grass is all but unstoppable. Fountain grass, introduced by landscapers who thought it was pretty, is equally virulent.

"I think fountain grass is what's just recently, inexplicably appeared on our land," my friend Pat ventures.

"Kill it," Marilyn says, unequivocally.

During the past few months, I've lost myself repeatedly in images of wanting to kill myself, vivid thoughts of suicide crowding out anything else. It is hard for people to understand—especially those who love me, who see the blessings and privileges of my life, who know how much I would never want to abandon my young son, who have never felt, as Emily Dickinson so aptly put it, a funeral in their brain. I want to be able to explain the cause, to blame it on invasive grasses, but depression resists such tactile explanations. Perhaps it's genetics (my grandfather committed suicide; alcoholism, often a symptom of depression, runs rampant in my family); perhaps it's stress-related

(I have a toddler son, I'm the primary breadwinner, I'm in graduate school full-time); perhaps it's psychological (I don't like mothering, I feel I'm not the kind of mother I should be, I want to live alone, despite my love for my husband and son); perhaps it's spiritual (Do I really believe I'm acceptable to God?).

The group moves a few more steps down the path, Marilyn continuing to answer questions about invasive grasses, until finally my friend Sandy interrupts.

"So what about the future?" she asks, eager perhaps, as we all are, to hear the good news.

"Well, you'll see us out toward Old Tucson tomorrow," she says. "The Sonoran Desert Weed Whackers." She and a group of other volunteers spend at least one Sunday afternoon a month working along side roads where the non-native grasses have grown particularly thick. You do not belong here, they say, as their shovels dig deep, flipping the patches loose. You do not belong here, they say as they gather the grasses in bags and toss them in landfills.

"But," she continues, "invasive grasses are hard to eradicate."

She explains that fire moves rapidly across grass, but because nine-tenths of the plant lives underground, it simply sprouts again. The previous summer, one of Arizona's largest wildfires turned Tucson's air thick with smoke and destroyed thousands of acres of land. People gathered just outside the fire's perimeter, crying as their wooded refuge burned ten thousand feet above them. But not even a year later, observers have reported that green is sprouting again, shoots of baby aspens already visible.

But what worried Marilyn, she says, was watching the flames snake down the Catalina Mountain range, coming perilously close to the desert floor.

"Desert plants," Marilyn explains, "have never had to adapt to fire." Cacti carry water in their pads, for example. "Fire," she says, using her hands for emphasis, "heats that stored water and the plant explodes." Regeneration is much more uncertain.

I find a shady spot where I can sit down, not too far from the group, while Marilyn continues to walk that delicate line between despair and hope. She exclaims that the current administration has the worst environmental record in history. She laments the fresh wells drained to water private golf courses in the middle of the desert.

"Mesquite trees," she says, "will push roots down a hundred feet looking for water, but many just aren't finding what they need." She pauses. "We're taking more out of the land than the land can replenish."

And then, in the next breath, she bursts out with information about the amazing survivability of the landscape she loves. The creosote bush stores moisture in its resin and can live for two years without water. Its roots send out underground runners that sprout genetically cloned babies. Botanists have found a circle of creosote bushes that date back eleven thousand years. Palo verde trees produce bacteria in their roots that take nitrogen out of the air, creating natural fertilizer for its soil and ensuring its survival. Prickly pear cacti turn their pads at an angle to avoid the full brunt of the sun. The sharp thorns of many desert plants discourage the browsing of animals. The slender spines on the saguaros and barrel cacti create natural shade for their more tender centers.

I wonder if it is the same with my brain, its delicate ecosystem assisting my survival with adaptations that prick and spear. Depression halts my life, my brain malfunctioning whenever I work too hard, or don't eat right or quit exercising regularly, or stray too far from some essential part of myself. I drop leaves like the leggy ocotillo when it gets too hot, waiting until a capricious flush of rain to sprout again. Is this apparent faultiness in my brain a tactic to help me survive, a way my body has of telling me that something in my life has to change? It's the more spiritual approach to the illness, one I consider and long to believe. But then there are all those invasive grasses—the sluggish receptors and shifting neurotransmitters and empty synapses that no one, really, knows how to fix—the ones doctors assure me aren't "natural," are something they can "fix." So I take the pills they prescribe and hope for some miraculous clearing, but no one is really sure they'll work, that they'll eradicate the pervasive feeling that I just can't, or don't want to, survive.

It is a stretch, the metaphor of it all. And yet as Marilyn talks, botany becomes brain chemistry, and survivability becomes as much about the psychological and spiritual life as the natural world. Marilyn says that after the glaciers receded from this area, the desert vegetation in front of us today spent four thousand years figuring out ways to survive—or die—before it finally stabilized. She's smiling as she explains this, her appreciation for the desert's majesty, for the miracle of nature's intelligence, palpable. I am rapt with attention, then wonder if I'm just too eager to believe that it exists: some map, some instruction, some landscape from which I can take my cues and heal. I'm not sure why grace would appear here, in front of a cactus, say, rather than inside a cathedral, but here is where I find myself: in a landscape whose most stunning virtue is survivability.

EL RETORNO

Gloria Anzaldúa

All movements are accomplished in six stages, and the seventh brings return.

I CHING

I stand at the river, watch the curving, twisting serpent, a serpent nailed to the fence where the mouth of the Rio Grande empties into the Gulf.

I have come back. *Tanto dolor me costó el alejamiento.* I shade my eyes and look up. The bone beak of a hawk slowly circling over me, checking me out as potential carrion. In its wake a little bird flickering its wings, swimming sporadically like a fish. In the distance the expressway and the slough of traffic like an irritated sow. The sudden pull in my gut, *la tierra, los aguaceros.* My land, *el viento soplando la arena, ellagartijo debajo de un nopalito. Me acuerdo como era antes. Una región desértica de vasta llanuras, costeras de baja altura, de escasa lluvia, de chaparrales formados por mesquites y huizaches.* If I look real hard I can almost see the Spanish fathers who were called "the cavalry of Christ" enter this valley riding their burros, see the clash of cultures commence.

Tierra natal. This is home, the small towns in the Valley, *los pueblitos* with chicken pens and goats picketed to mesquite shrubs. *En las colonias* on the other side of the tracks, junk cars line the front yards of hot pink and lavender-trimmed houses— Chicano architecture we call it, self-consciously. I have missed the TV shows where hosts speak in half and half, and where awards are given in the category of Tex-Mex music. I have missed the Mexican cemeteries blooming with artificial flowers, the fields of aloe vera and red pepper, rows of sugar cane, of corn hanging on the stalks, the cloud of *polvareda* in the dirt roads behind a speeding pickup truck, *el sabor de tamales de rez y venado.* I have missed *la yegua colorada* gnawing the wooden gate of her stall, the smell of horse flesh from Carico's corrals. *Echo de menos las noches calientes sin aire, noches de linternas y lechuzas* making holes in the night.

I still feel the old despair when I look at the unpainted, dilapidated, scrap lumber houses consisting mostly of corrugated aluminum. Some of the poorest people in the U.S. live in the Lower Rio Grande Valley, an arid and semi-arid land of irrigated farming, intense sunlight and heat, citrus groves next to chaparral and cactus. I walk through the elementary school I attended so long ago, that remained segregated until recently. I remember how the white teachers used to punish us for being Mexican.

How I love this tragic valley of South Texas, as Ricardo Sánchez calls it; this borderland between the Nueces and the Rio Grande. This land has survived possession and ill-use by five countries: Spain, Mexico, the Republic of Texas, the U.S., the Confederacy, and the U.S. again. It has survived Anglo-Mexican blood feuds, lynchings, burnings, rapes, pillage.

Today I see the Valley still struggling to survive. Whether it does or not, it will never be as I remember it. The borderlands depression that was set off by the 1982 peso devaluation in Mexico resulted in the closure of hundreds of Valley businesses. Many people lost their homes, cars, land. Prior to 1982, U.S. store owners thrived on retail sales to Mexicans who came across the border for groceries and clothes and appliances. While goods on the U.S. side have become 10, 100, 1000 times more expensive for Mexican buyers, goods on the Mexican side have become 10, 100, 1000 times cheaper for Americans. Because the Valley is heavily dependent on agriculture and Mexican retail trade, it has the highest unemployment rates along the entire border region; it is the Valley that has been hardest hit.

"It's been a bad year for corn," my brother, Nune, says. As he talks, I remember my father scanning the sky for a rain that would end the drought, looking up into the sky, day after day, while the corn withered on its stalk. My father has been dead for 29 years, having worked himself to death. The life span of a Mexican farm laborer is 56—he lived to be 38. It shocks me that I am older than he. I, too, search the sky for rain. Like the ancients, I worship the rain god and the maize goddess, but unlike my father I have recovered their names. Now for rain (irrigation) one offers not a sacrifice of blood, but of money.

"Farming is in a bad way," my brother says. "Two to three thousand small and big farmers went bankrupt in this country last year. Six years ago the price of corn was $8.00 per hundred pounds," he goes on. "This year it is $3.90 per hundred pounds." And, I think to myself, after taking inflation into account, not planting anything puts you ahead.

I walk out to the back yard, stare at *los rosales de mamá*. She wants me to help her prune the rose bushes, dig out the carpet grass that is choking them. *Mamagrande Ramona también tenía rosales.* Here every Mexican grows flowers. If they don't have a piece of dirt, they use car tires, jars, cans, shoe boxes. Roses are the Mexican's favorite flower. I think, how symbolic—thorns and all.

Yes, the Chicano and Chicana have always taken care of growing things and the land. Again I see the four of us kids getting off the school bus, changing into our work clothes, walking into the field with Papí and Mamí, all six of us bending to the ground. Below our feet, under the earth lie the watermelon seeds. We cover them with paper plates, putting *terremotes* on top of the plates to keep them from being blown away by the wind. The paper plates keep the freeze away. Next day or the next, we remove the plates, bare the tiny green shoots to the elements. They survive and grow, give fruit hundreds of times the size of the seed. We water them and hoe them. We harvest them. The vines dry, rot, are plowed under. Growth, death, decay, birth. The soil prepared again and again, impregnated, worked on. A constant changing of forms, *renacimientos de la tierra madre.*

> This land was Mexican once
> was Indian always
> and is.
>
> And will be again.

SACRIFICE TO PROGRESS

Patricia Wellingham-Jones

Like a German shepherd at ease
on a hearth rug, he reclines
by the side of the road.
Propped on forelegs,
ears pricked, snout raised,
he inhales exhaust, his lower limbs
stretched helpless and still.
Threats roar from behind, his view
the stream of taillights ahead.
Wild coyote eyes focused inward,
he waits in dignity to die.
At freeway speeds under a sky gray
and gravid with August, I sweep past,
seared by the picture of yellow eyes grown dull,
head lowered, shoulders sliding,
his body lying limp on hot tarmac.
I carry his image engraved
in the bone of my braincase,
in the civilized curl of my mind.

THE POND

P. J. Pierce

*S*itting at my desk in Austin some three years ago, I couldn't
bear to think of that bulldozer, sixty miles away, uprooting an
acre of towering loblolly pines. The trees had stood in that spot
in the Lost Pines region of Texas for centuries, perhaps for mil-
lennia. The same trees had sheltered me from the sun. Only a
few days before, the wind had played its tune through the high
branches, imitating a waterfall as I hiked on the thick, springy
bed of pine needles below.

When we made the decision to build the pond, my husband
Jack and I had owned the twenty-four-acre wood for less than a
year. Having grown up on the treeless plains of the Texas Panhandle, where each cherished tree is hand-planted, neither of us
could bear to think of tearing healthy trees out of the ground.
But we wanted to have a small fishing lake that we could see
through the trees from the porch of our home-in-the-woods. It
was clear: some of the trees would have to go so our pond could
become a reality in this natural dip in the landscape. It's only
a couple of hundred trees, I kept telling myself, only a fraction
of the thousands of loblollies in our forest. But I knew I was
allowing a rape to take place.

When I finally got the nerve to drive the hour from Austin to
assess the damage—or rather, to view the "progress"—I steeled
myself. There, where the forest had been a few days before,
was a shocking brown crater, a clearing uncharacteristic in this
thick forest. The crater was backed by an earthen dam the bulldozer operators had built from the clay soil gouged out of the
forest floor, deepening the natural valley. When I climbed to
the top of the dam, I discovered behind it the huge felled pines,
pulled out by the roots and left there to die, eventually to be
milled into lumber.

My stomach lurched at this eerie transformation of the landscape. But then I noticed a shallow aqua-blue pool, filling the

crater's low center. Seeing that puddle took some of the sting from the mass destruction we had caused. The bulldozer had unearthed a natural spring that was seeping gradually up at the bottom of the pit.

Over the next months, the dammed pond did fill with rainwater. Just after a heavy rain, the water turned brown and our pond became a small lake, seventeen feet deep at the center. But when drought came the following summer, the seeping underground spring remained a constant, its Caribbean-blue water keeping the pond alive. It invited me often to swim on hot afternoons, and I always obliged.

On this June evening, three years after the trees were felled, I lie on the dock studying the surrounding pines mirror-imaged on the quiet water of a full pond. The bulrushes and cattails line the water's edge. Just before the stars come out, bats dart above me, having emerged from their daytime sleep in an undisclosed location somewhere in the woods. From time to time a bat swoops to the water's surface to retrieve a gnat or mosquito, and concentric circles radiate outward, barely discernible in the fading light. Suddenly one frog launches into his loud serenade, and a thousand more frogs and their tiny offspring join in. Crickets add to the chorus. The pond's daytime inhabitants—the dragonflies and water gliders—have gone to bed. I imagine the big turtles have called it a day as well.

And I ponder: how did these creatures and plants know about our pond? As the brown hole filled with rain and springwater, how was it that they appeared? Maybe it's like the baseball diamond in the cornfield: if you build it, they will come. I suspect that the birds have dropped cattail and bulrush seeds—or maybe the seeds have come in from other nearby ponds when they overflowed during a Central Texas deluge. But the dragonflies, the turtles, the frogs? How did they know to come? The only creatures Jack and I have intentionally put in the pond are the hundreds of bass and perch we brought in big water-filled plastic bags from Larry's Fish Farm in nearby Giddings. The fish seem to have adapted well to the ecosystem that has developed naturally over these three years. In fact, both perch and bass are producing fry that swim along with the tadpoles and baby turtles.

It's dark enough now for me to distinguish the Big Dipper—and yes, the Little Dipper, too—from the place where I lie here on the dock. If the moon isn't too bright tonight, the Milky Way will be visible after the western horizon has disappeared into blackness. A family of deer appears on the dam to munch on the new grass sprouts and to quench their thirst after the long, hot day spent resting in the woods. They make their way past the head-high loblolly seedlings that have sprouted on the dam and around the water's edge. And I smile. For in spite of the destruction we humans caused a few years ago, these hopeful pines have found their way back from the seeds of their parents and grandparents.

Nature is patient. Perhaps she has forgiven us.

the sustaining land

. . . I rise of earth and wind
to the height of one woman
and cup my breast to the hollow-gourd vine
to feed the place that has sent me songs
to grow from the ground that bears me . . .

WENDY ROSE, "LOST COPPER"

SUSTENANCE

Teresa Jordan

*O*verindulgence is a sin, but Aristotle thought it impossible to take in too much beauty. On the river, I found myself drunk with visual excitement, engaged in a gluttony of looking. Among the few possessions that I had stuffed into the grocery-bag-sized dry sack that carried my belongings, I packed a small box of water-colors, and I stole away from our group for a few moments each morning and afternoon to paint. Often I would try to recall something I had seen on the river. Other times I would focus on something directly in front of me: a family of barrel cacti in the late afternoon sun, a single cube of Zoraster granite. On the rafts I found myself looking with an engagement that made me blind to everything else, often forming a peephole with the crook of my little finger, trying to isolate, to understand, the purity of that particular gold of morning light on the ridge, or the muddy claret of the red wall limestone. Once, when I turned away from my own looking to take in my fellows, I realized that our boatman for the day, Scott, had set up his video equipment; Keith, a Missouri farmer, was taking notes for his book; Kathy, a Portland therapist, was photographing; and my husband, Hal, a radio producer, was recording the murmur of flat water and the roar of approaching rapids.

The children's author and artist Maurice Sendak once told an interviewer about his favorite piece of fan mail. A young boy had sent him a particularly charming drawing; Sendak sketched one of his wild things on a card and posted it back. A few weeks later, the boy's mother wrote that her son had loved the card so much he had eaten it. "That to me was one of the highest compliments I've ever received," Sendak told National Public Radio's Terry Gross. "He didn't care that it was an original drawing. He saw it, he loved it, he ate it."

What feeds us, and what do we merely consume, insatiably hungry for more? As we floated off early one morning, I gazed upriver at receding lines of cliffs and talus slopes as they met the banks in the interlace of fingers in prayer. That evening, as I tried to recall the spectrum of blues, from the almost translucent cerulean of the slopes closest to me to the misty indigo of those farthest away, I yearned, with my tiny sketch, to ingest the blood and body of river and rock, not only to take it in, but to enter into it, to transcend, if only for a moment, the tissue that divides us from that which is not us, the mundane as much as the mystical and sublime.

I had climbed the steep hillside above our camp to paint, and when I finished I hiked down to join the easy conversation around hors d'oeuvres that had become the nightly habit of our group. That night, we talked about Princess Diana; her death had been the last news to reach us before we put in. The event had accompanied us these days on the river, a partner to the extraordinary power and beauty that swept us downstream, and now we wondered about the insatiable fascination that had hounded her literally to death, and our own part in it. Many of us were grateful for the distance the Canyon gave us from the media orgy that we knew had erupted around the tragedy, and the titillated addiction we would have given into if we had access to the news. What did we—the world at large, and our own small selves—need from her? What hunger did we think she could satisfy? How full must we be before we cease to grab what glitters, just because it's there?

I asked myself this last question again a few mornings later when a small king snake crawled along a half-inch crag in the limestone behind our camp. We gathered to watch him and he grew perfectly still, aware of us but not, apparently, much disturbed. He was a beautiful thing, only two feet long, striped black and white with the precision of fine painted porcelain. I made a move for my camera and startled him. He jerked perceptively and then slithered away. I still wonder what I thought a photograph might have captured that a longer moment of stillness would have failed to reveal.

Late in the afternoon of the eleventh day, shortly before we made camp for the last time, we stopped at Travertine Falls. We climbed a narrow slot in the limestone and shimmied up a sheer wall of gleaming black schist to reach a small travertine cathedral under a forty-foot waterfall, lit by a single shaft of sun. Each day on the river, embraced by such wonders, I had thought: This is the most magnificent sight I have ever seen. Surely, nothing can exceed this. A few miles later, the canyon would prove me wrong.

On our final morning, as I sat on my sleeping mat to sketch, I thought I would try to capture some essence of Travertine Falls. Instead, I found myself painting our black rubber dry bags: dark, amorphous shapes that nonetheless held, in the clarity of attention, a beauty as surprising as sunlight on schist. The bags were right in front of me; such mundane objects had been in front of me every day of my life. In awe, I realized I had never seen them, *really* seen them, before.

A river trip is a journey. If the current is strong, you don't go back, only farther along. On noon of the twelfth day, we reached Pierce Ferry, the end of our trip. We gathered with our river friends for one last meal—turkey sandwiches laid with dark green leaves of romaine and glistening jewels of cranberry sauce—and talked about how to hold onto the many gifts of the Canyon. We talked, too, about the news that had greeted our landing, the death of Mother Teresa. After lunch, Hal and I packed our car to drive twelve hours straight home; Hal needed to catch a plane to New York in the morning.

Late that night, as the long yellow beams of our headlights cut across the black Nevada desert, I fell asleep and dreamt of gauzy white cotton backlit by sun, billowing under a deep azure sky. Just as I realized I was dreaming of India, I woke to hear Mother Teresa's funeral on the radio. The reception was poor and full of static; it drifted in and out and came from very far away, a dream itself perhaps, or a sacred invocation.

I reached out to my husband. "Are you okay?" I asked. "Do you want me to drive?"

"I'm fine," he answered. "I'm good." He squeezed my hand, then put his own back on the wheel. We drove on through the night toward the comforts of home, looking for the courage to change our lives.

GATHERING AT THE RIVER

Joan Shaddox Isom

*P*eaches are ripe, and the great-aunts are once again at their summer place on the river. A thin voice on the telephone summons me. "Joan, Wade sent you some garden stuff. Come and get it."

My family has a communal garden and orchard on the aunts' property in eastern Oklahoma, where anyone who wants to ("long as you're fambly") can grow vegetables and fruit in the soil rich from the Illinois River overflow. But I know that the produce from my cousin Wade will be different: striped watermelons from the sandy fields around Shawnee, maybe, or Indian peaches that bleed burgundy juice when bitten into. I'm wrong on both counts. Two bulging grocery sacks block the hallway when I arrive. I peer inside one. Okra. It has a fuzz that stings like nettles. After gathering the innocent-looking pods, people have been known to break into a full gallop from the garden to the house, seeking a cool shower. The other sack holds purple hull peas. Remembering that I once spent an entire morning trying to shell enough peas for lunch, I struggle to put on an appreciative face as I enter the kitchen.

All three of the aunts are there, but only Nina, the youngest at eighty-one, is working. She's the practical one. The other two, both in their nineties, sit at the kitchen table watching the procedure and telling stories. Eleanor has made her annual trip all the way to Oklahoma from Amarillo to oversee the picking and preserving of the fruit. Dressed in a designer pantsuit, she sits like an ancient dowager with her cane in hand, regal, still beautiful. "I think someone is raiding my orchard," she rasps. I try to imagine peach pirates scaling the banks and lowering their contraband to waiting canoes. But this is a quiet place. Any peach thief would be a neighborhood child grabbing a snack on his way to swim in the river.

Still, Eleanor reflects the thinking of most of my family. Food is paramount. Grandmother M. was known for her huge, late suppers cooked on the wood stove long after company arrived. In the 1940s, air conditioning was nonexistent, so waiting until the heat dissipated before starting the evening meal was a sound idea. As a kid, I would doze on a kitchen chair, listening to the talk and the clatter of pans, smelling the scent of green beans cooking with new potatoes mingled with the smoke from the cedar firewood Grandmother kept feeding the enormous range. By the time the meal was ready, most of the younger kids would have given up and gone to sleep on one of Grandma's bright quilts spread in the living room, but she would roust them. "Get up, get up, you childr'n! Come and eat!"

An unspoken agreement in the family dictates that each time we meet, we trade gifts that are food or food-related—half a pecan pie, or freshly picked blueberries, or gritty sand plums from the plains around Anadarko (good for jelly making), or a jar of sourdough starter. Ancestral faces peering reproachfully from the past, I try to summon the courage to uncover the lemon cake I've brought, hoping that the great-aunts won't notice how it slopes to one side, praying that I'd succeeded in fishing all the lemon seeds out of the batter before I baked it.

Iona, the philosopher-storyteller (who, I suspect, doesn't enjoy cooking and canning any more than I do), is in her usual talkative mood. Given to salting the conversation with historical non sequiturs, she informs us, "Grandpa Lynch used to peddle peaches in the summer time. Once a lady came to the door in just her petticoat, and it was so short he could see her britches."

Eleanor broaches a more important subject: who could cook and who couldn't. "Now take Emitar," she says. "She may have been named after someone in the Bible, but don't let that fool you!" Emitar's name surfaces often in our family. She is not a positive role model. It seems that the woman, a distant and long-deceased in-law, could cook, but wouldn't. On the other hand, Grandma Lynch, wife of Mose, held up as an icon for the rest of us, habitually cooked huge meals and fed them to anyone who wandered by.

"And Grandpa Mose and I would always sit at the kitchen table and talk. I liked him," Iona says, clearly absorbed in the past.

"And he liked you because you'd listen while he rattled on about the stars and the universe," Eleanor declares. "I don't give a flip about the universe." She accentuates her words with a thump of her cane and hoists herself out of her chair to peer into the cupboards. With a satisfied grunt, she finally locates her cast iron pot and plunks it down on the stove, while Iona, whose doll-like face reminds me of a good fairy in an Arthur Rackham illustration, smiles beneficently from her perch in the corner where she peels an occasional peach.

Nina has figured out how to assemble the food processor and she's whirring up the fruit. It's impossible to have a conversation over the noise, but Eleanor and Iona continue to talk anyway. Eleanor's lips are moving. I think she's saying, "Don't turn that stove up too high—you'll scorch those peaches!" but I can't be sure. Then the processor stops and her voice is loud in the sudden calm. "It'll take a chunk of your time to shell those peas," she tells me, her thin lips on the verge of a smile.

She's just doing this to rankle me. You have to understand that in this family's mind-set, letting any fruit or vegetable rot on the ground is sacrilegious. Anyone not buying into that philosophy is considered a renegade. Eleanor knows me too well, and that's why she's about to grin.

But only one other thing rivals the fondness for food and cooking among my relatives: storytelling. Above the clamor of peeling and preserving, the aunts continue to pull stories out of the past. Most of their anecdotes are centered on food: how to fry fish (get the grease so hot it will light a match tossed into it), how to make wild huckleberry pie (throw in a few green huckleberries so the filling won't be too bland). I ask for my favorite tale, something that happened long before I was born. Eleanor obliges. It seems that the adults were eating dinner and the children were all playing chase around and around the dining table, which was perched precariously over a trapdoor that led to the cellar. As the game became more rambunctious, the catch on the trapdoor loosened and the dining table and all the dishes and food fell into the cellar.

Iona listens to her sister and nods sagely. She has developed a let-it-be attitude as she grows older, probably imagining an afterlife where other philosophical fairies will welcome her with sugarplums and honey cakes and everyone will sit around and discuss lofty topics, with or without Grandpa Lynch.

It's time to go. I bid the aunts goodbye as they pile sacks of peas and okra into my arms. I totter to the car. Afternoon is turning into evening, and the cicadas' song is not as shrill. Bees and wasps buzz sleepily over the fallen fruit in the orchard. I sit for a moment, trying to absorb the hot, dry season that I had wished would end. Weary of the fierce heat, tired of dragging hoses to water newly planted trees on our own acreage, scrambling to keep the blueberry and black-berry bushes alive with generous buckets of water every evening all during July and August, I'd thought I craved a change. But now that summer is about to be swallowed by autumn, I'm inclined to mourn its passing.

I look at the tomato plants, tall, caged in wire, still producing green fruit that will never fully ripen before the frost. I think of standing in the middle of the patch, just after the Fourth of July, and picking a sun-warmed tomato, rubbing it on my jeans to get the dust off, biting into it, juice running down my chin and onto my shirt, the tanginess of the first mouthful making my jaws ache, only to relax when the sweetness of the center soothes my taste buds. I remember how I chewed and swallowed and felt the sun burning on my shoul-ders, all the while listening to the rattle of the rain tree pods in their parody of a real downpour we were all longing to hear.

Taking one last look at the river, its level at a summer low, I know the vacationers will soon go back to their routines of work, football, soccer, and band. The fall rains will wash clean the pollution they've left behind, and farmers along the banks will check their cattle, pick up litter in the fencerows, and nod complacently at the sight of a solitary heron fishing in the shade of a willow tree. At twilight, local moms will once again bring their toddlers to splash and squeal in the shallows, not worrying about getting mooned by revelers canoeing by. Country boys will eye the native pecan trees with entrepreneurial eyes and start counting the days until they can fill their baskets to sell at roadside stands. And the land and the river and the natives will heave a great sigh and settle down to enjoy the too brief Indian summer.

A swirl of blackbirds in the orchard. They have not yet begun their squabbling, sputtering chorus that portends cooler weather, but they are restless. And it's late, and I'm loaded with produce. I get into my car and pull out of the drive. My wrists start to itch. I suspect that some of the okra fuzz must have worked its way inside my sleeves, and longing for a cool shower, I take a curve too fast. A thump tells me one of the sacks has overturned. I'll have to grabble under the seats to find elusive peas or worse, spiny okra pods. Emitar comes to mind, the scorned one, the Woman-Who-Would-Not-Cook.

Finally home, I douse my hands and wrists with cold water before I start the shelling and chopping and frying process, vowing to fix the stuff and feed it to anyone who'll eat it: the hay balers in the neighbor's field, still working at twilight in an effort to get the hay in before a summer storm sweeps through, joggers who find our country road a good place to run, my husband, anyone is fair game.

I may not be the best cook in the world, but I'm no Emitar.

For Maura Luna Squash Blossom

THE COLLECTION

Margo Tamez

*C*hile pods wintered over,
shriveled like old toes in a bath—
their stems brittle as amber
that would snap apart at the touch.
They will save in Tarahumara baskets
for seed and grinding.

Aztec blue corn, dried on the stalk.
We let the weeds get away.
Rodents and crows had their share.
I rub each cob in a wringing motion,
old calluses wake up.
Kernels fall into the pan,
pinging like hard rain
on the metal roof.

Saving these seeds, I feel a peace
that many lives got what they needed
and gave back.
A micro-landscape was fed and enlarged.
When these night-blue kernels
rub my fingers raw,
when I am tired of doing this
and it hurts,
I'm mad
that I want to quit.

People's faces appear. I go on.
This corn came heirloomed,
grandmothered and grandfathered,

to me, us.
The corn breathed air, drank water,
smaller lives ate the compost,
their shit and heat and life made the humus
that fed it.
I will eat.

The soreness will go away.
My hands twist and rasp
one cob against another.
I reach for two more
from the basket piled high
with a day's full work.

CHILE TALES: THE GREEN ADDICTION

Sandra Ramos O'Briant

*I*n Texas, when my parents were still married, we ate fried chicken, mashed potatoes laden with cream gravy, green beans flavored with bacon, and buttery, light biscuits. Every item on the menu had its own serving dish, and cloth napkins were always used.

"May I have another biscuit, ma'am?" I would say.

"You surely may, Sandra Mae," my daddy's mother would reply, and everyone would smile. If it was just Mama and me at the dinner table, we might have fried pork chops and suck on the salty bones.

In Texas, there were black-eyed peas and ham, and all manner of greens and put-up preserves. And we had watermelon and homemade ice cream. Daddy held a bourbon and water in one hand and turned the handle of the ice cream maker with the other, while Mama and Grandma drank iced tea on the back porch and exchanged polite insults.

My grandmother didn't like it that Daddy had married a *Mexican.*

"Don't forget your manners out there, Sandra Mae," Grandma said after the divorce, right before Mama and I set off for New Mexico. Glaring at my mother, she bent down to whisper in my ear. "Remember what you learned here and act like a lady."

In Santa Fe, we ate pinto beans muddy in their own gravy at Mama's parents' house. My aunts, cousins, grandparents, and sometimes neighbors ladled the beans into their bowls from the pot in the middle of the table. No other utensils were in evidence. Instead, tortillas wrapped in a dishcloth were passed around.

Each diner split her tortilla, usually into fourths. Then the tortilla was rolled into a half-moon scoop, and eating commenced. Dexterity and speed were required to fill the tortilla scoop and stuff it into your mouth before the bean juice had a chance to run out the back and down your forearm. I leaned over my bowl, like the adults, and soon shoveled like an expert.

"Hand me another tortilla," Aunt Frances would say, not at all unfriendly, pointing her chin in the general direction of the tortillas.

The only green vegetables offered at my grandparents' table were chiles. Meat, usually pork, was a rarity reserved for the green chile pods. If I wanted meat or vegetables, I was going to have to learn to eat chiles.

Mama started me off slow. She would pick up a chunk of meat and suck out the chile juice before placing the morsel on my tongue like a sacrament, then sit back and wait. I chewed tentatively, fearing the bite of the treacherous chile pod. Occasionally, a seed would sneak through to make my eyes tear and my nose run. My face contorted in pain, I'd swallow glass after glass of icy well water. Then I would ask for more.

By the end of that first winter, my yearning for the green was established. I was an addict.

"Chiles from Hatch," the boy yelled from the back of the pickup that drove slowly down our street, pausing whenever a homemaker ran out to negotiate. He sat atop a truck bed piled high with shiny green pods, some plump and beginning to turn red, others long and thin or curled into a defiant C. I scooped up a handful of pods and breathed in their spicy promise—Hatch was an area in New Mexico where the best and most flavorful chiles were grown—while my grandfather sniffed and then bit into a pod to judge its heat—mild, medium, or hot. He bought a bushel judged to be medium. Yeah, right.

In Texas, my father's new wife and his mama might be putting up figs, strawberries, tomatoes, or pickled okra. But in New Mexico, the women put up chiles for the winter. A certain *macha* bravado was necessary for this task.

The chile pods were laid on cookie sheets and roasted under the broiler. Periodically, my aunt would reach in and turn the pods over. Soon the house filled with the acrid scent of burned green. Next, she dumped the black-mottled pods onto the newspaper-covered table in the dining room. The roasted pods' black skin lifted easily as my aunts, Mama, and I sat around the table peeling chiles.

Soon our fingers burned. We began to sweat and sniffle. Too late, Mama warned me not to touch my eyes. She refused to rush me to the emergency room, flushing my eyes with cold water instead. We returned to our task. By the end of the day, two hundred peeled chile pods were laid to dry across the lines strung up in the screened porch off the kitchen. Adults and child alike gazed red-eyed, noses and fingertips smarting, at our day's work.

I looked up at the glistening faces of the women in my family, each content with her contribution. I too had suffered, wept, and done my share. For the first time since my arrival, I felt full and at peace. The manicured hands of my Texas relatives might master a pecan pie or even divinity, but they didn't have the *cojones* to deal with the sultry heat of chile. Feminine wiles and prissy manners had no place in New Mexico. *We* were the real women.

POEM IN WHICH I GIVE YOU A CANYON

Sandra Lynn

Notice that this canyon is comprised of
two strata of volcanic origin:
a dark bitter chocolate and an airy vanilla.
The vanilla is light-hearted, grainy,
like the sugary dust suspended
in the slope of each morning's sun
as it first pours into the Basin.
The chocolate beneath is stubborn
and grumblesome
and continually hums a low tone.
But together they make a nice duo,
for you, a double-dip canyon to sample.

And for a fillip, my love,
two ravens playing loud wings
and a white cove stuffed with black bees
    on a honeycomb.

DUMPLINGS COME TO TOWN

Patricia Nordyke Pando

*O*ur bright blue 1949 Buick eased to a stop under the bois d'arc tree that dwarfed the tiny white bungalow. It seemed strange to be visiting Grandfather and Grandmother Nordyke at their new house in town. Always before we'd driven down a dirt road to their farm, stopping for Mother to open the gate to another world.

Those dry two hundred and forty-seven acres plopped in the center of Texas might have seemed forlorn to random passersby, if they were able to see that far back from the county road. But it was a place of wonder for my dad, his sisters and brothers, and all their children.

During our visits, Uncle Clarence, a Texas Ranger, sometimes lifted me in front of him for a horseback ride. Daddy often took us to the top of the ridge, to scout for arrowheads and see the grave of the old Indian chief.

"Whatcha doing down there?" he'd ask.

Silence.

"See," Daddy laughed. "Just like I told you. He said, 'Nothin' a-tall.'"

"But, Daddy," I protested. "He didn't say anything."

"Nothin' a-tall," my father repeated.

Later, we hunted for eggs with Grandmother or watched Aunt Alda milk the cows or took a bucket of scraps to the pigs. The girls always helped with the dishes. Whatever we did, we always gathered on the front porch after supper. In the soft glow of a kerosene lamp, we watched Grandfather pull his fiddle from its case, lift it to his shoulder and create magic.

But today was different. Unable to manage the farm any longer, my grandparents had moved to town. Though Daddy bought the country home, we weren't going to live there. Other children would. I never again would fall asleep to the lullaby of the creaking windmill. Maybe never hunt for arrowheads or eat a snack under the long shadows of the cedar tree. Already, I missed it.

Daddy glanced at his wristwatch. "Just in time. They'll be sitting down about now." Of course, he meant the men would be sitting down. We'd driven over two hundred miles to have Sunday dinner with the family. It was our first visit since the move. I held a gift-wrapped box full of fluffy pink towels for Grandmother's first real bathroom.

"She promised chicken and dumplings." Daddy rubbed his hands together.

Mother wore a pained expression. Chicken and dumplings had always been a sore point between them. No matter that Mother copied the recipe exactly from the notes she took as a bride, watching Grandmother make them. No matter that she followed it exactly until the recipe card was smudged and torn. "Don't stir," was written firmly in black pencil and underlined. "Don't put lid on!" Underlined twice.

But it did matter. Mother's dumplings were never as good as Grandmother's, at least not to Daddy.

We trooped in the front door. After all the hugging and kissing, Daddy pulled out the one empty chair at the table. "Pass me those chicken and dumplings."

Mother and I fled to the kitchen where she eyed a fresh batch of dumplings and slumped. Dusty with flour, they were laid out on a towel made of neatly hemmed, cotton feed-sacks.

Daddy stuck his head through the kitchen door. "Mama! You've done it again. Moving to town doesn't make one whit of difference. Those chicken and dumplings—" He looked at Mother, who looked away.

After dinner, the men gathered under the bois d'arc tree outside to talk about men-things. They admired Daddy's new car and Uncle Jewel's new pickup, then discussed horses, peanut prices, politics. They all loved Harry Truman.

The women's turn to eat came after quickly washing and drying the dinner plates. Unbuttoning the top button of their flowered rayon dresses and rolling their stockings down around the tight garters worn during church, they could enjoy life for a few minutes. Choice pieces of farm-grown chicken and slices of pie, somehow overlooked by the men, made their way to the table. But both batches of dumplings were gone.

I kept quiet and listened to talk about new babies, long-lost nephews, and naughty Aunt Thelma, who had moved to Phoenix.

Later, Mother took a few extra minutes to dry the last set of saucers and coffee cups. "Mrs. Nordyke," she said, "I'm still trying on the dumplings. I just can't get them right."

"Did you stir them? I told you, never stir."

"No, ma'am. I only stirred that one time."

"And the lid?" Grandmother asked.

"Not once."

Grandmother patted Mother's hand. "To tell the truth, Dottie, I changed that recipe as soon as we left the farm, and Lewis didn't even notice."

"What do you do different?"

Smiling, Grandmother walked to her shining new refrigerator, opened the door, and pulled out a can of Pillsbury biscuits, handing it to Mother. "Roll 'em out with lots of flour, till they won't hold anymore, then cut 'em in strips. Hide the can at the bottom of the trash."

"Mrs. Nordyke!" Mother's jaw dropped. "Not canned biscuits!"

"I lived without electricity or even an icebox for fifty years. I've got 'em now, and I'm never going to make a biscuit or a dumpling from scratch again. Never." With that, Grandmother stuck the can way back behind the eggs in the refrigerator, took off her apron, and headed for the front porch.

She sat down beside me on the swing as Grandfather pulled out his fiddle. "You know," she said, "I don't miss that farm one bit."

More than fifty years have passed since that night. The farm belongs to me now, and I return there occasionally to sit in the shadows of the cedar and remember my family.

Mostly, I remember Grandmother.

WISH LIST

Rosemerry Wahtola Trommer

All I want is to linger with you
in a meadow above tree line
steeped in pink paintbrush
hushed below the gray ridge.

To lie there with you,
below midsummer sun,
paintbrush pink blushing,
our limbs barely stirring,

your elbow, my thigh,
warm where our skin meets,
goose bumps where wind strokes.
Below the pink paintbrush

my limbs seek your skin—
amber as high desert honey—
bare, we lie stirring,
my elbow, your thigh.

    To steep into morning.
To linger below. To yield
to the meadow's pink blush.
Stroke of wind. All I want. Hush.

LOST COPPER

Wendy Rose

Time to tend the fields again
where I laid my bone-handled spade to earth
and dug from its dirt the shy child-songs
that made my mouth a Hopi volcano.
My hands retreat dusty and brown
there being no water pure enough
to slide the ages and stones from my skin,
there being no voice strong enough
to vibrate the skin and muscle apart.
Like a summer-nude horse I roll on my back
and fishtail my hips from side to side;
then on my belly, my navel gone home,
I scrape my cheek and teeth and ride.
From there I rise of earth and wind
to the height of one woman
and cup my breast to the hollow-gourd vine
to feed the place that has sent me songs
to grow from the ground that bears me:
this then my harvest
    squash-brown daughter
    blue corn pollen
    lost copper

THINK NOT OF A TECTONIC PLATE
BUT OF A SUMPTUOUS FEAST

Ellen Meloy

*I*magine the Colorado River Basin as if it were a grand banquet spread before you, your dining room chair bellied up to the Grand Canyon, your left elbow resting on Hoover Dam, your right elbow on the Sleeping Ute's nose, your fork poised somewhere above Canyonlands National Park.

Think not of a tectonic plate but of a sumptuous feast. Mesa tops of thick-headed piñon-juniper broccoli, meandering banks of lush cottonwood celery and tamarisk slaw, a tangy salad of hackberry, coyote willow, and other riparian greens. Rich, teeming eddies of catfish bouillabaisse and carp carpaccio. Slickrock pools of quivering green Jell-O, sage-freckled Uinta Basin custard, Book Cliffs tortillas, frybread rolled from the yeasty mounds of Nokaito Bench. The cool slake of a pothole martini, garnished with tadpole shrimp and a Russian olive. Wingate Sandstone tarts steaming beneath a latticed cryptobiotic crust. North Rim cutlets breaded in mountain bikers. A jumbo helping of Moenkopi mud pies piled high on your sectional plate, buttressed with brave volcanic dikes to dam off the gravy of Chinle Wash. A thin ribbon of café au lait river that carries a tiny speck of a human being, although the lusty feast distracts your notice.

You gulp succulent brachiopods embedded in limestone fruitcakes, gnaw the bony ribs of Shiprock, spoon up sun-ripened tomato-Red House Cliffs, and ice your tongue with the San Francisco Peaks' pale sherbet. You swallow Navajo Mountain like a plump muffin and bite off that potato chip of a dam on Glen Canyon. A faint tease of gluttony numbs your palate. Or is it indigestion? Still, you must eat, for each year the Colorado Plateau menu diminishes, the diners grow more numerous and their appetites ravenous.

Munch that meatloaf of a mesa, that most tender loin of Comb Ridge. Wash down Monument Valley with foamy drafts of Lava Falls. Crunch those toad bones, devour the lizards, ravage the Triassic cephalopods. Never mind the desert bighorns, who are endangered, or the ravens, who taste awful. Avoid the datura. Spit out the dung beetle. Relish bite-size canyon wren appetizers, impaled on yucca toothpicks. Slurp the dark sauces of Black Mesa coal, fend scurvy with Lime Creek, and scald your tongue on Mexican Hat's gravel-capped uranium tailings pile, that broad, glow-in-the-dark, blue cornmeal mush wedge sprawled below and beyond the Moki Dugway, insane and forever.

After-dinner Cigarette Spring in hand, plate clean clear down to bedrock, you push back your chair and loosen your belt. You pluck a few B-52s from your teeth and launch a sated burp toward Denver. If we gourmands truly love this river basin, you sigh, we shall never go hungry . . .

the key is in remembering

GROWING UP ON THE LAND

Sand still blows wild
as mesquite, shadows prickle like cactus piercing
the horizon and eyes still tear from the sun, but
courage rooted deep here, gushed high and fierce here,
and generosity still sprouts sudden as an
*   occasional elm.*

DAVI WALDERS, "BIG SPRING, FIFTY YEARS AFTER"

THE TRICK IS CONSCIOUSNESS

Paula Gunn Allen

I must have been mistaken.
Taken for a ride, an eternity of them,
masked strangers driving me hundreds of miles in
unidentifiable cars down nameless highways,
dark side roads of a thousand tales and thoughts—I
must have misunderstood the terms of the agreement
between time and place, identity and surmise, those roads
led somewhere, I thought, and those someones would take me
swiftly there. I must have been wrong.
It has, I suppose, to do with temporality—
sensation, duration, whatever we know of time:
with how waves swell and break, how sand blows from one
county to the next, how light blooms pale and deep
one year from another, yet still remains the light.
I think about long ago
as they say or said *humma ho* when the tale began,
and wonder how the earth has changed, not I but
it in twenty years, wonder at the completeness of it,
getting, forgetting, sudden realization, no
excuses, no surprise,
there it is.
I remember the corral behind the house,
the wooden stairs up to it, chicken house, stall, rabbit pen,
pigeon pen, the high rocks shading.
It was full during the war. My father
didn't want us to want—there were chickens, rabbits, a cow
that gave enough for the whole village, sheep, pigeons,
a huge pig.
They made *chicharrones* when they slaughtered it.
I was maybe four.
Later the corral was empty.
Used to wander around in it, wondering.

I still do, at night, at dream.
And I remember Grandma's mulch bed—
the crazy lily pond she ran us out of,
the tamarisk tree behind the coal shed, deep
shadows there, spider webs, trumpet vine, I
dream about them now, sound, smell, shade and light
so complete—I have changed nothing.

The key is in remembering, in what is chosen for the dream.
In the silence of recovery we hold
the rituals of the dawn,
now as then.

RED DIRT: GROWING UP OKIE

Roxanne Dunbar-Ortiz

I was nearly three, and we had almost finished more than a year on the farm a few miles south of Piedmont, in a nice area down by the creek with cottonwoods, when one day in January Daddy came home and announced we were going to move ten miles northwest, out on the flat plain, and caretake a horse ranch. In the deal we would be allowed to have a vegetable garden, cornfield, and some stock and chickens. My brothers and sister and mother were relieved about not having to chop cotton anymore, and I was happy I wouldn't have to when I was older . . .

The day we moved to the Barnes Ranch was Groundhog Day, a day that felt like springtime. The air was soft and warm, the sky the color of the bluing Mama used in the wash and without a cloud. For a week rain had fallen and melted the ice and snow. The roads were no longer muddy but still ruby red from the rain. The wheat fields on the plains had turned pale green overnight . . .

The landlord had promised to provide two milk cows, two hogs to breed, and two dozen chickens, and he did. Laurence and Hank milked every morning, and Mama and Vera made butter and buttermilk. The women fed the chickens and collected the eggs and slopped the hogs. Soon we had a litter of pigs and slaughtered the hogs for bacon and loins to sell in town, keeping only fatback for ourselves. As the chickens multiplied we had fried chicken for Sunday dinner and Mama had plenty of eggs to sell, but mostly we ate the squirrels and rabbits and possums and coons that Laurence and Daddy shot. Mama and I did not like the wild meat. I disliked biting into the shot. So I was content with beans, fried potatoes, raw onions, and cornbread, like my mother. Soon the garden gave us radishes and green onions, tomatoes and lettuce, snap beans and peas. Mama canned what we couldn't eat or sell . . .

The summer of 1941, just before I turned three, came in hot and dry on the Barnes Ranch. By the Fourth of July the land was parched. For a month the temperature had rarely dropped below a hundred degrees even at night. The horses suffered. Daddy, reading the natural signs, scared us: "There's gonna come a bad wildfire." . . .

Another month passed without rain.

"Just like '36, sure am glad I ain't working no cotton," Daddy said. The cotton and wheat crops in the county had withered and been plowed under, making even more dust to blow.

And then it happened just as Daddy had predicted. One night I woke to a strange sound, a sound I had never heard before, a kind of roar and crackle almost like sharp thunder, but I did not smell rain, only more dust, which was no longer a smell but a presence. Yet I hoped that the racket foreshadowed a downpour. I lay listening as the sound grew louder and felt the room grow hotter. Suddenly the room lit up, almost as though the sun were rising close by, or closer than usual.

"Roxie, run!" a voice boomed from the dark. At first I thought it was God's voice but it was Daddy's.

"It's the end of the world," Mama yelled.

"Ain't no end of the world. Worse than that, a wildfire," Daddy said.

Suddenly we were all outside. The horses screamed. Mama yelled out a verse from the Book of Revelation: "And the devil that deceived them was cast into the lake of fire and brimstone, where the beast and the false prophet are, and shall be tormented day and night for ever and ever."

"Why I'll be doggoned," Daddy said. The wall of fire turned and headed south. "The road stopped her but she could come back." He told Mama to pump water and fill the tin bathtub and buckets. Daddy and Laurence ran to the barn to get the horses out. I followed them. They took all the quilts and a big tarp and soaked them in the horse tank. They put them on the roof of the barn but there weren't enough to cover it or the house.

"Let's get that hay out of the barn," Daddy said.

I went back to the house to find Mama stuffing the picture albums, letters and her Bible into a gunnysack. She took me by the hand and led me to the fence around the horse corral and said to stay there and hold the gunnysack, then went to take the chickens out of the chicken house and the cows out of the barn.

I sat on the fence watching the wall of fire recede south. I had heard about prairie fires but never seen one. Balls of fire shot off from the main one and ignited a new area. Oil wells exploded on the horizon, sending rockets of flames into the red and black sky. Soon a wall of fire loomed on the horizon in every direction. The heat and smoke were nearly unbearable. I pressed the wet rag Mama had given me over my face. I watched Daddy and Laurence blindfold and hobble the horses, tying rope around their front legs. Daddy said the horses would panic and run into the cauldron if the fire returned.

But the fire did not return. At nine in the morning we all sat, exhausted, around the table in the yard, gazing over the charred fields. Smoke hung acrid in the air. The horses pawed the ground and nuzzled each other.

We were too jittery to go back to bed and by the time the fire left, the sunrise appeared only palely. Then the landlord's sleek black Cadillac emerged like a hearse from the smoke. Mr. Barnes did not get out but honked his horn. Daddy walked slowly over to the car. After a few minutes the landlord drove away. Daddy stood in the same spot and watched the car disappear. Then he walked back and sat down at the table in the yard.

"Reneged. That ol' boy says he's gonna get rid of the horses, says there's oil beneath this land."

"He can't do that, can he, Moyer?" Mama pleaded.

"Sure the hell can, do whatever he damn pleases—he owns the land," Daddy said.

And so we went back to being tenant farmers.

JEWISH OIL BRAT

Davi Walders

*i*magine
> *her*

looking through the dusty window, sand cyclones swirling in
the distance above ten thousand men sleeping in tents, the endless tracks of the Texas Southern Pacific and a two-day honey-
moon long past, her eyes large above her swollen belly
imagine
> *longhorns*

snorting at windows she tries to keep clean, an elm so rare she
waters it growing through the warped floor, sandhill cranes
pecking at lizards coiled in caliche pits, dogs slower than arma-
dillos crying in moonless nights
imagine
> *fifteen*

miles from Big Spring, fifteen miles from nowhere, fifteen frame
cottages resisting the wind, the Settles family happy to lease to
oil squatters banking green between cactus and cattle strag-
gling along rutted roads
imagine
> *fifty*

thousand fenced acres, the Conoco gates opening for a skinny
immigrant of a man, his shtetl Yiddish buried in scholar-
ships and a deep Texas drawl, his brow already creased from
sun, breaking the rule of dusty boots, the door slamming
behind him
imagine
> *the two*

of them, ignoring the spotless sky, the worsening war, whirling
through sand, cactus, and rattlers, holding on to each other in

an old Studebaker, bouncing by derricks pumping like mules and
you, a *sabra,* about to be born here
  imagine.

Sabra means cactus in Hebrew and is uscd to describe the first generation
born in Israel.

BIG SPRING, FIFTY YEARS AFTER

Davi Walders

That a skin-and-bones boy climbed down from
the rafters after the Cossacks spit, kicked,
and left little of the shack, the shtetl

and a terrified mother, and stumbled, hatless
and mapless, leading a fragment of family out
into bitter nights and a fetid ship to Texas.

That a young woman sweated days in a laundry
in the Bronx, labored year after year in night
school for the diploma she tied to a stack of love

letters and dreamed her way five days on the Texas
Southern Pacific to a depot in the desert, that her
dimples appealed to his skinny honesty, that his

gravel-kicked boots and roustabout hands skidded
into her romance-starved heart, that the two found
a circuit rabbi to marry them, a drilling camp

willing to take them, that there among a thousand
oil boom tents, one night in the bosses' ten-by-ten
bedroom, when the blow-your-brains-out gusts of west

Texas dust hid the stars and left them nothing else
to do, that in a moment of tender whispers, they
huddled, caressed, and careened towards me like

tumbleweed, that together we were buffeted down
rougher-than-a-cob rutted roads, shaken and popped
like grains from arroyo-ridden land until their trail

left only half-buried tracks to a camp on the desert
of memory where I stand. Sand still blows wild
as mesquite, shadows prickle like cactus piercing

the horizon and eyes still tear from the sun, but
courage rooted deep here, gushed high and fierce here,
and generosity still sprouts sudden as an occasional elm.

OKARCHE, 1961

Janie Fried

*M*y mother holds a broken beer bottle streaked with red dirt. Somebody smashed it and tossed it into the weeds. She drops it into the barrel where we burn our trash once a week because there is no garbage pickup in Okarche. The air feels like the coils of our electric stove when they turn orange with heat. Wearing Bermuda shorts and a sleeveless cotton blouse with the print faded from too many washings in the sink, Mother isn't sweating. She's used to the heat now. Since my father went up north to crop-dust for the summer, she's spent more time outside. Lifting the handle of the push mower, she steers toward another tangle of weeds.

Why does she pick up smelly old beer bottles? I wonder, sitting on the steps in front of our trailer house. In 1961, the year John F. Kennedy moved his family into the White House, my father moved a blue-and-white metal house on wheels to the center of town in Okarche, Oklahoma, where our family was to live. Mother, a gracefully thin woman, looks like Jackie Kennedy but with red hair and green eyes. She can dress real snazzy, too. When we lived in Oklahoma City, before my father became a crop duster, she wore pearls, suits, and hats. So I can't figure out why she's wearing old clothes and getting so dirty now, even if she doesn't sweat.

We are new in a town where Mother says, "People have to size you up, for sure." That's okay with me, because I'm sizing up Okarche, too. The town doesn't have a movie theatre or even a dime store. The main street has a post office, an IGA grocery store, the *Okarche Chieftain* newspaper office, and a bar called Eischen's that is famous for its fried chicken, white bread, and sweet pickles.

My father's good intentions often turn out wrong. He has the lean, tanned looks of an aviator, and Mother always hoped he'd become an airline pilot. But he can't tell the difference between red and green, and color-blind pilots can't fly for the airlines. He's adapted, thinking he can earn a living in places like Okarche where prosperous farms have green bug problems. "Green bugs are money," he says, although the bugs must look gray to him. Acres and acres of wheat and the green bugs that ate it brought us here. It was a big mistake. Harvest was almost over by the time we arrived, so my father went to Nebraska, where the wheat hadn't been harvested yet. "Next year will be better in Okarche," he says.

But I am beginning to doubt his promises, this summer of my eighth year.

We don't got no money, I think that afternoon. "Don't got no" is a double negative that means, the way I said it, we *do* have money. We don't, no matter how I say it. My father's been gone a month, and we don't even have a dollar to buy Twinkies and Cokes at the IGA grocery store.

Mother says she can't do anything about that. We have to wait for him to send us more money. What Mother has is a push mower that she pushes over weeds in a vacant lot in the middle of town while we wait. When rocks, tin cans, or beer bottles get in her path, she stoops to pick them up, carries them to the trash barrel, and goes back to her mowing. She doesn't look happy. But she doesn't look sad, either. I'm afraid. Afraid my father never will send money.

"Why are you mowing the weeds?" I ask as Mother spreads peanut butter on Saltines that evening. The sky has turned pink, and the air is cooler.

She's arranged the crackers in a circle on a plate so they look pretty. There's one too many for the circle, so she hands it to me. She says, "I want to clean up the park."

"What park?"

"The park across from our home."

"You mean all those weeds are a *park?*"

She smiles. "Well, it once was a park, I imagine. Helen at the IGA told me the town of Okarche owns the land." Helen is the sturdy, dark-haired lady at the cash register. She is the kind of person who can see to the bottom of things, which is what I want to do.

"Why not let the town clean up the park?" I ask. "Why do you have to pick up those smelly old beer bottles?"

Mother gives me a look that tells me she can't understand how I could be her daughter, and that makes her sad. "I want to do it," she says, setting the plate of crackers on the coffee table in front of the long black couch in the living room. A gust of wind blows through the kitchen window, swirling the steam rising from a pan on the stove where two eggs are boiling. "The eggs are ready. Let's have our dinner."

While we eat, my mother tries to explain. "This is a farm town. Maybe people in farm towns don't have time to make things nice."

"Why not?"

"Maybe they are so busy planting wheat or raising cattle that they don't see the land."

After dinner, I get dressed for bed so we can watch *Mystery Theatre* on television before I get sleepy. The trailer has two bedrooms, one at each end. My room is at the back, next to the bathroom, with a wooden sliding door that sticks if there's too much steam from the shower. In my room, there are bunk beds and a brown desk that folds into the wall. I look forward to doing my homework at that desk when school starts in a few months. Mother says I'll meet friends at school. I hope she's right.

During the middle of *Mystery Theatre*, the wind begins to blow so hard that the television picture goes fuzzy. Something hard and heavy smashes on the roof, and the lights go out. Whap, whap, whap—someone's pounding on our door. "Come on! You've got to get to the basement!" a man yells.

Mother wraps a blanket around me, and we hurry into the storm. The man hustles us into a pickup truck that smells like beer. A few minutes later, we are following him down concrete steps into a basement filled with people in bathrobes and overalls. Someone leads me to a cot, where I fall asleep.

That's all I remember about my first tornado in Okarche, in that summer of 1961.

Later, Mother told me that Helen from the IGA had sent her husband to rescue us. "I guess they sized us up," I said. Maybe people in Okarche let vacant land get weedy and ugly, but they sure don't neglect each other.

Our trailer house didn't blow away in the tornado. The next afternoon, I sit on our front steps and watch my mother dragging tree limbs away from her park across the street. We went to the post office earlier, but there was no mail from my father.

About sundown, Helen and her husband pull up in their pickup truck. A couple of skinny boys climb out of the truck bed. "Hey, squirt," Helen says. Handing me a basket of fried chicken, white bread, and sweet pickles from Eischen's Bar, she tells my mother to let the men haul off the tree limbs. The chicken is the best I've ever tasted. While we eat, Mother tells Helen she wants to plant Shasta daisies in flowerbeds around the trees in the park. Helen says she doesn't know much about Shasta daisies, but if we have room in our freezer, she'll give us half a side of beef.

A week later, we make another trip to the post office. This time, we find a white envelope with a check for over two hundred dollars from my father. We buy Twinkies, Cokes, and a basket of food at the IGA. Then Mother says we're going to Oklahoma City. We drive thirty miles down a two-lane highway to a nursery on the outskirts of town, where she buys daisies and periwinkles that fill the backseat of our Plymouth with enormous fragrance.

By the time my father comes home from Nebraska, Mother's park is beautiful. The editor of the *Okarche Chieftain* has written about her mowing, weeding, and planting flowers. Her name has appeared in his "Over the Fence" column five weeks in a row—a record for a town that doesn't piddle much with its history, except for what's in the weekly paper.

I begin to understand that there are people like Helen, who can see to the bottom of things. And there are people like my mother, who can imagine what things could be and make them happen.

BLOWOUT

Mary Bryan Stafford

In the middle of the great South Texas drought of the fifties, hope leaped beyond the cracked, hard earth of my uncle's ranch: the promise of a gas well. Exploratory geologists had researched the underground formation on Tío's land for over a year. When I asked what exploratory geologists were, Tío said they were diviners of squiggly sonar maps, which could predict whether oil or gas might lie underground. "Like diviners of water wells who walk around with a Y-shaped stick?" I asked. I'd read about those guys.

Tío laughed. "Yeah, Izzie . . . yeah, as a matter of fact. Sooth-sayers, *oooooo*." Tío rolled his eyes and made the sounds from *The Shadow*. "They conjure visions of great wealth!"

"Cyrus York!" Aunt Carmen chastised. "I wish you'd take this more seriously. It's going to be a wonderful well. And you can quit worrying about all those ol' cows."

THE RIG CAME OUT on huge trucks that rumbled over the road in great white clouds of caliche dust, bearing names like Schlumberger and Halliburton. In the afternoons, Tío would pack us all in the Cadillac—he, Aunt Carmen, and Mama in front and my cousin Junior and I in the back. We'd drive the few miles to the well site, we kids hanging out of the car window, our mouths open in awe at the size of the project.

"Whoa, look at that!" The astonishment in Junior's voice said it all. The derrick lifted into the sky like a great metallic erector set.

We begged every day to go to the well. "Just let the men do their work now," Tío responded, patiently resisting our pleas. "Y'all go swim or find that poor old mare." But finally he'd relent and call Mama and Aunt Carmen to load up the car and go.

We sat perched on the seat, our fingers wrapped over the car window rims, watching while the roughnecks added another joint of pipe. Up close, you could see roughnecks in heavy boots and dirty Levis and hear them hollering at each other over the roar of two engines. Sweat soaked into the seats of their britches. Black grease and mud smeared their sweaty biceps, the veins looking as if they might burst as the men wrestled with the pipes.

After supper, Junior and I often climbed on top of the house to look toward the lighted drilling rig. When the wind was right, we could hear the heavy clang of pipes and motors churning, but mostly the rig was quiet from that far away, like a sparkling fairy tale castle. Even in the silence, it promised happily ever after.

The last night of June, we didn't go to the well. We were watching the only television station with good reception. *Hit Parade* was on and none of us wanted to miss it. Then, just after Giselle McKensie crooned "impatient to be *freeeee*," thunder rumbled—not from the clear night sky, but from deep in the earth. I covered my ears and pivoted to find an answer in Tío's face. Like the whip crack of a lightning bolt, a huge finger of light zigzagged across the window. We froze.

"Blowout!" Tío was on his feet and out the door. "Call the fire department!" he yelled over his shoulder. We heard the Cadillac's tires squeal on the driveway and rattle hard over the cattle guard.

Mama ran to the kitchen for the phone. I could hear her voice calm and steady, giving a quick account to the Volunteer Fire Department of Duval County. We could still hear the rumble, like one of the big oil trucks coming down the road too fast.

"I wanna go! Let's go see!" I shouted.

"The roof," Junior mouthed, and I nodded.

"We're just going to go sit outside," I said to no one in particular, as we backed out the door. We climbed to the roof in record time. Junior led the way as we scrambled to a point where the view wasn't blocked by pecan trees.

Breathless, I choked out, "See anything?"

"Man, I'd say so!" he breathed. "Wow! Look at that!" He stood hypnotized. I looked into his eyes, then turned. But in his eyes' reflection, I had already seen the bright orange flare of the well, engulfed in flames. It lit up the sky.

THREE DAYS HAD GONE BY and we were on our umpteenth visit to the well site. The same scene was replayed time after time. "You are looking at thousands of dollars going up in flames. *Hundreds* of thousands," Aunt Carmen mourned. We stood agog at the image of hundreds of thousands of one-dollar bills with wings aflame, lifting like ashes in the breeze. Having seen the fire from miles away, people started showing up, carloads of them, bumping down the road to get a closer look. They made a picnic of it. In addition to the rough-necks' junk, Dairy Queen cups and Lone Star Beer cans littered the ground in a half-mile radius around the flames.

On our next trip to the blowout, we all stood beside the car, watching the inferno. You could tell Tío was angry.

"These cowboys can't drill a well to save themselves," he growled. "And those geologists, they're nuttier than fruitcakes! I can't tolerate damn geologists who don't anticipate gas pockets." He gave the car door a hard jerk. "Get in."

"What exactly went wrong, Cy?" Aunt Carmen asked, staring bleakly through the window at the fiery scene.

Tío grasped the steering wheel with both hands and leaned his head on them. "Bottom line," he said, "it was the drilling mud. It's supposed to be thick enough to hold back any gas that may start to bubble up. Here in Duval County, there're lots of high-pressure gas pockets, so the drillers gotta use the heaviest mud they can. Of course, that costs money. And you know what?" He raised his head and shook it in disgust. "These wildcatters thought they'd save the heavy, expensive mud till they were closer to the mother lode. When that mud started to buck, there was no holding it. The mother load spit in their face."

Tío sat up straight, started the Cadillac with a roar, and gunned it hard. Aunt Carmen and Mama jumped a little but didn't say a word. We rode back to the house in silence.

Night after night, the evening sky east of the house glowed with never-ending fire. The flames burned into late August until Red Adair could get there. He'd been working for two weeks when we heard the dynamite blast one night during supper.

"Good lord, what's going on out there, Cyrus?" Aunt Carmen asked.

"Well, I hope Adair just shut down the fire." Tío sawed at his steak and popped a piece into his mouth. We waited. "If he's lucky, he can get in there and tighten down the valve, and that'll shut down the flow of gas. Pass the green beans, please."

"And if he can't get it shut down, Cyrus?" Aunt Carmen's voice was a pinched whisper.

"Then the well burns till it burns itself out. Months, maybe."

"Oh, lord." Aunt Carmen looked out the window, shaking her head. "The well, gone up in flames. Gone! You're just gonna let them walk away from this?"

"We can't lose what we never really had," Tío said. "What we really lost was just the potential."

Aunt Carmen looked him straight in the face. "The potential was everything, Cyrus."

It was long past sundown when I made my way to the roof. The flames were out, and the night silent except for a few squawks of the last cicadas. I couldn't tell whether it was the gas explosion or the drought, but the flat lap of earth to the east looked as though an old, sad dragon had heaved his last hot breath across the land. The mesquite was singed and the cactus shriveled. My sparkling castle was gone, as though the fairy godmother had waved her wand in a fit of pique. If there was to be a happily ever after, it wouldn't come from this well.

CREPE MYRTLES

Rebecca Balcárcel

*T*hose in full sun have
cracked open their round cases
and flounced out their ruffles,
hot pink *vestidos*.
They sway under *el sol*—
whole bunches!—and unfurl their fiesta frills
from June to September.
We watch their salsas, their boleros,
their cha-chas. "*Mira!*" my aunt shouts
every time we pass.
And every time we pass, they bob and curtsey;
they twirl their sizzling fringe.

This was my introduction to passion:
the flowers, the way they explode
into curls of crepe, and my aunt,
the way she soul-sings the old *canciones*,
right through drought,
through those long, tangled days after the accident,
sometimes through clenched teeth.

This is what I knew of spirit, *espiritu*,
that molten stream,
before I ever wrote a poem,
before it turned me inside out,
    like the blossoms.

BELONGING PLACE

Jackie Woolley

The north Texas cotton farm where I was born during the post-Depression days was near the little town of Odell, a few miles from the famous Doan's Crossing on the Red River. Underground water was plentiful in this area, and windmills dotted the landscape, groaning and creaking as they turned into the wind. Awakening to hear them in the night, Daddy could rest easy, knowing his storage tanks would overflow by morning, and the stock could belly up to the tank and drink their fill. Mama knew the cooking and washing could be done, and we kids could take our Saturday night baths. To us, the sound of windmills was the sound of life.

We lived in a wood-frame house surrounded by cotton and grain fields. Daddy's neatly plowed rows stretched in every direction from the house like spokes on a wagon wheel. Daddy had a crippled leg due to polio, so Lucien, our hired hand, did all the heavy work. Every day Daddy sat in the rocker on the porch, but his thoughts were out there with Lucien—cutting stalks, deep plowing, planting, and picking cotton. In the cool of the evening, after the milking was done, Lucien came and sat on the porch while they talked about crop rotation and rainfall and the war news. If the tractor was down, Lucien would pull it up alongside the porch, and Daddy would talk him through a repair job.

Our whole lives revolved around the seasons. Spring, we plowed and planted. Summer, we weeded the cotton and watched the skies for rain. Fall, we harvested. Winter, we caught up on our chores and planned next year's crops. I felt a part of everything on that farm. It was my belonging place.

We lived off the land and made just about everything we needed. We had a large vegetable garden every year, a family project which started in early spring when we turned under the soil and planted onions, potatoes, carrots, and peas. Throughout the summer months, we picked green beans, tomatoes, corn, black-eyed peas, squash, okra, and cucumbers. When the first frost threatened, we made green tomato chow-chow and added that to our storehouse. Our fruit trees produced apricots, pears, peaches, and plums for preserves, jellies, and fruit cobblers. What we couldn't eat we canned for use during the winter.

Mama even made our own soap. She poured hot water over wood ashes to make the potash. Her neighbor sometimes used cans of lye from the store, but Mama considered that extravagant when you could make your own. She'd measure a quart of water into a black pot, put in six pounds of lard, and let it come to a boil. Then she'd add the lye or potash and three more gallons of water. I'd help by stirring the pot until the soap was thick; then Mama poured it into wooden molds.

On Mondays, before the sun came up, Mama would go outside and start our family washing by building a fire under the wash pots. When the water boiled, she shaved small pieces from a bar of lye soap, then added the sheets and towels and stirred them with a stick before rinsing them in tubs of cool water. By the time I got up, she had the first clean sheets on the line, popping and snapping in the wind.

Mama's chickens, Rhode Island Reds, gave us plenty of eggs to eat and some to sell in town. The money from the sale of eggs went into a large teapot on the top shelf of the cabinet and was used for school supplies, an occasional new dress, or an Easter bonnet.

When Daddy said he was growing feathers from eating so much chicken, we'd buy a hog, usually a Duroc, to fatten up for slaughter at the first frost. Hog killing was a full day's work for everyone. Lucien stunned the animal with a blow on the head and hung it by its hind feet from the top rail of the corral. Daddy cut the carotid artery in the thick neck, and after all of the blood drained out, Lucien scraped the hide clean with a sharp knife.

Our dog Bob always watched the procedure from a safe distance while all of the squealing and grunting was going on, but his interest quickened when the noise abated, and the men began to cut up the fresh meat, working fast in the cool open air. Daddy sat on a stool at a table made of boards laid across two wooden horses, cutting the ribs with a hacksaw while he sang, "The eyes of Texas are upon you, all the live-long day." Lucien trimmed off strips of fat, cut them in chunks, and tossed them into the black pot for rendering down into lard. Mama mixed a curing solution of salt, sugar, and brine, and rubbed the spices into the bacon slabs, shoulders, and hams. We carried these to the smokehouse for curing. She ran the trimmings through a meat grinder to make pork sausage, seasoning it with garlic, hot pepper, and sage, and finally stuffing the mixture into long cylinder casings sewn from feed sacks. She fried some of the sausages in the black skillet on the kitchen stove, placed them in their own grease in quart fruit jars, and processed them in a pressure cooker. When they cooled, we stored the jars in the storm cellar on the shelves next to the jars of fruits and vegetables that would feed us through the winter.

As the chunks of fat melted in the black pot, Lucien poured the grease into buckets and set them aside to cool. The lard was saved for baking, frying, and making lye soap. After washing and rewashing the intestines in numerous tubs of water, Lucien cut them into bite-size pieces and tossed them into the pot of boiling fat. While the chitterlings fried, he kept an eye on the low-burning fire in the smokehouse. By sunset, the hog butchering was finished, except for the slow curing and smoking of the hams and bacons. Lucien washed the bloody tables, and Mama spread a feast of fried pork steaks, red-eye gravy, and buttermilk biscuits.

Life on the farm wasn't all work. We kids played tag or Annie Over in the yard until it was too dark to know who was *it*. On rainy afternoons, we rocked our dolls to sleep in the porch swing while we giggled over the neighbor boys' antics. We carried our work to the porch on hot afternoons and watched the clouds build up while we snapped green beans or shelled peas, dropping them like BBs in the pan. Mama took up hems, mended blue jeans, and darned socks, occasionally warning us to quit playing in the hot sun before we cooked our brains. Visitors dropped by, were invited for supper, then sat in the swing and talked until the food was ready. The porch was the perfect place for drinking lemonade, eating watermelons, and turning the ice cream freezer.

But such perfection couldn't last.

My father died when I was seven, and we laid him to rest in the small neighboring cemetery. On the other side of the fence, a Jersey cow solemnly chewed her cud and watched the intruders. The minister, swatting at a honeybee buzzing around his head, kneeled to say a prayer, and then it was over.

A few days later our landlord would order us to move. Although Mama wanted to use the remainder of Daddy's life insurance to buy a boarding house in Vernon, my uncle insisted that we move to a place close to his own farm near Lockett. He made us leave Lucien behind as well, because "it wouldn't look right for a black man to live way out in the country with just white women." This pained me almost as much as losing my daddy because Lucien had been with us all my life. Before that, he'd been with Daddy ever since he was a boy back in Kansas.

We packed up and left the only home I'd ever known, moving to a place twenty miles farther west. I wedged in behind the sofa in my uncle's open truck and watched the cottonwood leaves dance in the breeze. When the engine started, I held tightly to Bob, who wasn't happy about riding in the back of the noisy truck. As the truck pulled out on the road, I stood up and waved to Lucien as long as I could see him. Then my pasted smile collapsed, and I buried my face in a basket of clothes, with the clean smell of sunshine still clinging to the hastily dried sheets and towels.

Already I missed the sound of Lucien singing in the barn as he milked the cow, Bob barking at the grackles and meadowlarks, and the comfort of the creaking windmill. I missed our old home, my belonging place, with its familiar odor of green, growing things, the smell of life itself.

"NOT YOU," HE SAID

Leslie Marmon Silko

I spent a great deal of time with my great-grandmother. Her house was next to our house, and I used to wake up at dawn, hours before my parents or younger sisters, and I'd go wait on the porch swing or on the back steps by her kitchen door. She got up at dawn, but she was more than eighty years old, so she needed a little while to get dressed and to get the fire going in the cookstove. I had been carefully instructed by my parents not to bother her and to behave, and to try to help her any way I could. I always loved the early mornings when the air was so cool with a hint of rain smell in the breeze. In the dry New Mexico air, the least hint of dampness smells sweet.

My great-grandmother's yard was planted with lilac bushes and iris; there were four o'clocks, cosmos, morning glories, hollyhocks, and old-fashioned rosebushes that I helped her water. If the garden hose got stuck on one of the big rocks that lined the path in the yard, I ran and pulled it free. That's what I came to do early every morning: to help Grandma water the plants before the heat of the day arrived.

Grandma A'mooh would tell about the old days, family stories about relatives who had been killed by Apache raiders who stole the sheep our relatives had been herding near Swahnee. Sometimes she read Bible stories that we kids liked because of the illustrations of Jonah in the mouth of a whale and Daniel surrounded by lions. Grandma A'mooh would send me home when she took her nap, but when the sun got low and the afternoon began to cool off, I would be back on the porch swing, waiting for her to come out to water the plants and to haul in firewood for the evening. When Grandma was eighty-five, she still chopped her own kindling. She used to let me carry in the coal bucket for her, but she would not allow me to use the ax. I carried armloads of kindling too, and I learned to be proud of my strength.

I was allowed to listen quietly when Aunt Susie or Aunt Alice came to visit Grandma. When I got old enough to cross the road alone, I went and visited them almost daily. They were vigorous women who valued books and writing. They were usually busy chopping wood or cooking but never hesitated to take time to answer my questions. Best of all they told me the *hummah-hah* stories, about an earlier time when animals and humans shared a common language. In the old days, the Pueblo people had educated their children in this manner; adults took time out to talk to and teach young people. Everyone was a teacher, and every activity had the potential to teach the child.

But as soon as I started kindergarten at the Bureau of Indian Affairs day school, I began to learn more about the differences between the Laguna Pueblo world and the outside world. It was at school that I learned just how different I looked from my classmates. Sometimes tourists driving past on Route 66 would stop by Laguna Day School at recess time to take photographs of us kids. One day, when I was in the first grade, we all crowded around the smiling white tourists, who peered at our faces. We all wanted to be in the picture because afterward the tourists sometimes gave us each a penny. Just as we were all posed and ready to have our picture taken, the tourist man looked at me. "Not you," he said and motioned for me to step away from my classmates. I felt so embarrassed that I wanted to disappear. My classmates were puzzled by the tourists' behavior, but I knew the tourists didn't want me in their snapshot because I looked different, because I was part white.

THE HILLS OF SUMMER

Joyce Sequichie Hifler

Times were hard. Summer drought had ravaged the land, the well had gone dry, the chickens no longer laid eggs and the cows gave no milk for lack of grass in the meadows. But water was a necessity for drinking and bathing. Mama, in her usual efficient manner, set out to use what was at hand to get it.

A half mile or so from our house was a hand-dug well that always had water. It was situated on low ground and was probably spring-fed. Mama made a sled out of scrap lumber, loaded a barrel on it, and harnessed the horse to pull it. We were off to get water—but it had to be drawn up bucket-by-bucket to fill the barrel, and this was no small effort.

Our Cherokee allotment land lay in the crest of three hills. Almost everything that had anything to do with our lives was played out on those hills. Storms, when they finally came, would come from the west. The school bus came over the north road, and coyotes slipped over the east hill in sly efforts to catch one of our hens. Other things happened over the east hill as well. British cadets were making training maneuvers there, diving and turning as though they were in combat. With Papa away in the Engineers, stationed in Virginia, Mama and I were on our own—so much of my time was spent riding my horse, Figger, over the east hill where everything could be observed.

The hill was not a particularly friendly place—except to snakes, hawks, and rabbits. All I had to do was walk across the pond dam and I would be at the base of the hill. There were many trees around the hill, but my favorite was a wild holly with red berries. Though I was not allowed to eat the berries, the birds loved them. The lower limbs of the tree drooped down to the ground giving me a hidey-hole when I needed it. Bread and butter and green onions made a nice little picnic for my dog and me, away from anyone that might want to intrude. (Of course, no one ever did.)

I was on intimate terms with every other part of our land, knew it like the back of my hand and loved it as my very soul. Like all Cherokees, I felt that the land was a part of me. It was integral to my spirit, from the wet-weather streams with sandstone bottoms to the huge ash trees and elms and the lush wild strawberry beds that hugged the sides of every moist ravine. Like a house painter uses two different paints to decorate, the Decorator had used two different stones here. There was limestone on top of the east hill and sandstone at the bottom. What truly amazed me was that two different rocks could be so near to each other and never together. I courted and wooed the hill—invited it to be my friend—and it ignored me like the sought-after girl ignores the young man in pursuit of her company.

The east hill was unlike all the others. I rode my horse at full speed across all the others because they were free of rock, except for a few flat limestone boulders that were white in the twilight and shied the horse unexpectedly. Whenever that happened, we would stop and check out the strange enemy. Soon Figger was quiet, and I'd hear him pull at the prairie grass, and it would squeak through his teeth.

But the east hill was not hospitable to Figger. Here thick slabs of limestone lay flat and only inches apart so that even my foot could not fit between them.

There were no expanses of prairie grass, only a few wild persimmons growing here and there and clumps of wild pink verbena. Even these few isolated flowers looked like they had a temporary foothold among the great limestone boulders. More times than not I was barefoot and it was impossible to walk on the rocks because of sharp fossils that proved an ancient sea had once covered the hill.

So many complicated things for an Indian child to understand. Why did everything have to be so hard? Why did my mother not have the things she needed?

In a way, the hill told me. Life had its hard places and its comforts. It had flowers and cactus—sometimes a rainbow and sometimes a storm cloud. But I had love, my mother, my horse and my dog—and I had these hills.

MERCURY RISIN'

Paula Stallings Yost

*g*rowing up, I already knew that Texas women were tough and resourceful. They had to be, to survive the torrid Texas summers and plagues of insects and critters. I first understood this as a nine-year-old girl in the 1950s, visiting my grandmother Murdee in the piney woods of East Texas, where survival was defined in the simplest of terms.

Marathon heat waves challenged even the heartiest locals, with temperatures climbing above a hundred degrees for weeks on end and air so thick with humidity that you could almost drink it. But Murdee, an auburn-haired, petite woman with hazel eyes that spoke their own language, always kept her cool. "Daylight's wastin', honey," was my standard wake-up call. "Best be climbing outta that bed, 'less you'd rather be pulling weeds in the heat of the day." Tossing a fresh pair of cotton shorts and red-bandana shirt on my bed, Murdee would whistle her way to her tiny kitchen to whip up a lumberjack breakfast.

"Ain't gonna get many chores done on an empty stomach," she'd preach. Across a table laden with biscuits, bacon, sausage gravy, and scrambled eggs, we'd watch the sun rise over the pine trees outside the open, screenless window. "Them 'maters got a case of the wilt this morning," she might say between bites of biscuit and vigorous fly swats. "You need to haul some water up from the pond."

"But, Murdee, I did that yesterday—"

"Yeah. But it's already hotter than blue blazes outside, so we've got to soak 'em again. The only thing that's gonna grow without water is them durn weeds. Our weedin' oughta go a little easier today since I sharpened the hoe last night. Gotta pick cucumbers, too. They're just the right size for pickling. You know how prickly them things are, so grab your gloves." Murdee would smile. "With a little elbow grease, I 'spect we might finish in time to take a dip in the pond before lunch." She was great at dangling carrots of motivation.

So my days began. Balancing a hickory limb across my shoulders with a bucket hanging from each end, I hiked a million miles between our garden and the stock pond by summer's end. Dry buffalo grass tickled my bare feet each morning and scorched them in the afternoon. If I moved quickly enough, the Kamikaze mosquitoes and horse flies had trouble keeping pace. Of course, I had to watch the ground closely to avoid cow patties, fire-ant hills, and mole tunnels. There was no faster way to become one with the land than to stumble over any one of those obstacles.

If the weeding was accomplished early enough, and the veggies gathered and properly stored, my grandmother and I would race each other to the stock pond for a cooling swim. "Last one in's a rotten egg!" We'd float on black truck-tire inner tubes and chat about everything from God to *I Love Lucy*. Afterward, we'd make our way home for lunch and a nap.

With no air conditioning, sleep didn't come easily in the heat of the day. Murdee had a solution for that, too. While I put away the sandwich fixings and cleared the lunch table, she would hose down the roof of her white clapboard house. Then we'd doze on the cushioned front-porch swings under a lazily turning ceiling fan.

By three o'clock I was in the yard again, trimming hedges, mowing grass, raking, or burning brush. Mowing the grass was the absolute worst. Murdee's small push mower required a lot of that prized "elbow grease," and it seemed to take forever to cut even the smallest areas. And no matter where I mowed, bug armies attacked en masse—hordes of gnats, flies, mosquitoes, wasps, dirt daubers, and grasshoppers. The grasshoppers especially loved to fly in my face, down my shirt, or up my shorts as I pushed the clacking mower. Finished, I'd take an iced tea break in the shade of a mimosa tree. Amusing myself by rolling doodlebugs into minuscule black balls, I was pestered occasionally by bagworms, asps, and bird poop falling on my head or into my tea. I eventually learned to wear a wide-brimmed hat and cover my glass with a sycamore leaf.

When we were caught up on the yard work, Murdee and I sometimes trekked to the dewberry patch a mile down the road. Wearing long-sleeved shirts and jeans tucked inside our socks to protect against thorns, snakes, and chiggers, we filled our buckets and our bellies. Back home, berry-stained, chigger-bitten, and sweat-soaked, we'd strip down to our undies in the backyard and hose each other off. Berry picking was a hot and arduous chore, but we were rewarded with the unmistakable aroma of a dewberry cobbler baking in the wood stove that evening.

The stock pond held different perils. My Uncle Paul once swore that a twelve-foot mama alligator, especially partial to tender little girls, lived beneath the lily pads. One morning, wading through the hydrilla to fill my water buckets, I stepped on something large and slimy that nipped my big toe. I broke all previous speed records in my screaming dash home.

"Murdee, help! The alligator got me!"

"Land sake's alive," my grandmother sighed as I slammed the screen door and fell to the kitchen floor to check for missing toes. After listening to my tale of woe and Band-Aiding my wound, she said, "Now, honey, you know your uncle loves to get your goat. I've told you a thousand times, there ain't no alligators round here."

I wasn't convinced. Against my better judgment, we marched back to the pond to investigate. As we approached, Murdee giggled and pointed to my deserted bucket on the bank. Basking in the sun atop the bucket was the apparent culprit: a grumpy snapping turtle. He glanced up at the sound of my grandmother's laughter and slid back into the water with a smirk. (I swear.)

Though the alligator may have been a bogus threat, the cottonmouth water moccasin was not. Highly venomous, a cottonmouth is an aggressive water snake that attacks with the resolve of a mad bull if someone comes too close. Even Murdee didn't go near the water without a hickory limb or hoe. She left many headless, writhing serpents behind.

Copperheads, a less poisonous breed, preferred the woods and were considerably more polite. You almost had to step on one before it would strike, which gave a new meaning to the expression, "Walk softly and carry a big stick." My cousin Flay Don actually tripped over a copperhead in the woods. When the offended viper sank its fangs into his ankle, Flay Don jumped a yard straight up and hollered like a stuck pig. He was bedridden for a week.

We occasionally saw diamondback rattlesnakes, which denned in rockpiles in the sunniest fields. But chicken snakes showed up everywhere, huge, menacing, and harmless. Murdee used to tell me, "Now, honey, if you come upon an old chicken snake, just say howdy and leave him alone. He eats mice and rats. In my book, that makes him a friend."

Since our ponds, lakes, woods, and fields were such popular habitats for these creatures, it wasn't easy to avoid them. So I gladly granted them all the space they required—except once. When I discovered a copperhead slithering across the kitchen floor one night, I quickly ended his adventure with my grandmother's iron skillet. Though her polished hardwood floor suffered a couple of permanent dents, Murdee didn't complain.

I thrived on the challenges of those summers and delighted in a multitude of simple things. The juice of a freshly picked tomato dripping down my chin. A newly mown lawn to play on at the end of the day. Murdee's pantry filled with rows of canned tomatoes, black-eyed peas, dill pickles, peach jam, dewberry jelly, and more, all sealed with love.

Five decades and several big-city careers later, I have returned to my East Texas roots. Some things have changed for the better—central air conditioning, riding lawnmowers, and underground sprinkler systems, for instance. The summers still sizzle, however, and the critters have multiplied quite nicely.

I wouldn't have it any other way.

eagle inside us

I make a prayer for us.
That we'll be singing like Inca doves,
that we'll be watching swallows on a thermal flow,
that we'll be the swallows eating dragonflies on
    the wing
when the herd returns.

MARGO TAMEZ, "ON THE WING"

EAGLE POEM

Joy Harjo

To pray you open your whole self
To sky, to earth, to sun, to moon
To one whole voice that is you.
And know there is more
That you can't see, can't hear,
Can't know except in moments
Steadily growing, and in languages
That aren't always sound but other
Circles of motion.
Like eagle that Sunday morning
Over Salt River. Circled in blue sky
In wind, swept our hearts clean
With sacred wings.
We see you, see ourselves and know
That we must take the utmost care
And kindness in all things.
Breathe in, knowing we are made of
All this, and breathe, knowing
We are truly blessed because we
Were born, and die soon within a
True circle of motion,
Like eagle rounding out the morning
Inside us.
We pray that it will be done
In beauty.
In beauty.

ALAMO CANYON CREEK

Kathleen Dean Moore

We found the first rattlesnake no more than a hundred yards from the foot of Alamo Canyon. At this point, the Ajo Mountains form two parallel ridgelines, tending north and south. Alamo Canyon breaches the first ridge and gives access in both directions to the valley between them, a valley clogged with saguaro, palo verde, yellow mounds of coreopsis, mesquite with thorns two inches long, and huge blocks of volcanic rock, black rock heaped against a bleached sky . . . The trail cut between rock ledges and brushed past thickets, detoured around slab-sided prickly pears and dropped over boulders, forcing us to walk altogether too close to vegetation that often hides snakes.

Sure enough, a western diamondback rested in leaf litter under a mesquite that brushed across the trail. It was coiled as perfectly as a Zuni pot, with its neck poking out the middle like a lily and its broad head resting on the top coil. The snake lay in easy striking range of the trail and could have picked off hikers one after another if it had chosen to, but apparently it had not. Instead, it sat quiet and cool, shining as if it were freshly waxed, while we inspected it from a decent distance.

After the first snake, we hiked on full alert, peeking under the bushes, then scanning the trail, then inspecting the margins, flinching whenever a cicada rasped in branches overhanging the track or a lizard dodged from rock to rock like a gunfighter. Even so, we didn't see the second snake until I stepped just off the trail to get a better look at the rock foundation of a cowboy's line cabin, if that's what it was—I never did get a closer look. A rattlesnake set off an alarm buzz and I whooped, leaped away, and froze in place, all before the thought of a snake had time to cross my mind.

I used to worry quite a lot about whether I would recognize the sound of a rattlesnake in time to take evasive measures. Would I stand there wondering *Is that a cicada, or is that a rattlesnake?* until the rattlesnake decided I wasn't going to get the message and nailed me? *Is the sound more like a rattle?* I would ask people, *or more like a door buzzer?* Useless questions, all of them. The sound of that snake had not entered my consciousness before I was gone; some part of my brain recognized the rattlesnake, and that was all it took.

From a safe distance, I watched the snake raise its heavy body and sway like a cobra, darting its head around branches to get a clear shot at me, or maybe, as Frank said, to taste the air on its tongue. The snake was as thick as a man's arm, but what I had never figured out about that cliché is that anything as thick as a man's arm could also be as strong as a man's arm, and this snake broadcast strength. Rearing back to strike, drawing up to full height as if it wanted to arm-wrestle me, the snake was five long feet of power and menace and fury, but mostly power. I could see his rattle sticking up in the air like a finger, vibrating so fast it blurred, making a terrible racket. He was hot, he was mad, and I was afraid—for the first time in my life, afraid of a snake, afraid in my muscles and bones. I backed away down the trail . . .

After the second snake, we moved even more carefully up the Alamo Canyon and made a wide detour around the old ranch buildings baking in the sun. Just at the point where the canyon intersects the valley between the ridges, and two sandstone rocks lean toward each other across the trail, we thought we heard water—an insistent, fluttering sound, soft as seeds sifting in a sack, a sound that might as well have been leaves falling through dry branches or wind in cottonwoods. Great loping strides brought us to the sound, and we looked down on a thousand rivulets trickling under gravel into a rock-bound basin. Has anyone ever heard water in the desert and not turned toward it, glad, shouting aloud and climbing over rocks to the source of the sound?

Like the snake's warning, the sound of the water lodged somewhere near the muscles in my back—a lovely wash of comfort and safety, the simple assurance of something good, unmediated by any thoughts. How could anyone explain an emotion in the muscles? As far as I know, the only person who comes close is Thomas Hobbes, an English philosopher dead now for four hundred years, a materialist who thought that the body is a collection of particles. The way Hobbes described it, desire is the movement of all those particles toward an object of desire, particles simultaneously surging toward what is good. Aversion is movement away, a million particles recoiling. I used to think the whole idea was silly, imagining a microscopic chorus line of dots. But I don't think it's so silly anymore. In the desert, I felt all the parts of my body leap away from that snake, every molecule, every nerve fiber in full retreat from the slam of intracellular fear. And the joyous movement toward water was prickly, every cell responding. I dropped my pack on the gravel and knelt over the water.

Where Alamo Canyon Creek pools up under a boulder, the water carried clouds of brilliant, bilious green algae, dotted with—of all things in the desert—polliwogs, the young of the spadefoot toad. You wouldn't think an amphibian could survive a desert summer when all surface water evaporates and temperatures reach 125 degrees. You'd think that all you'd find in the way of desert amphibians would be little dried-up toadskins, tough and dark under the desert sun. But the spadefoot toads show up in wet years, digging themselves out of the sand.

Thunder brings them out. The rolling vibrations of sand pounded by thunder, the echoing *pap pap pap* of hard rain, the low-frequency waves of the heaviest storms, startle them to life after a long time of torpor, and they start to dig. Toad after toad, they pop out of the sand and hop to water for their first drink of the year, or two years, or three. They lower their hindquarters into cool, ozone-soaked water and suck up moisture through their skin . . .

I took off my boots and socks and arranged them in the sun. Then I dropped down onto the rock and stretched my feet over the water, leaning back into the shade of the sandstone slab, scattering polliwogs that soon regrouped in the shadow of my right foot. I was feeling most satisfied by the progress of this hike. We had set out to encounter the desert, to find the animals that bring the landscape alive, or maybe to find the animals that enliven us to the landscape by raising our heartbeats and focussing our attention. Encounters with animals are a gold mine of interest because the more you learn about an animal, the more improbable it seems, and you realize suddenly that there is more than one way to skin a cat, more than one way to live a life. The characteristics possessed by humans—five senses, daylight vision, a certain moral compunction about eating relatives, a daily schedule, and nowhere near enough time to wait for a good storm—are facts that restrict the way humans live. But they do not necessarily impose any such limits on an animal's life. Rattlesnakes can see pictures drawn by heat. Toads can go underground without any more fuss than going to the grocery store and live a life that would be, for a human, the most exquisite, brutalizing torture, buried for years, deprived of every sense but touch.

Observing animals, you also learn that some of the characteristics that enrich human lives—self-righteousness, reflective thought, empathy, planning to a purpose—are utterly absent from the experiences of the animals, or at least that's what I am assuming from what I know about the structure of their brains. Snakes and toads have a primitive brain, hard-wired for fear and the detection of prey, for sex, hunger, and thirst. We primates have that brain too, and on top of that, the layered accretions of the cerebral cortex. So I come the closest to thinking like a snake, to seeing the world through the brain of a toad, when my body reacts to a stimulus with terror or elation and leaves my conscious mind out of the process.

I study the issue: What was I thinking about when I was thinking with my reptilian precursor of a brain, when I was frightened by the snake and yowled, and leaped back, and froze? In the effort to remember, I reconstruct the sequence of events in my mind, and at the point where the snake buzzed, I find . . . nothing. Nothing. No visual images. I don't even find a memory of the first sound of the rattle. No memory of jumping. A step off the trail toward the adobe bricks, a blank space (maybe a dark space), and then I'm ten feet behind where I was before, my shout echoing against the rock, my mind ablaze with interest in a snake that is still ripping off a buzz to terrify the world.

So maybe I know what it is like to think like a snake, because I know what it is like to think not at all—to act with no memory, with no decision, with no awareness, to do the appropriate thing at the appropriate time and nothing more. In a vacuum, in unawareness extended through time, a toad may live out its life, eat its sisters, absorb its tail, lay its eggs, hop out of the pond, and in increasing heat, paddle backwards into the sand, one foot down, two feet, and wait for the storms.

Or maybe I don't know what it's like to think like a snake.

Maybe snakes and toads feel emotions that I can't even imagine. Why should I think that the range of human emotions has exhausted all the possibilities? Maybe the sensation that washes over a toad when he eases his rump into a desert pool is in a category of feeling entirely unknown to me.

Or maybe what the snakes and toads lack is not emotion, but consciousness. Maybe cresting waves of anger and fear and pleasure pass over a toad, unfelt—just as a human being, sleeping, may not hear a wind that slides through the canyon, bending back the branches.

Sometimes, in a desert landscape, a landscape without consciousness, emptier of intellect than any other landscape I have ever seen, I think I can feel emotion lying like heat on the surface of the sand and seeping into cracks between boulders. There is joy in the wind that blows through the spines of the saguaro, and fear in bare rocks. Anger sits waiting under stones. Exhilaration pools in the low places, the dry river beds, the cracked arroyos, and is sucked by low pressure ridges up into storm clouds that blow east toward the Alamo Canyon.

ON THE WING

Margo Tamez

The blue martins snatch
damselflies and stinkbugs
as they drift an evening thermal.
The largest of swallows, their size
all in the tail.

I'm hanging laundry in autumn
late in the day,
stiff shadows of clothespins,
their oblique angle to earth,
and their large V-forms
oddly like martins
dipping and braiding for food.
With the blue martins' return,
I surrender all my fear
to a past I can't dismiss.
I won't speak, nor forecast,
nor ask for a thing,
but just watch them
as they pull lavender-plum threads of evening
through the fiery kiln of sundown.

Tonight I'm praying for the buffalo
trailing that aurora,
a sky where night is day
and day is night and

what we say is dust
and what we can never say
goes into a prayer,
where I am you

and you are me
and we move this
into a spirit of the herd.

And when the herd returns
we'll be hanging laundry on the line,
we'll be watching sparrows and doves,
we'll be listening to the children,
when the herd returns
we'll be painting the ancestors,
we'll be teaching under ironwoods in blossom,
we'll be suckling on our mothers' soft breasts,
when the herd returns
we'll be asking for peace,
we'll be asking for a blessing,
we'll be making peace with our mothers,
when the herd returns
we'll make bread for our fathers and learn to plant corn,
we'll share our bounty with those who didn't plant,
we'll eliminate poverty and hunger,
when the herd returns.
we'll live with less,
we'll birth babies at home,
we'll sing them welcome songs when they crown,
when the herd returns
we'll be singing to bring rain,
singing to heal our grief,
singing to the moon.

I make a prayer for us.
That we'll be singing like Inca doves,
that we'll be watching swallows on a thermal flow,
that we'll *be* the swallows eating dragonflies on the wing
when the herd returns.

HUMMINGBIRDS COMPETE FOR THE TOBACCO TREE

Margo Tamez

How can I understand that what is absent is not gone,
that what has ended is not finished,
that what is taken is returned
as more than memory?

SUSAN HANSON, "WHY WRITE ABOUT NATURE?"

Their flute-bodies wind the trunk
of a tobacco tree shading me
as I clean some seed from the chaff.

The tobacco's yellow flowers,
tassels gathered at each stem,
heave and swell
on waves of heat.
I show my children how
to clean the nectar from the delicate tube,
ripe for sucking.

The hummers,
like tiny missiles under my arm.
I reach to them,
arms and hands to hold,
carry. Gather me to loved ones.

The hummers skim the wide wood footholds
near the mud-splattered spigot.
I laugh at their chase,
surprised by their precision,
how they attack without thought
for their own hunger.

Under this tree
the shade is a loose lace
of blank eyes
quaking on July's baked ground.

The hundred yellow bugle-blooms
shrug off summer.

Outside the fringe of shade,
Earth shifts a scorched shoulder,
plunges, eyes away from the hot god.

Cool above in the vault,
thin strands of lately gone souls
stretch out above us. My father,
who lately made his journey,
is out there too.

I wave to him.
He wears vintage clothes,
Leans against a spotless
teal '57 sedan, smiling.

He tells the dearly not-departed
to keep cooking eggs and potatoes,
make tortillas in a good mood.
Bathe the kids and comb the knots from their hair . . .
Look at my eyes in the mirror longer.

Forgive. Make love.

Go to the desert and howl
the body's compressed grief.
Gather ironwood kindling
to make a fire. Look under decaying
cholla or mesquites for mulch
to catch the flame.

Blow steady breaths on the fragile glow.
Feed it, stay there.
Look at the eyes in the fire.

Before it's over,
when maybe everything almost is,
offer little branches
to crumbling coals
    of naked wanting.

THE RAVEN

Marie Unini

One of our ravens is dead. I saw its body, an undefined mound of blue-black.

The desert serves up its dead like cuisine, on a large platter, light on garnish. Animals that die seem to end up out in the open. They appear to have simply dropped, stricken with heart attacks and incapable of dragging themselves to the shade of a juniper or scrub oak to struggle for a last breath in the comfortable shade.

The raven was on its back, lying just outside the ring of large rocks surrounding an elephant grass bush and the main power pole on our property. Noticing dust on its belly, I thought it must have been nosed over by some curious, perhaps hungry, passerby. When I touched it, the body moved easily, although it was no longer warm. Voracious ants already covered its back, and a faint odor was obvious. Another few days and it would have been gone except for the bones and scattered feathers.

Looking up, I saw the tangle of wires in the transformer box and wondered if we really needed the infrastructure. I cursed it and cursed our intrusion on this place, although being here has made me happy. I hope our raven died quickly, painlessly—the way you hope your grandmother will die in her sleep.

I say *our* raven because we fancy ourselves a multispecies commune here in Juniper Hills. We arrived two years ago with a mare, four dogs, two cats, and too much stuff. Since then, another dog came to stay and two more dogs have passed through on their way to other homes. Hosts of cottontails, jackrabbits, quail, owls, finches, robins, thrashers, doves, pigeons, hummingbirds, chipmunks, lizards, and toads have discovered our fertile, welcoming oasis.

We've named some of these animals. The goldfish are the de Milles, a general name for a subgroup that we have to remember to feed; the toads are all Prince So-and-So. Beyond that, naming the hordes seems unnecessary. We are acquainted with them the way we were acquainted with people who walked by our city home each day on their way to the bus stop, or the way a supermarket checker recognizes the folks who shop regularly. Maybe she gets to know some individuals better than others because they stand out. They're friendly, or they dress unconventionally. Or they are few among many. Rare. Like the ravens.

The raven pair arrived with fanfare this spring, our third in this place. *Awk-awk*ing, swooping dramatically from deodar to cottonwood, from power line to barn roof, they moved in. They splashed in the fountain. They washed their kill and left the unwanted guts in our mare's water trough under the cottonwood. They picked apart the black rubber insulation around our outdoor pipes, adding it to their cleverly camouflaged nest. Since they hunted everyone else's young, they were wise about protecting their own.

Each morning, we came outside to greet the ravens. They *awk*ed. We *awk*ed back. We loved to watch them flap-flap and soar. And we didn't even mind their hanging out in the cottonwood tree where they scouted for tasty morsels that might cruise by, conveniently close to their washing sink. We admired their audacity, the way they made themselves at home.

When I called Bob at work that day to tell him about the dead raven, he said, "Oh, no." I heard his grief in the spaces between the words.

"I'm sorry to tell you," I said. "It was just important, and I didn't want to feel it alone."

"I know," he said, and wondered if it had been electrocuted. "They have big wings. Touch two of the wrong wires at the same time, and it's over. Of course, it could have been the sharp-shinned hawk. Leave it there. I want to see it." Bob always wants to examine things like this, as if to divine some mystery from the evidence.

Late that afternoon, I went to change the mare's water and spotted the remaining raven perched high in the tallest juniper just beyond the barn. It scanned the area, balancing against a gentle breeze with soft lifts and drops of its wings.

"*Awk, awk!*" I yelled, wanting to do something. Wanting to take back this event, but helpless to do so.

"*Awk, awk!*" I yelled again.

Then I thought, *Oh shit. What if my awks are misinterpreted by the raven?* It might think I said something like, "Your mate had to leave quickly. Said to meet him in Modesto in July."

Defaulting to human tongue, I finally just said it. "Your mate is dead. I don't know how it happened. It's over there by the pole. I left it so you could know. I hope this won't ruin things for us. Hope you'll consider staying. I'm so sorry."

Late that afternoon, Bob buried the dead raven as its mate watched silently from the cottonwood. Then that raven, too, was gone.

FISHING

Joy Harjo

This is the longest day of the year, on the Illinois River or a
similar river in the same place. Cicadas are part of the song
as they praise their invisible ancestors while fish blinking back
the relentless sun in Oklahoma circle in the muggy river of life.
They dare the fisher to come and get them. Fish, too, anticipate
the game of fishing. Their ancestors perfected the moves, sent
down stories that appear as electrical impulses when sunlight
hits water. The hook carries great symbology in the coming of
age, and is crucial to the making of warriors. The greatest warriors are those who dangle a human for hours on a string, break
sacred water for the profanity of air, then snap fiercely back
into pearly molecules that describe fishness.

THEY SMELL ME as I walk the banks with fishing pole,
night crawlers, and a promise I made to that old friend Louis
to fish with him this summer. This is the only place I can keep
that promise, inside a poem as familiar to him as the banks of
his favorite fishing place. I try not to let the fish see me see them
as they look for his tracks on the soft earth made of fossils and
ashes. I hear the burble of fish talk: "*When is that old Creek
coming back? He was the one we loved to tease most, we liked
his songs and once in a while he gave us a good run.*"

LAST NIGHT I DREAMED I tried to die. I was going to look
for Louis. It was rather comical. I worked hard to muster my
last breath, then lay down in the summer, along the banks of
the last mythic river, my pole and tackle box next to me. What
I thought was my last breath floated off as a cloud making an
umbrella of grief over my relatives. How embarrassing when
the next breath came, and then the next. I reeled in one after
another, as if I'd caught a bucket of suckers instead of bass. I
guess it wasn't my time, I explained, and went fishing anyway

as a liar and I know most fishers to be liars most of the time. Even Louis when it came to fishing, or even dying.

THE LEAP BETWEEN THE sacred and profane is as thin as fishing line and is part of the mystery on this river of life, as is the way our people continue to make warriors in the strangest of times. I save this part of the poem for the fish camp next to the oldest spirits whose dogs bark to greet visitors. It's near Louis's favorite spot where the wisest and fattest fish laze. I'll meet him there.

LEAVENING

Penelope Moffet

The sun's up somewhere east of the grove
not much above the parched hills
and the moon's gone from the skylight over the bed.
On the orange table a green metallic fly does a fly-walk,
  speeded-up, jerky.
Quail in oak leaves pick after insects, scold phantoms.
I'm no longer silver-shoed
descending through sleep the endless cabin stairs.

Noon. A dust-colored moth quivers up a window screen
above the table, confused by some imagined glow
where all heat, all light swirl in. In T-shirt and underwear
I survive, survive rather well despite the baking.
Had I been deft at suicide I'd be eight years dead,
wouldn't know a quail call from a finch's,
or have watched, just this morning, a rufous towhee
talking to itself—not the querulous hillside flaunt to scare off
  scrub jays,
but complex music saved.

The fly's larger cousin arrives with evening, multicolored and
  pugnacious.
His striped back and red eyes speak business.
Lasciviously he rubs forelegs, trying to choose between
red wine, waterglass and me. It's almost cricket time,
time for oil lamp and praying mantis.
Time to sauté fish with onion, garlic, ripe tomato.
What's sweet grows sweeter
like the man who waits a hundred miles away.

Five hummingbirds hover in fountain spray.
Green and purple, with lacy wingtips, coming in for midair
  gulps,

they chase each other off and circle back. Had I better
    understood
pills and carbon monoxide
I wouldn't rise in these hot rooms.
Moths mob the screen.
Something transparent rasps against bamboo.
Up at the pond
frogs are calling all the water beings in.

WATER

Terry Tempest Williams

*A*t first I think it is a small leather pouch someone has dropped along the trail. I bend down, pick it up, and only then recognize it for what it is—a frog, dead and dried. I have a leather thong in my pack, which I take and thread through the frog's mouth and out through its throat. The skin is thin, which makes a quick puncture possible. I then slide the frog to the center of the thong, tie a knot with both ends, and create a necklace, which I wear.

I grew up with frogs. My brothers and cousins hurled them against canyon walls as we hiked the trail to Rainbow Bridge when Lake Powell was rising behind Glen Canyon Dam.

I hated what they did and told them so. But my cries only encouraged them, excited them, until I became the wall they would throw frogs against. I didn't know what to do—stand still and soften their blow by trying to catch each frog in my hands like a cradle, or turn and run, hoping they would miss me altogether. I tried to believe that somehow the frogs would sail through the air in safety, landing perfectly poised on a bed of moss. But, inevitably, the tiny canyon frogs, about the size of a ripe plum, quickly became entombed in the fists of adolescents and would die on impact, hitting my body, the boys' playing field. I would turn and walk down to the creek and wash the splattered remains off me. I would enter the water, sit down in the current, and release the frog bodies downstream with my tears.

I never forgave.

Years later, my impulse to bathe with frogs is still the same. Havasu. It is only an hour or so past dawn. The creek is cold and clear. I take off my skin of clothes and leave them on the bank. I shiver. How long has it been since I have allowed myself to lie on my back and float? The dried frog floats with me. A slight tug around my neck makes me believe it is still alive, swimming in the current. Travertine terraces spill over with turquoise water and we are held in place by a liquid hand that cools and calms the desert.

I dissolve. I am water. Only my face is exposed like an apparition over ripples. Playing with water. Do I dare? My legs open. The rushing water turns my body and touches me with a fast finger that does not tire. I receive without apology. Time. Nothing to rush, only to feel. I feel time in me. It is endless pleasure in the current. No control. No thought. Simply, here. My left hand reaches for the frog dangling from my neck, floating above my belly, and I hold it between my breasts like a withered heart, beating inside me, inside the river. We are moving downstream. Water. Water music. Blue notes, white notes, my body mixes with the body of water like jazz, the currents like jazz. I too am free to improvise.

I grip stones in shallow water. There is moss beneath my fingernails.

I leave the creek and walk up to my clothes. I am already dry. My skirt and blouse slip on effortlessly. I twist my hair and secure it with a stick. The frog is still with me. Do I imagine beads of turquoise have replaced the sunken and hollow eyes?

We walk. Canyons within canyons. The sun threatens to annihilate me. I recall all the oven doors I have opened to a blast of heat that burned my face. My eyes narrow. Each turn takes us deeper inside the Grand Canyon, my frog and I.

We are witnesses to this opening of time, vertical and horizontal at once. Between these crossbars of geology is a silent sermon on how the world was formed. Seas advanced and retreated. Dunes now stand in stone. Volcanoes erupted and lava cooled. Garnets shimmer and separate schist from granite. It is sculptured time to be touched, even tasted, our mineral content preserved in the desert.

This is the Rio Colorado.

We are water. We are swept away. Desire begins in wetness. My fingers curl around this little frog. Like me, it was born out of longing, wet, not dry. We can always return to our place of origin. Water. Water music. We are baptized by immersion, nothing less can replenish or restore our capacity to love. It is endless if we believe in water.

We are approaching a cliff. Red monkey flowers bloom. White-throated swifts and violet-green swallows crisscross above. My throat is parched. There is a large pool below. My fear of heights is overcome by my desire to merge. I dive into the water, deeper and deeper, my eyes open, and I see a slender passageway. I wonder if I have enough breath to venture down. Down. I take the risk and swim through the limestone corridor where the water is milky and I can barely focus through the shimmering sediments of sand until it opens into a clear, green room. The frog fetish floats to the surface. I rise too and grab a few breaths held in the top story of this strange cavern. I bump my head on the jagged ceiling. The green room turns red, red, my own blood, my own heart beating, my fingers touch the crown of my head and streak the wall.

Down. I sink back into the current, which carries me out of the underwater maze to the pool. I rise once again, feeling a scream inside me surfacing as I do scream, breathe, tread water, get my bearings. The outside world is green is blue is red is hot, so hot. I swim to a limestone ledge, climb out and lie on my stomach, breathing. The rock is steaming. The frog is under me. Beating. Heart beating. I am dry. I long to be wet. I am bleeding. Back on my knees, I immerse my head in the pool once more to ease the cut and look below. Half in. Half out. Amphibious. I am drawn to both earth and water. The frog breaks free from the leather thong. I try to grab its body but miss and watch it slowly spiral into the depths.

Before leaving, I drink from a nearby spring and hold a mouthful—I hear frogs, a chorus of frogs, their voices rising like bubbles from what seems to be the green room. Muddled at first, they become clear. I run back to the edge of the pool and listen. Throwing back my head, I burst into laughter spraying myself with water.

It is rain.

It is frogs.

It is hearts breaking against the bodies of those we love.

A PASSING

Pattiann Rogers

Coyotes passed through the field at the back
of the house last night—coyotes, from midnight
till dawn, hunting, foraging, a mad scavenging,
scaring up pocket gophers, white-breasted mice,
jacktails, voles, the least shrew, catching
a bite at a time.

They were a band, screeching, yodeling,
a multi-toned pack. Such yipping and yapping
and jaw clapping, yelping and painful howling,
they had to be skinny, worn, used-up,
a tribe of bedraggled uncles and cousins
on the skids, torn, patched, frenzied
mothers, daughters, furtive pups
and, slinking on the edges, an outcast
cowdog or two.

From the way they sounded they must have smelled
like rotted toadstool mash and cow blood
curdled together.

All through the night they ranged and howled,
haranguing, scattering through the bindweed and wild
madder, drawing together again, following
old trails over hillocks, leaving their scat
at the junctions, lifting their legs on split
rocks and witch grass. Through rough-stemmed
and panicled flowers, they nipped
and nosed, their ragged tails dragging
in the camphorweed and nettle dust.

They passed through, all of them, like threads
across a frame, piercing and pulling, twining
and woofing, the warp and the weft. Off-key,
suffering, a racket of abominables
with few prospects, they made it—entering
on one side, departing on the other.
They passed clear through and they vanished
with the morning, alive.

MY ANIMAL LIFE

Ellen Meloy

*M*y husband and I live in a small, remote desert town where a bit of discomfort is a virtue. The distances to commercial centers are considerable, and thus far the place has avoided the fate of many overtouristed western towns that have become parodies of their own clichés. There is no numbing spectacle of consumerism. There is less than the most basic of services. But there is a river, and the river absorbs our lives and our souls. Between April and November very little time passes without a boat in the water, a float through the deep-walled wilderness of home.

One day I return from a solo trip on the river, a long string of days in a canyon lit with primordial radiance. Looking back at a logistical error involving the raft, I am convinced that I nearly died on that trip. The brush with danger so exacerbates a chronic restlessness, I unload the gear and clean up, but I cannot stay at home. The town feels as crowded as a Kurdish refugee camp with newcomers from Kosovo. On a long stretch of days off from work, Mark hangs around the house and putters, totally *pu,* a Japanese term that describes a person who is at home and unproductive, perhaps between jobs. At first I thought *pu* (pronounced "poo") translated somewhat fittingly as "wet leaves," but I was confused and mistaken.

Suddenly, I feel the urge to roar through my house and yard like a fury of locusts: Clean up this place, quit living in dust and sand and bugs and lizards, weeds and prickles and everything bone-dry and shaggy. Within a few minutes the compulsion passes. However, the brain fog that arose with the animal insurrection fails to subside. I still feel like a mental patient, wrongly discharged. It is time to seek psychiatric help.

The wild geese rise high above the house, pushing me in an easterly direction. I gas up the truck at the local inconvenience store. The bulletin board lays out a busy social calendar. A Head

Start parade, tribal government chapter house meetings, the hours of worship at the Church of Jesus Christ of the Latter-day Saints, the minutes of the Mosquito Committee. "Overweight, pooped, and bored?" queries one message. Another message announces activity on the rodeo grounds. "Woping invitational," it reads. "Calf wopers' purse $200."

A tour bus overwhelms the parking lot with its sleek mass of chrome and ebony windows and the acrid exhaust of its idling. The bus is making a pit stop between official sites of scenic interest. Since we are not officially scenic, none of the tourists looks past the gas pumps to the drop-dead beauty of the town. The restroom doors at the inconvenience store face the outdoors; about a dozen bus passengers line up in front of them. A Navajo man threads his way through the crowd to his truck. In his best low-register Tonto voice he greets them as he passes. "Hello, rich people."

At the post office the velvet grandmothers—older Navajo women in long, fluted cotton skirts and velveteen blouses—give me the News of the World: lots of headaches this year, time to pick crane's bill and buffaloberry. Broken-faced sandstone cliffs embrace the river. Bright sun, no clouds. Only a hard squint can swallow the distances.

On the road to the psychiatrist the desert is everything there is of the world. Red rock and coral sand, silver rain and gilded river, the immense dome of turquoise sky—the land coalesces into flesh. Every particle of place reincarnates as fur, feather, and fin, heart, lung, leaf, and wing. Every life form carries the desert within it. Colorado pike-minnow, kit fox, desert bighorn sheep, leopard lizards, and other natives grew to this place, graceful and specific in their fit. The generalists arrive with the luggage that makes it their own: flexibility, adaptation, the ability to expand or alter, in whatever possible way, their repertoire of behaviors in order to survive. The sandhill cranes that needed the active floodplain and marshes of an undammed river diminish in numbers or go to wetter elsewheres. Eager exploiters of cultivated land, the Canada geese stay put. Without a reliable supply of dead meat and live human entertainment, surely the ravens would drop dead of boredom.

The back road slips off rocky tablelands into a gentle valley and crosses the Utah border into Colorado. Mixed stands of sweet clover, bunchgrass, and wild mustard spill from the farmlands and line the roadside fences. At several points of higher elevation the land breaks into uncultivated, ungrazed stretches. One of these stretches grows a forest of cliffrose, the desert shrub whose fragrance in spring will make you feel as if you are free-floating but tethered. Today I pass cliffrose well past bloom, but I know their power and always note their presence. No matter how often you travel home geography, the familiar roads, you cannot take the locals for granted.

A person's animal life can become high-maintenance, I think as I turn into the shrink's driveway. Nature constantly revises and rearranges itself in the face of novelty and surprises, its imperative of "order" demands a ragged, healthy turmoil, the compulsions of diverse and complex creatures trying to stay alive even as circumstances change. I would like to think that our scrubby patch of desert has opened new niches to the domestic wildlife. I hope that the whirs, chirps, quorks, peeps, rustles, and slithers are the sounds of dynamic adaptation.

For some species the pressures of humans are simply too overwhelming—the elimination of an entire food supply or habitat comes to mind—and they disappear, leaving an absence as palpable as their presence, a hollow emptiness in the human spirit. More tolerant creatures cling to verges and vacant lots, the "unofficial" ecosystems that are neither countryside nor places of wild earth but patches of real estate on what is swiftly becoming the weed planet. One of these days the starlings will have no bluebirds among them. Then, even though they are opportunistic pests, the starlings, too, might succumb to a diminished world, relegated to oblivion or the rafters of a hockey stadium. These thoughts invite images of a sludgy, sterilized planet devoid of birds and other life, a *Silent Spring* gloom so dense that arrival at the mental health clinic is fortuitous and timely.

The doctors—there is a pair of them—crop grass, twitch the skin on their muscular flanks, and amble over a rough field at the mouth of a box canyon. They are plump and happy, and they barely turn their big heads when I park the truck and walk over to their fence. They ignore the passing traffic and outpatient visitors like me, but they never ignore one another. Physically, the mules are identical, a perfectly matched set. It is their nature to form two halves into a whole, a union into intractable muleness.

The mules are nearly as husky as Clydesdales—sleek, breathing barrels of muscle and flesh and bone atop stocky legs built like pile drivers. The afternoon sun burnishes their silky coats into a deep red-gold. Their legs and bellies are nearly white. This same paleness surrounds black nostrils and dark brown eyes. The white eye patches make you watch their faces with mindful love, as you would a clown's face. Most of all I adore their blond tails and the blond, roached manes that bristle along their heavy necks. The roaching gives them the blunt angles of punk weightlifters or blue-collar workers with crew cuts and chests the size of a walk-in freezer. As if they were the last two bachelor proletarians on earth, their comfort with one another is nonchalant but needy.

For years I have passed the mules on supply runs from home to a larger town. When I do not have the time to stop, I make sure as I pass that both mules are still alive. Sometimes one mule stands at the opposite end of the field from his brother or both have been swallowed up by the pool of black shade under a cottonwood grove, and I will panic until I spot them, nearly driving into the ditch with the distraction.

As is usual when I park and linger for a full therapy session rather than a reassuring glimpse of them, today the Mule Brothers largely ignore me. Only occasionally has one or the other come over to inspect the palm of my hand with velvet lips and a rush of warm breath blown from the nose.

Their polite indifference does not infer poor psychiatry. The cure they offer is simple mammalian empathy. I find contentment in the company of these two huge strawberry blondes. Perhaps because all three of us have hair and body heat and warm red blood, the Mule Brothers help me feel the presence of the world.

When I am in the need of calming, when the mind fevers rage with particular ferocity, my preferred psychiatrists are a certain band of desert bighorn sheep that live deep in the Colorado Plateau wilds. Putting myself in their presence requires more effort—no vehicle access, a long, hot hike, the possibility that I will look in the right places but will fail to find them. To be among bighorns I must also overcome a reluctance to disturb them or in any way jeopardize their precarious existence. To spend sheep time, time among the wildest of the wild, there is distance, physical rigor, and the anguished compromise between their needs and mine, all of it rewarded by the great solace that comes when you join your own breath to the vibrant, resonating breath of living creatures.

In this light it is perhaps less strange that two old mules—common, domesticated, a couple of reproductive dead-ends—would serve as a frequent mammal-empathy substitute for wild sheep. The mules nuzzle one another. Both of them rest their standing weight on their left hind legs, then in unison lift their haunches and shift their weight to their right legs. They will not do anything without one another. They are so . . . so *spherical*. Because they are sensitive I cannot let on that I know this. I also keep the sheep secret to myself, reluctant to admit that these equine therapists are second-string guys. I don't want to hurt their feelings.

The Mule Brothers don't work. They are off duty. They are *pu*. They hold down the world when I pass this way; they offer a constant against reckless spin. Their box-canyon pasture opens to a narrow green valley and a creek lined with shady cottonwoods and Russian olive trees. Flies buzz. The mules shake them away with their punk manes. Their long, velvety ears angle to the sun, backlit with halos of molten gold. There are two of them, I remind myself. There will always be cliffrose and two mules, and they will always be here. I could not endure the heartbreak of one mule gone and the other mule looking, always looking, toward the place he last saw his brother. The sorrow of a single mule would be harder to bear than no mules at all.

PRESENCE

Penelope Moffet

Something sings so high we cannot hear it.
Not the long descending trill of canyon wren,
not hawk call or goldfinch whistle,
not scrubjay chatter.
The singer has a snake's discretion,
sounds less often than the poorwill flies,
spreads over hills like wild cucumber
tendril by tendril, root big as a man
buried deep in the earth.
Bees droning wide in their nectar quest
will never find it.
Above fly buzz and tick scritch,
beyond coyote yip and the grind
of bulldozers and earthworms
persists the fluctuating note.

SNAKE

Kelly Tighe

The buzzing interrupts my daydream, slams me back to the present. In a split second, I realize that my horse and I are in a precarious position. An agitated rattlesnake is coiled on the left of the narrow trail. To the right is a two-hundred-foot drop-off.

The snake has apparently been dozing beneath a bush, whiling away the heat of the day in a pool of shade. The horse and rider ahead of me probably jolted it from its reverie as rudely as it, in turn, rouses me. Perhaps it has just begun to calm down, to relax its loops and coils and settle comfortably. Has its soundless mind picked up the vibrations of my horse's feet? Or perhaps the ancient heat-sensing pits below the snake's eyes have alerted it to the large, two-headed biomass ambling up the trail.

My gelding and I move quickly up the trail, out of harm's way. When we stop to rest the horses, I tell my husband about my close encounter. As we relax for a while, I think about a young deaf woman, Belinda, who recently moved to our small town. She is a poet and artist, and her work sometimes reflects the special kinship she feels with snakes. Like the snake, she survives in a silent world, depending on vibrations to identify a slamming door, footsteps, or music. Perhaps Belinda has influenced the way I view rattlesnakes. Though the fear is still there, the revulsion is gone. I see them now as creatures trying to survive, like the rest of us, in a frightening world.

In the Huachuca Mountains of southeastern Arizona, we are at the southern end of the Arizona Trail, a 790-mile, nonmotorized pathway soon to span the state from Mexico to Utah. It is a warm and beautiful October day and the cloudless sky is a deep, clear blue as we climb one of Arizona's southernmost "sky islands," mountain ranges that are isolated from one another by valleys of desert or grassland. We are on our way to one of my favorite places, the 9,466-foot-high Miller Peak.

This outing was my idea, but my husband leads on the trail. His gray mare loves to be in front of everyone else and sets a rapid pace. Ears forward, neck arched, and eyes bright with anticipation, she surveys the route ahead. When the mare is not at the front of the group, she's a different girl. Her ears hang dejectedly and she stumbles along, heaving huge sighs of discontent. We usually let her lead.

The trail makes a steep ascent from the desert chaparral of Emory oak, piñon pines, yuccas, and cactus, toward the impressive pines and firs of the mountaintop. The temperature cools as we gain elevation. After a scramble through granite boulders, we find ourselves traveling along the highest ridgeline of the Huachucas. On the final half-mile climb to Miller Peak we pass the first aspen trees, their gold-tinged leaves shimmering in the breeze. They remind us that winter snowstorms will soon come. Miller Peak is rocky and windblown, with a 360-degree view of the world below.

On our way back down the mountain, the horses move faster in anticipation of their home corral and supper. Shadows fall across the trail, and there is a chill in the air. We watch for the snake, but the bush is abandoned.

The snake has fled, I hope, to a less-traveled place.

WORKING CATTLE

Carol Fox

The sun beats down on the shabby corral
pieced together with baling wire and old boards;
dust and the noise of bawling cattle thicken the air.

The old squeeze chute works, and my unused fingers slowly
  remember.
I am the only woman as I was once the only girl.
Today my son is the neophyte, a city boy trying not to
  show it.

The heifers are easy: one man works the squeeze,
scissoring calves at the neck,
another slips the needle in under the tough skin.

My son and I alternate: we brad the insecticide tag into the
  left ear,
slice the right ear (to mark the blackleg inoculation),
and spray deep into both ears for ticks.

Once when the heifer bawls and throws her head,
my son jerks back, but then he holds steady.

It's different for the bull calves.
The men throw them, pinning them to earth while
my brother cuts off the end of the leathery sac,
pulls out the testicles until the vas deferens is exposed.
He scrapes with careful strokes,
sealing the blood vessels as the strands part,
and then tosses the balls into the grass.
I put them in a bucket.

The calves do not struggle or bawl:
they lie stunned and unbelieving.
My brother is silent, concentrating.
My son still slashes the ears.

I stand to one side, thinking.
From earliest childhood I worked cattle,
smeared tar-like medicine into open wounds
crawling with maggots—there were no sprays then.

Before plastic ear tags, I pressed
a hot iron into the calf's hip
until the stench of scorched hair filled the air.

I have broken off needles in a calf's neck and started over
    again.
I have slashed an ear in two with my pocketknife
while the blood ran down my arm into the grass.

I have been covered with blood and manure
and dirt and calf snot,
sweating under a hot sun.

But I have never cut the balls from a calf,
carefully scraping the vessels so that its
life's blood did not seep into the
ground along with its manhood.

One small calf's testicles are undescended.
My brother works and works but cannot get them down.
My father gives the signal: Let him go.
"You lucky, boy," one of the men says,
whacking the calf out of the pen, and they all laugh.
My son is silent, but he wears the colors of his initiation:
blood and manure and purple tick spray streaked with sweat,
and he stands near the men.

What is this mystery my son is entering into
and I am excluded from?

Mutilating mutilated manhood, emasculating masculinity,
slicing open the sac to pull out the entrails of the self,
with dull strokes paring away procreative power
to leave a gaping bloody hole
and a pile of fleshy nubs in a bucket.

The men gather up their things:
empty syringes, ear tags, knives, tick spray,
and put them in the shed.
I gather up the bucket of huddled lumps of flesh
which was left behind in the grass,
leaning against the weathered fence post.

KNOT

Pattiann Rogers

Watching the close forest this afternoon
and the riverland beyond, I delineate
quail down from the dandelion's shiver from the blowzy silver
of the cobweb in which both are tangled. I am skillful
at tracing the white egret within the white
branches of the dead willow where it roosts
and at separating the heron's graceful neck
from the leaning stems of the blue-green
lilies surrounding. I know how to unravel
sawgrasses knitted to iris leaves knitted
to sweet vernals. I can unwind sunlight
from the switches of the water in the slough
and divide the grey sumac's hazy hedge
from the hazy grey of the sky, the red vein
of the hibiscus from its red blossom.

All afternoon I part, I isolate, I untie,
I undo, while all the while the oak
shadows, easing forward, slowly ensnare me,
and the calls of the wood peewees catch
and latch in my gestures, and the spicebush
swallowtails weave their attachments
into my attitude, and the damp sedge
fragrances hook and secure, and the swaying
Spanish mosses loop my coming sleep,
and I am marsh-shackled, forest-twined,
even as the new stars, showing now
through the night-spaces of the sweet gum
and beech, squeeze into the dark.

COYOTE LOVE MUSIC

Nancy Owen Nelson

Light streams in from the east,
just as coyotes leave the den
for the day. In the dead of night
they were near, outside our window,
insistent, harmonious yes, insistent
that the world hear them.

Our house cats growl and hiss,
do jiujitsu on the end of the bed.
In the midst of chaos, you touch,
you find your way of awakening,
your own song.

MASTODON TEETH

Sybil Pittman Estess

*O*range coral, tan sea-cork, fishnets
hang in curves over the Formica bar
of his hermit hut, the man from Racine,
a curator who's lived for seven years
on this beach-cliff in south Texas.
He scavenges the coral from the Caribbean,
perhaps Cancun. He shows us petrified wood,
as we fight off troops of mosquitoes,
the fields of Texas expanding beyond us,
the "Danger"-marked sea below . . .
Three pieces he holds off until the end—
two five-inch mastodon teeth, one mammoth's bone.

The teeth are encrusted with nipple-like cusps
that make them bumpy and ugly and odd.
They aren't at all like teeth of a toy elephant,
or glassed, dated relics in some museum.
No, real mastodon teeth simply lie
in my quaking hands—casual remains of a monster,
picked up on an inaccessible shoreline
near Brazoria. The man keeps them with
a foot-long piece of the old pachyderm's bone.

Dear old beachcomber, you loosed fear in me
on that hot and itchy night under an August moon.
Fangs gnawed in my kneading nightmares,
and I waked knowing this: of all there was
of these beasts, only their teeth remain.

MONARCHS

Alison Hawthorne Deming

I've come, for the third time, to see the monarch butterflies that migrate here to overwinter in the coastal eucalyptus groves. I've been reading for years about these little beauties, and the more I learn about their talents, the more beautiful they become. To see them and to contemplate the intelligence dwelling in their flighty bodies is to feel the force of heroic effort in nature—frailty and tenacity as one. Most of the monarchs living west of the Rockies in any given year journey thousands of miles to cluster high in these weeping branches. Their eastern counterparts travel to sanctuary forests in the central mountains of Mexico. This migratory flight is even more heroic when one considers that a monarch lives only for nine months. It makes the flight once in its lifetime, knowing innately how to navigate the distance because of a speck of magnetite in its head, coded genetic information, and a set of compound eyes that are among the most refined mechanisms in nature. A butterfly's eye has six thousand lenses. It looks like the seeded yellow center of a daisy. No one knows, of course, what it can see—whether images appear as a panorama, mosaic, or fragmented composite—or how far it can see, or how clearly. What's known is that it can perceive motion from all sides and a broad range of colors. The great blue morphos that live high in the tropical rain forest will respond to a scrap of blue silk tethered to a pole, a male attacking the fabric as it would a competing male. Butterflies can see light in the ultraviolet range—glittering opalescence—beyond the spectrum visible to us.

Lepidoptera, the second-largest order in the animal world, have been around for fifty million years—much longer than humans have—and the monarchs have been around for much longer than their California hosts, the eucalyptus trees. These

shaggy, fragrant giants were imported from Australia as a source
of timber (I once heard that they were brought to be harvested for
telephone poles) and have since filled in areas that used to be treeless.
The monarchs have found the groves hospitable. By accident, the im-
portation of eucalyptus resulted in this sanctuary. It's hard to imagine how much the monarchs must cherish the forest in which they
sleep after their migration. To cherish—not an idea or an emotion—
a physical intimacy, the fact of being in the one place they belong. It
brings to mind a story my father, an inveterate New Englander, used
to tell about the cross-country road trip he and my mother made in
the late thirties. There were no interstate highways, few other travelers, barely enough gas stations and cafes to keep them and the old
blue Plymouth convertible rolling. He remembered best the places
that humbled them—the dirt road through Rabbit Ears Pass in the
Rockies, the fearful desert expanse that went on day after scorching
day. When they finally got home to the damp and leafy Connecticut
forest, he fell to his knees and kissed the ground.

"You're not here to see the monarchs are you?" asks the ranger,
after I've snaked along the heavily populated coves to the entrance
of Natural Bridges State Park. "They're gone. Only fifteen percent
of the normal population showed up, and they left by the end of
December."

Usually the monarchs stay into February or March. I drive on—
no point in looking at the empty trees—and decide to consult the
local expert. John Lane's office in the basement of the Santa Cruz
Natural History Museum is a kind of bowerbird nest of books, tropical butterflies mounted in exhibit boxes, computer hum and glow,
papers and files—the friendly clutter of a well-used working space.
We go outside to talk, leaning against a life-size statue of a blue
whale. We talk about our childhoods, the many places we've lived,
how few of us get to stay in the same place for more than five years,
yet how much we need to feel we're in the right place, connected to
the land—rooted, as we say in our tree envy. And how we have to
relearn the natural world each time we move—how strange the saguaros and paloverde of the desert are to people like me raised under
hickories and maples.

He tells me that some fluctuation in the monarch population is
normal. But this year's combination of low population and early
departure is not understood. He wonders whether low population

itself might be the reason for the departure. Maybe they perceived that a critical mass was missing and said, "Hey, let's get out of here." Like many scientists I've met, he seems to have an abiding faith in nature's unexpected periods of profusion and decline—no catastrophist here, but a pragmatic student of the big picture.

"Is it light sensitivity that normally tells them when to leave?" I ask.

"No, because they do so at different times each year. It's some combination, perhaps having to do with an accumulation of light in their bodies, having to do with the weather, the temperature."

Nevertheless, threats to the shrinking islands of wildness that harbor the monarchs are significant enough that California will spend millions this year for habitat protection. Part of Lane's job is consulting on proposed developments to determine whether a planned building site is a monarch habitat. Chalk up one for the butterflies whose presence can ban a condo development. He urges me to go to the El Rosario site in Michoacan, Mexico. You have to go by cattle truck, but it's worth it. You swim your way through butterflies. That site too, however, is threatened. Illegal logging has caused the deaths of millions of monarchs—seventy percent of the 1991–1992 population. And by 1993, ninety percent of the original fir forest used by the monarchs had vanished. The remaining trees, though protected by a 1986 presidential decree, are being hacked away. Much of the bootleg logging is done by campesino farmers who use the wood for fuel, sell it, or build their homes with it, then grow crops on the cleared land.

Lane recommends for today that I drive down the coast to Point Lobos and walk the cypress grove before heading back north to the city. Fond of Robert Louis Stevenson's dictum "to travel hopefully is a better thing than to arrive," I drive on. Lobos is a gnarly, moss-draped, wind-stripped stand of trees—barely enough green hanging onto the boughs for photosynthesis. While I'm reading the trail guide, a carload pulls up, checks the billboard—"Oh, it's nothing but trees"—and pulls off. I take the loop trail along the cliff, pass a cobble of stones packed into sedimentary deposits (like pebbles mixed with cement) interbedded with solid rock, the shore crumbling into the hammering waves. I pass a grassy meadow, which the trees have encouraged by providing the shade that stunts more demanding vegetation. Trunks and branches listing away from the wind, gray

blighted ice plant collapsed into dormancy. Then patches of wild lilac, the petals of its flower cones so small that up close they look like
they're comprised of blue dust, but when I look back from a distance
the lilac bloom sprawls like localized oil slicks across the hillside.

Each piece of land can tell a story of grief and loss—forests turned
to waste and stone, lifeways dried up in spite of sacred ritual, the human heart ruined by war. And yet the land keeps telling another version of the story—that its cycles and processes are the final authority,
that our hearts are constructed to love its beauty. Some land seems
too beautiful—the images enter directly to the heart like a patch of
nitro taped to the chest. Life enhancing, but what a jolt. So much
of California has this effect—the liquid rippling of green grass on
the coastal hillsides; live oaks whose wood seems to weave through
air the way seaweed weaves through water; the cathedral forest of
redwoods, where scorch marks stripe the massive trunks and hollow
out the cores, yet the igneous convolutions of bark rise up to random
spokes, climb away from the dusk that they are creating, taper, and
bud in a slow, green reach for light.

SLEEP, MONARCHS, RISING AND FALLING

Alison Hawthorne Deming

Sleep, Monarchs, rising and falling
  with the wind, orange children tucked in your winter bed,
  teachers of patience and faith
     dreaming in the eucalyptus dark,
  accumulating in your cells the photons that tell
  you when to move, a sense
     I share in mind,
  that makes the blue world
     light up, electric. It's too late

     to just let the world be and think
  it will mend. Yet how you, little nothings, perfect my spirit!
     almost erasing
  the actual ruin of living and all its doctrines
     with your evolved sleep—
  delicate and frail as you are, the profusion of you
  awakening in me soundings of the past
     that name the future.

what we leave behind

Holding my sherd, I feel the substance of time, a place I can travel to while standing still . . . This moment is a thousand years ago and a thousand years ago is this moment and we are both the same, that woman then and this woman now.

SHARMAN APT RUSSELL,
"WHEN THE LAND WAS YOUNG"

WHAT WE LEAVE BEHIND

Joy Kennedy

*W*hump! *The explosion shakes the cave. White dust churns down the culvert-sized passage, tumbling like a cloud, swirling, unfolding and folding inside itself. Helmet lights shrink to pencil-thin yellow beams, weak and unable to penetrate the limestone dust, which smells like damp chalk. I can hear the scuffling of cavers squirming through the opening the blast has made, but they are invisible to me. The dust grows thicker, and as I pull my shirt over my mouth to breathe, I realize that I have been left behind.*

This land of sun-dappled Texas cedars has claimed my heart, but the depths of its caves and caverns have claimed my soul. Nancy Sather, an ecologist from Minnesota, has written, "There are places that own our souls because of the investment we have made in them—the days or years we lived there, heard their night sounds and watched their dusks; or the energy we invested getting to them, fighting to save them or documenting their creatures."

But if there are places that own our very souls, what else might they have of ours? Are there tree-lined hillsides that keep our secrets silent under their lattice-lace of shadows? Do we ever lose ourselves in the depths?

We certainly don't mean to leave anything behind in the caves. Responsible cavers collect their urine in a bottle, carry plastic bags for excrement, and use various pockets and pouches to keep trash. I pick up other cavers' used carbide, the discarded blue sprinkles that sometimes litter the rocks like lost turquoise. I try not to drop granola crumbs, which could encourage non-native animal life or poison the delicate troglobitic insects not accustomed to such rich fare. I try not to scrape the top of my helmet as I crawl, to not dislodge the delicate soda straw formations that have taken hundreds of years to dangle a single pinhead of water like a rainbow. I try not to take false steps, make sudden moves, or disturb the bats that cluster above in chittering masses, as soft and warm as winged dreams. But this is impossible. Even my lightest touch leaves skin oils on the formations, and the slightest light causes the bats to blink and become alert.

"Joy?"

"Here!" I shout with relief.

"It goes! Bring down the survey tape."

I roll up the stereo cord wires used for the charge and stow them in the battered mud bucket. I had mixed the mud for the explosion "up top," as the cavers say, beneath the blue expanse of Texas Hill Country sky. The mud was packed over the ammonium nitrate and methane mix, simply called "bang." A good mud packing and careful placement would ensure minimum damage to fragile formations.

It's hard to see where to go in the twilight of chalky dust and deep shadows. The narrow passage splits. My caver friend Mike compares his love of caving to taking an unknown road: "Sometimes you just have to see what's there—to find what you can't see from the main road." Like me and other members of the Texas Speleological Society, Mike volunteers to survey and map the caves in Hays County, a rocky area sandwiched between San Antonio and Austin. Like all of us, Mike is enthusiastic about caves.

I think of this and smile, deciding to choose the passage with the most airflow. Wriggling through an opening no bigger than an air-conditioner vent, I watch a cave cricket with its elongated antennae clamber over a smooth pebble inches from my eye. There are no sounds except my ragged breathing and a single drip of water as loud as a kettledrum. No one has been here before. My elbow makes an arc through the sandy yellow dirt. A mark where there was none before. An impression.

The motto of the National Speleological Society ends with "Leave nothing but footprints." But the terrible secret is that this is impossible. Lint scrapes off visitors' clothes to float like germs, eventually sticking to formations and generating organic acids that can dissolve the calcite, the bone of the formations. Each year "lint camp" volunteers in Carlsbad Caverns in New Mexico pick or wash away five pounds of lint, the same bluish-gray fluff that you pull from your clothes dryer's filter. Our hairs—we lose about two hundred a day— can introduce foreign microbes and bacteria.

As an example of how important it is to leave a pristine cave environment, scientists look to Lechuguilla in New Mexico. Explorers can enter this cave only by invitation and must take extreme measures not to contaminate it: they cannot comb their hair, disturb the water, move off the trail, or leave anything behind. Why? Among many things, some of the microbes collected from its depths have been shown to "eat" breast cancer cells. Such extromophiles may hold the key to saving our lives, but contamination will ruin them forever.

There are, however, "sacrificial caves": caves with few formations or difficult passages used by the National Spelcological Society to train beginners. Their crawling passages are worn smooth, their walls are stained dark from beginners' fumblings for handholds. "Sacrificed for the good of the others," Mike says, shaking his head regretfully. But such caves are needed—a caver can get her cave legs there before trained volunteers take her to more delicate caves. If she's clumsy or irresponsible, she won't be invited to others. Sacrificial caves can be fun, but there is a sad, shy victimization about them, as if they know that they were once beautiful and whole.

Some caves are sacrificial because the damage done to them is too great to reverse. There are muddy footprints on white calcite, the glare of graffiti. There are broken formations as jagged as teeth and sinkholes filled with rusty car parts, cans of used motor oil, barbed wire. What goes into a cave goes into the aquifer's water, like the flow of blood straight to a heart. In this part of Texas that heart is the Edwards Aquifer, which supplies water to numerous cities, including San Antonio.

Some have tried to restore sacrificial caves, but with mixed resulsts, for even when we try to save these places we damage them. The act of rubbing graffiti from a formation, for example, is like trying to erase pencil marks from paper. The paper looks clean, but we have removed layers of the delicate paper fiber. Betsy Hilbert expresses this concern in "Disturbing the Universe," in which she writes about trying to save loggerhead turtle eggs: "None of us knows the final outcome of any action, the endless chain of ripples that we start with every movement. We walk in the world blindly, crashing into unidentified objects and tripping over rough edges. We human beings are too big for our spaces and too powerful for our understanding. What I do today will wash up somewhere far beyond my ability to know about it."

Caving is like wandering into uncharted realms in our lives and trying not to make a misstep. I've had someone tell me, "See that formation above your head? It's at least a thousand years old and the rarest in this state. Be careful you don't bump it." I nearly had a heart attack. Similarly, I've seen friends at the altar told, "This person will be your partner for the rest of your life. Be thoughtful." Caving and life, love or work or faith, our embraces come with costs. One misstep is all it takes.

Sometimes, we can only hope our gracelessness will be forgiven. In a cave deep in Mexico I lost a lens cap. In a cave in Belize, a flashlight. Perhaps someone who comes after me will pick them up. I hope so. I hope they take away the jarring plastic from such wild places, plastic as incongruous as a laptop in a leaf-strewn jungle. Perhaps someone will come along and pick up all the things we have left—a heartache here, a lost friend there, a missed opportunity. Perhaps they will find places for them in their own lives, cradling them like prayers.

The passage I have crawled through has led to a room with limestone columns. Tiny plant roots grow down through hollow soda straws to dangle in mid-air, the moisture on them beading like diamonds in the beam of a helmet light. Cave crickets scatter en masse down a wall like a strange and beautiful waterfall. The others come after me, and want to "push" the cave even further. We follow the direction of the airflow, which is growing faint. Some have lit incense, and we watch soundlessly as the pungent smoke curls in protean shapes, drifts, perhaps points to a new passage, a new room, a new cave, a new hollow place hidden like a geode under the green Texas hills.

When Thoreau returned to his cabin after walks in the woods, he always knew who had visited in his absence by the things they left behind: "either a bunch of flowers, or a wreath of evergreen, or a name in pencil on a yellow walnut leaf or a chip. They who come rarely to the woods take some little piece of the forest into their hands to play with by the way, which they leave, either intentionally or accidentally."

Like Thoreau, we are drawn to wild places. Texas features show caves like Natural Bridge Caverns, Wonder World Cave, and Inner Space Caverns; they have thousands of visitors per year. The city of Austin's biggest tourist attraction is the evening flight of the Congress Avenue Bridge bats. Further south you can watch forty million of these free-tailed bats—the largest accumulation of mammals in the world—fly out of Bracken Bat Cave near San Antonio. The bats' emergence creates its own wind and a vortex of invisible swirls of warmth and coolness from the cave.

And like Thoreau's visitors, we leave things behind. Once while surveying a cave I saw specks of dirt all over my clothes, like pepper. I was ankle deep in guano when the dirt began hopping and jumping. It was fleas. In my haste to get away, I left behind a notebook, which I returned for the next spring. It was wet, soiled, and smelled sour and musty.

After being in a cave all day you can find yourself disoriented when you come out. A thousand smells greet you. Sounds descend upon you. Long after the cave blast, I finally poke my head outside. A blackness has fallen, sirens are blaring, and a large white circular object is poised, ready to roll down on top of me.

"Keep going. What's the problem?" the cavers below me shout.

But I'm frozen in fear, staring at the white object only feet away. The sirens slowly reveal themselves to be cicadas. The blackness softens; it is only night, and a white smattering of stars appears in the purple twilight. The circle is a full moon, pock-marked and white.

Well. When Mike became sick with a mysterious illness, doctors were concerned that his illness could be histoplasmosis, a fungal infection caused by spores in the bat guano found in caves. They checked for rabies. In the end, it was discovered to be lymphoma. And in the end, it was too late. There are things we don't want to leave behind, but must. Something or someone will gently push us away, or take our hand in a hospital room and say it's time to go. There will come days when the places you love grow dimmer and faint in your rearview mirror. Days when dark passages retain no light. At his wife's request, and with a landowner's gracious permission, I placed Mike's ashes in a cave that we had explored together. His dust was sterile, reduced to the barest elements, but I had never gone to a cave to deliberately leave something behind. I did this time.

Can we really move softly and carefully through such passages in our lives without tripping? Can we "leave nothing but footprints" without causing damage? The caves have taught me that we can't. But perhaps the beauty and the grace lie in our willingness to try.

Called to explore difficult places, we will hear our bedroom curtains rustling like bat wings. Umbras of moon shadows and paths will be waiting for us. Home and hill and horizon will be singing for us then, and sacrifices must come. We leave behind what we must. We chart our topography and step outside lightly to see the white full moon waiting, so low and large on the horizon that it could roll into our waiting arms, settling like a stone.

THE BONE-MAN'S APPRENTICE

Susan Cummins Miller

*b*etween Route 66
and the Old Spanish Trail
we hiked serrated ridges, discovering
a cache of fossil bones preserved
on a limy sandstone ledge
in the heart of the Mojave.

Under your watchful eye
I chiseled away the barren, protective strata,
exposing teeth and dimpled bone—a horse's skull
no longer than my hand, concealed
for eighteen million years. With clear drops
of Glyptol, I sealed the fragile fragments.

You showed me how to swaddle the delicate palate
in layers of TP, how to mix plaster of Paris.
I poured tepid canteen water into the dented basin, added
pale gray powder that smelled like kindergarten, warmed
numb fingers in the exothermic reaction, dipped strips
of rough brown burlap in the thick white soup.

Laughing, we smoothed the hardening paste
on fossil and rock pedestal, our fingers
and forearms taking on the chalky hue until
neither of us could identify
where our bodies ended
and the sun-bleached hills began.

STONES AND JAWBONES

Kathryn Wilder

I'm tiptoeing through cryptogamic crust, ever so careful not to damage the velvet-like, moss-covered soil with heel or toe. I step from rock to stone, to cowpie to bare spot to stick, heading toward a curve of redrock that swells into a higher rock and then another, ocean waves caught in their surging rhythm and cast to sandstone. At times I feel frustrated, wanting simply to stride freely down a path, cryptogam be damned, but there are no paths here and I'm not willing to make one.

I'm forty years old, and have lived four times longer than some of the fungus at my feet, and not nearly as long as others. In these four decades I have been well weathered: dried by sun and wind and pain, moistened by tears and rivers and rain, polished smooth, roughened up, worn, discarded, pieced back together, and now my buckskin dress is just that in which nature has clothed me—brown white skin textured with scars and wrinkles and stretchmarks: the stories of my life.

Reaching the slab of red stone that tilts sideways toward the sky, I climb it on all fours. Through the pads of my feet and my fingers, desert warmth spreads upward, meeting the sun's rays on my back and the blood pounding in my veins and I want to revel in it, to curve my body to the earth's, let the sun in, and become prayer. But I must get to the top first.

Maintaining cat-like posture as I scramble, I am closer to the earth than usual. My eyes dart back and forth across the rockface, scanning for special objects as if I were a pack rat or a raven. I stop to touch a small stone, to pull it in for closer examination, to redeposit it in its place like a puzzle piece. I pause for glitter, for anything shiny that resembles quartz or aluminum, as in the innards of geodes or scraps of foil or poptops. White stops me in my tracks—which, with relief, I am not making on this solid rock—and bleached bone compels my fingers earthward.

Straightening up, I fondle the lower jawbone of a desert snake (the teeth lining the inside of the jaw offer me only this general identification). I have found many jawbones in my wanderings—of mule deer, wild burro, beaver, skunk, coyote, cat—and pondered at the meaning. Leaving this snake jaw in a shelter of sage, I continue my ascent toward the perch I decided upon from our campsite downstream. The rock is steep and rough, and I feel both pain and exhilaration as my toes and fingers grip the sharp etchings of wind and propel me upward.

Perhaps cat-like in posture and destination, I am not so cat-like in fearlessness, and I am grateful when the rock rounds out in front of me and I can sit safely on the edge of the world. As my panting ceases, my gaze spreads like cloud shadow over a desert aglow with slanted sunlight. Desert details, from the tiniest filaments of cryptogamic soil to the vast expanses of red rock and blue sky, stretch before me. The Canyon is out there somewhere, and through it threads the mighty Colorado, while here within my reach is a half-foot square plot of land encrusted with a soil so delicate I could wipe out years of growth with a mere thumbprint. One huge rock over, a lone juniper clings for its life to more such soil, a testimony to implantation by wind or wing, to the workings of the system.

I, too, am testimony, as is the dirt road carved between rock wall and streamside, the contrail bisecting bright blue overhead sky, the orange flash of a tent downcanyon. I wince, and for a moment curl in on myself in despair—there is no true wilderness left here, there, anywhere—but then I feel the sun nudging my shoulder. Like the touch of my purest love, who has disappeared into redrock crevices far upstream, sun is irresistible to me. I unfold, lie back, feel rock pockmarking my body from beneath, sun penetrating my skin from above, breasts rising in velvet air with each deep breath I take; I spread my limbs and hair across time, close my eyes, and feel the earth carrying me . . .

Drifting, I see raven feathers and fossilized shells, twisted sticks and obsidian chunks, sprigs of sage, owl down, rocks rough as canyon walls, stones polished river-smooth, sun-whitened femurs and jawbones and pelvises lined up like stairways to the sky.

Drifting, I think how the totems I see in my wanderings I also find in the dwellings of those I recognize as clan, how I am far from alone in this activity of constant scrutiny and sometimes collection of the organic gifts that lie upon the land.

Drifting, I wonder just what it is that speaks to us as we stoop to pluck these treasures from sand and stone, from redrock and riverbed. And what is it that propels us to leave this one in its place, to borrow that one from the earth to be returned later, at some right time?

What voices do we hear, truly? Is it the Earth Mother, saying *Come, lean close. Listen and you will hear me breathe. See the glitter in this stone? Move closer now to touch it, pluck it from my skin and hold it to your cheek, your heart. Like the shell taken from the shore in which you can hear the ocean, through feather, stick, and stone you can hear me. And—if you listen close enough—I will tell you stories. Stories old as me, wise as women, tales you need to know to do your work, to pay attention, to pass on.*

Lying on slickrock, cradled by Earth, caressed by Sky, I know no greater contentment. A soft breeze wanders over my skin, gentle fingers. Drifting, I turn my head so my ear touches stone. I listen.

Like scars, stretchmarks, and wrinkles, the landmarks of the earth's surface are altars upon which tradition, ceremony, memory, and story are placed. And in this land where the earth's covering is so sheer, so simple, the stories read close to my soul. As I listen, it comes to me that the talismans I find in the form of rock are reminders to stay grounded; feathers teach me to feel the stirrings of spirit air; porous lava and solid obsidian tell me of the power of fire; common driftwood takes me to the river, Earth blood.

The sum of all the parts says again: *Listen. Earth and her creatures have much to tell.* And then, with the clarity of the fine white line on the horizon before me where desert earth meets desert sky, I know that the jawbones carry another message. *Speak,* they say.

ASHES

Beth Paulson

What is there to do about wind that blows ashes
from the white-hot smoldering
remains of gathered brush?

My own thoughts leap into the heaped ash,
my few words kindle new flames
until all that's left, smoke.

The box I carried in July was so small
for a father I placed in a grave
that now watches spread maples go red,
cornfields dry to brown.

This is what you think when you watch a fire burn.

See against the dark firs
how smoke plumes into a fragrant cloud?
And see there the ghost woman
who keeps me company,
her long hair blown back like flame?
She says,

Make of these bones a shelter.
Over it hang the night.
Keep one small fire against wolves
and when dawn tenders the top peaks,
your sorrow will be gone.

LAND OF THE GAPING MOUTHS

Lisa Swanstrom

I didn't know the dead woman, but I remember what she looked like when she lived: slender legs and short Pippi Longstocking braids. Freckles, pale skin, interesting, bright sort of eyes. I certainly noticed her, the same way one is forced to notice all things that contrast: a field mouse in the shade of giant sequoia, a thistle in a lily field. For the kids who came through Yosemite, she was a raft atop a fickle river; a paddle to poke at the churning water; or the dark tannin that holds such things together. Joie Ruth Armstrong was important. But I didn't know her. I never even spoke to her.

I'm confessing this so I won't sound callous when I admit that I didn't carry on too much when I saw her face on the cover of the *Times,* followed by the headline, "Naturalist Murdered in Yosemite"—the face of a dead girl I had once seen living. Woman, technically; but you'd say girl too, if you'd seen her.

I didn't cry, but from that day I've felt a dull ache in the middle of my belly, as if my navel were a scar from a bully who couldn't stop digging into my skin, his fierce whisper and sullied finger grinding like a cheap corkscrew. And this bully, this murderer—he's changed the way I look at pine trees. From tall strong lines of cone and branch they've turned to slanted shadows, heaps of slag where strangers hide, better off cut and delivered as cordwood.

The only thing to do with such a bully, of course, is to fight back with his own rough tactics, to dig and turn things right back at him, in order to see the other side again.

So I'm going back to Yosemite, Land of the Gaping Mouths, to revisit Joie Ruth Armstrong, even though I didn't know her, never spoke to her, and was jealous of the girlish legs that loped over piles of broken sugar pine. Because she, a tiny woman, was a custodian of our trees, our rivers, our thrumming birds.

A keeper of wings, beaks, and spidery caves. A woman killed in the berth of redwood boughs, on the edge of wild flowers. A woman who should not have died.

WHEN OUR SIXTH-GRADERS ARRIVED at the Yosemite Institute last spring, Joie and the other guides lined up against a stage, a crudely fashioned platform of splintered wood. They grinned at our students, their teeth even and white, their hair coarse and thick.

The bear expert looked our children up and down suspiciously, sizing them up for litterers, city slickers, and bear feeders, and lectured them for fifteen minutes as they shuffled in the dirt. When she finished, our guides stepped forward: one wiry man, one woman in overalls, and Joie.

Imagine shaving the bark from a redwood tree, straight thin sweeps of it. That was the color of her hair, plaited into shoulder-length braids. Imagine a patch of snow, freckled with pine needles. That was her skin. Imagine a well-worn trail after the rain, where two dark pools stand, reflecting all the movements of the forest until you cannot decide if the pools are green, brown, black, or red, or clearer than the wind, and you will see her eyes.

We hiked miles that first day, stopping only to splash in Mirror Lake and learn the Indian names of Bridal Veil Falls, El Capitan, and Yosemite.

Joie made maps of their bodies. She made them lie down, then put their arms above their heads, tucked a bend to their knees, and pointed to their armpits while they giggled and squirmed in the dirt. "This is Tisse Yak," she explained. "Woman turning into stone. El Capitan is here." She pointed to their shins. "Yosemite Falls here." Their kneecaps. Their arms became vernal falls, their trunks a river, their butts Glacier Point, and their fingers pointed to Tuolumne Grove. She waved her hand over the whole of their bodies. "And you are Yosemite, the land of mouths, of gaping holes."

It was easy, after that, for them to see their bodies as valleys, coursing with rivers and falling rock. Hair of branches, skin of earth and grass. Hearts like granite, warm as nests. A place where bears and birds would rest out winter.

And it was easy for me, when I read the newspaper, to see her body as a map of gaping wounds. Where he had cut her flesh, marred her freckled skin, removed her head from her neck. Her dead fingers against the grass. Clean, simple things, now sullied because she'd ripped his skin with her own nails, trying to fight.

It reminds me of a game she taught us to play one night in the starlight. We hiked in the dark to the grass fields that edged the forest, huddling in a circle as Joie explained the game of Predator and Prey. Some of us were owls and some of us were mice. She told the mice to hide in the brambles and in the thickets, under the logs of felled pine. She told the owls to fly over the grass, across the river, just above the brush line. The mice were quiet in the dark, with breath like smoke, waiting for the owls to swoop down.

Perhaps it was a lesson she never learned, how to run and cower. She did not hide from him, and perhaps that led to her capture. She tore his skin, screamed, and kicked. She was no small scrap of fur. She fought with nails and pounding fists.

Our roles were defined when we played the game, but for Joie, the rules were inverted. Twisted. And it is this night that I keep coming back to, chewing on. Because there must be rules to govern nature, us, and owls. And I keep thinking of her body, torn and filled with holes, and asking, is this what it's come to mean? A land of wounds and gaping skin?

The images seesaw in my memory.

There is her body, echoing with holes. The murderer, who hides in the shadows, waiting for dark.

Then there is the forest: a bowl of dirt, a cup of pitch, a brush pile that's never quite cleared.

But then there are high curving walls, crystallized granite, sweeping stone, and veiled falls. A place that hurts the neck, forcing one to stare up at trunks of pine, straight as flutes or Corinthian columns.

Then there are the children from Los Angeles, some who'd never stepped off pavement, who wiggled through redwoods and hiked at night, balancing on felled pine, helping each other climb through spidery caves.

And then there is Joie, before she died, who offered pine needles as if they were heaps of rough-cut emeralds. Who gave them the scent of vanilla on tree bark.

All of these images teeter back and forth, up and down, each one blurring into the next until I find it impossible to sort them out. The children are the only constant.

When it came time to leave, the kids pummeled Joie with their awkward embraces. Some wept on the bus ride home, as they watched Half Dome disappear; some snapped pictures furiously until the stretch of asphalt spoiled the shot.

And as we climbed down from the forest, a sort of silence came over us, sobering and heavy, as we returned to the land of pavement.

LAMENT AT DUSK

Lianne Elizabeth Mercer

a pair of ravens swoop and cry for me.
Names of those gone before rush
past on fierce winds:
    William Frederick, Elizabeth Ann, Huldah
    Martha Christina, Cleo Anna Helena,
    Theodore William, Robert John
        And—two days ago—Ileta Metha.

Encroaching darkness wraps me in its arms.
My body revolts. My heart mimics dusk.
Moon grins a seasonal story—
a time to be born, a time to die.

Mom climbed out of her life. I am unable
to climb steps on red canyon walls.

Did the world she knew lose focus?
Did the ground fall away beneath her feet?
Did she find places to step
until ancient ones took her spirit hand
and led her home?

TRAIL GUIDE

Erica Olsen

This is southeastern Utah, BLM land. There's no real trail through this canyon, just the wash, the canyon's narrow cleft. Fresh cowpats underfoot—who knew cows were such intrepid canyoneers? These must be part mountain goat, negotiating ledges, squeezing past boulders, dodging the spiky branches of old piñon pines.

We're looking for ruins, an Anasazi site. It's around three in the afternoon, and we suspect we're in the wrong canyon. Our directions are the kind that make sense when you hear them in town—*head straight in* (this for a canyon with three twisting forks), *look for a Y-shaped tree*—but turn out to be sublimely useless in the wild.

This canyon is one of dozens that cut into an enormous ridge that runs for miles north-south. The canyons are all roughly parallel. You can't get lost, if all you want is to find your vehicle again. From anywhere on the ridge you can look back down, see the dirt road that parallels the ridge, the wink of a windshield in the sun. But finding a particular site isn't easy. The canyons branch and fork. Pick one and you're committed, the walls rising to hundreds of feet.

Our canyon is V-shaped and narrowing at the bottom. Eventually, we're stepping heel to toe, picking our way between the cobbles. With the rock walls close at our ankles, but wider than our outstretched arms, things feel inverted. It's as if the world is doing a handstand around us. The air grows humid; suddenly there's grass, reeds, willows. We emerge to face a wide pool of water, dark, rimmed with sticky mud. On the other side of the pool, a wall of gray sandstone rises. Our path runs out here. There's no climbing the pour-off, which is high and smooth, polished by falling water.

Glenn sees it first. Not the ruins we were looking for, but a long, sinuous curve of moki steps, the traditional name given to the hand- and footholds that the Anasazi chipped into the cliffs. A series of lovely foot-sized ovals shows us the way, ascending the right-hand side of the canyon, around and above the pool and on to the upper canyon.

This is my favorite kind of backcountry hike: looking for traces left by people who were here long ago. A granary, snug on a ledge. Square-bodied deer, caught mid-leap on rock art panels. In an open field, bright flecks of potsherds and flaked stone. In and around this canyon, we're surrounded by signs of human habitation.

At the same time, as a responsible hiker, I know that my job is to leave no trace. To take only photographs, leave only footprints—and not even footprints if you can step on the resilient surfaces, on rock and sand rather than on the fragile cryptogamic soil.

We climb the steps.

It never occurs to us not to.

On the rock, I feel how perfect the steps are. Each oval slopes with the slope of the cliff, but the surfaces are pebbled—intentionally roughed up for traction, I realize. I'm grateful for friction. This is no mere artifact. Eight hundred, maybe a thousand years later, these steps work. My thick-soled hiking boots are functional enough, but the Anasazi would have gripped the nubby surface barefoot, or in sandals woven of yucca cord.

A few steps from the top, the cliff abruptly thrusts outward. The crux of the route: no way to reach the next step without moving into an unstable position, hands and feet pressed down on those now very sloping, widely spaced ovals, butt hanging out in the air high above the pool of water. I hesitate, searching for some move from the climbing gym to see me across. Ahead, Glenn calls back to tell me to undercling the slab. Another discovery—finger-size pockets concealed under a lip of stone. I tuck my fingers in, pull up and step. The precarious bulge of rock is transformed. It's as good as a handrail now.

A few days earlier and a few canyons away, we'd found a great number of grinding spots, slabs of rock worn down by the steady rub of *mano* against *metate*. The back wall of the alcove was covered with pictographs, red and yellow handprints that flickered like flame. Some of the hands were tiny, and low on the wall—toddler height. Rock art images often defy interpretation, but the context of the handprints seemed clear. In this alcove women had worked, grinding corn while keeping an eye on their children. You're not supposed to touch rock art—the oils in our skin degrade the images—but I'd wanted to match my hand to one of those prints. The alcove held soft pink sand underfoot; the light was dappled gold by cottonwoods in the late October sun.

Climbing the steps, we touch this world. A door opens. We climb into Anasazi time. The ancient steps choreograph our movement up the canyon wall, determine how we set our hands and feet. It's like hearing their language. This is a trail guide. Not one of those leaflets with a map and numbered guideposts, but a guide nonetheless, showing us how to move through the canyon.

The steps aren't an artifact, kept behind glass in a museum. We used this trail. If we wore it down a little deeper, it's a reminder that all human activity does leave traces.

And at the top? We thought we'd find a large group of ruins or a major petroglyph panel. The hiker's fantasy, the untouched site—something worthy of the climb. But everything's been touched. We find only the upper canyon, quiet, scoured by runoff, baking in the sun.

LIGHT ON THE WATER

Deborah K. Wilson

It is early spring in Central Texas. I am alone, and it feels good to be driving the "old way" to Pedernales Falls State Park. A busier road would not do on a day like this. I do not want to rush.

Traveling more slowly than usual, I roll down the windows and let the soft air rush around me. I glance down at bare arms, my fully freckled skin, and think that I am looking more and more like my father's mother. A farmer's wife, a rock of love and commitment, she wore all the hours she had spent at the gardens, the barns, the yard, the creeks and under the sun, right there on her skin.

The road dips across a low water crossing, then rises and curves as it runs up and along the ridge, offering sweeping Hill Country vistas against a backdrop of true blue Texas sky. I am surrounded by thick stands of green cedar with some live oaks mixed in. The oaks have just put on their new leaves, a lighter and brighter green, contrasting beautifully with the darker cedar. It all feels so much like home. Suddenly I get a whiff of exquisite mountain laurel, and my childhood senses come alive.

Where there is room to pull over, I stop to collect a few early wildflowers. Purple verbena, bluebonnets, and Indian paintbrush make a pretty bouquet. I admire their simple beauty. Farther down the way, I stop to look for fossils in a road cut and spot an ancient oyster shell. I can see only a portion of its rippled edge but manage to dislodge it, a nice specimen shaped like a human ear.

Continuing on, I soon reach the park road. I feel an aching longing. This was the last road my father traveled, on the last day of his life.

How appropriate it is that he spent his last day here. When we spoke about living and dying, of someone passing on or just going to a nursing home, he would say with his wry smile,

"Me? I want to live as long as I can go fishing." I never imagined it would happen so literally.

My father was all things Texas, as was his brother, just as much Texas as any rock, river, or tree. Formed out of the same raw materials, both men followed similar paths, shared similar natures. They were kindred spirits. It seemed somehow fitting that they died together that spring day on the Pedernales River.

I park in an area near the Pedernales Falls, and walk to the overlook. From here I can see the grandness of this awesome rock formation, over which falls one of the fastest flowing rivers in Texas. The rocks are exposed here in huge tilted beds, three hundred million years old, the dark gray-blue limestone masses standing high and proud as the river rushes over and through them. The carving and scouring action of the water has created marvelous textures and structures. There are strange angles, tilted beds lying beneath horizontal beds: angular unconformities that offer clues to dynamic earth movements, to missing intervals of earth history. Somehow, this geological description of missing time created by cataclysmic shifts expresses my feeling of a missing interval in my family's history. At the time of my father's and uncle's deaths, and for weeks after, there was a palpable sense of time standing still. Surreal, yet too real. Unbelievable, yet undeniable. They were gone, just like that. Time was suspended, although the clocks ticked on.

I gather myself now and walk below the falls, to the place where the water surges downward into a plunge pool, creating swirling eddies that gouge potholes in the rocks, some small, some as large as six feet wide and eight feet deep. Some are elliptical, like teardrops, here to catch the tears of those who come to the river to mourn. I am struck by the colors and textures, the angles and shapes meeting, contacting. Within these park boundaries, there are numerous visible examples of geologic contact, points where two different rock formations, two vastly different geologic ages meet, even overlap. At one location near these falls, I can put one hand on the youngest sand and the other on the oldest limestone, and my hands touch one another at the contact point. This idea of contact intrigues me, and I want to comprehend how, within me, disparate events and ideas can meet and overlap to create my inner landscape. Surely my life is varied and enriched by the inner contact of unrelated things, spiritual and physical. If only I could place one hand on the spiritual plane at the same time as I place one on the physical, as I can with the limestone and sand.

I walk downstream, passing Spanish oak, pecan, mesquite and sycamore trees. Prickly pear cacti and prairie grasses cover the ground. I reach the old wagon road that leads to Trammel Crossing, where settlers forded the river, and a stand of noble old cypress trees, battered and beaten, scarred by boulders and stones that remain lodged in their roots and trunks from the floods they have endured.

I am near the point where my uncle's body was recovered two days after he disappeared, two miles from the point he went in. He had been fishing with the others at the north end of the park, well above the falls, walking several hundred yards up the channel on exposed rocks in the river bed. There had been no warning of severe weather, and no alert issued to incoming park guests—standard practice if heavy rain was expected. My brother, who barely made it out, said they knew something was coming when the minnow bucket began to bounce. They had no idea how much of a rise to expect, but they knew this river can get fierce, so they gathered their gear and headed back. But in no time the rocks in the channel disappeared and a torrent was upon them, a torrent of churning, rushing water filled with boulders, limbs, and debris. They were good swimmers, but even good swimmers can't overcome such a furious force of nature.

I remove from my tote bag the fossil I found earlier, its grayish surface mottled with a crust of rusty brown chert. I place the ancient oyster shell to my ear, and then, remembering my uncle, I hold it to my heart before casting it into the waters that took him back to his source. And the rippling water is all that is left.

I return to my car, retrieve the wildflower bouquet, and head down the less-traveled trail that leads to the far north end of the park. The sun hangs motionless in the late cloudless afternoon, and I look up and across the broad expanse of the river to the steep cliffs on the other side. I am here to visit the rocky outcrop where my brother brought my father's body out of the raging water. I shed my shoes and dangle my feet in the Pedernales. The sun's light reflects on the water. It shimmers and dances before me.

At the time of the tragedy I lived in California. I came back to Texas to bury my father and uncle, comfort my grandparents, and try to understand that the two men I respected and adored were gone. As long as I was near my family I held up pretty well, but back in

California, I was in shock. Nothing seemed right to me. I dreamed of my father constantly, but they were distant dreams, dreams I could barely remember. I felt as if he were somewhere close by, but just out of reach. I would lie in bed, half asleep, thinking the phone was ringing and he was calling, but I could not hear what he was saying. My life was not moving. Time was standing still.

Then three months after my return, something happened. In California, I lived on a beautiful river. My father came to me in a dream, standing by my bed, telling me to wake up. He said he knew I had a heavy heart, and this would bring light into it. I got up, and he led me out to my back yard, to the edge of the river, and told me to look at the scene before me and tell him what I saw.

"I see the river and the mountain behind it," I said.

He said, "Now look at the sky and tell me what you see."

I looked up at the sky. "I see the stars in the night sky."

And he said, "Now look at the water, and tell me what you see now."

I looked at the water. "I see the reflections of the stars shimmering on the water."

"That is where I am," he said. "I am the light on the water. Whenever you see the reflection of light on water, know that I am here with you. I am always here with you, in the light on the water."

I rise, holding the flowers for a moment to my face to breathe in their wild sweetness. I untie the ribbon and scatter them across the light on the water.

WHEN THE LAND WAS YOUNG

Sharman Apt Russell

*O*n a spring afternoon, under a blue sky, in a cold wind, my husband and I take a family picnic. Perhaps we visit Massacre Peak, south of our home in southwestern New Mexico, where the petroglyphs are hidden in a rough tumble of pink fractured rock. On the floor of an alcove we can see the round holes, a foot deep. A thousand years ago women sat here to grind seed and admire the view of distant hills. Nearby a masked man has been pecked into a secret shelf of granite. From a lonely boulder my husband gives a shout. He stands before a macaw, a scarlet macaw among the scrubby creosote, gray mesquite, and devilish cholla.

Perhaps we go to Old Town instead, a village full of people in AD 800. This is another wonderful view of the Mimbres River winding through a green lace of cottonwood trees. Where the ledge drops off, we check the eagle's nest, abandoned now and cluttered with debris. The village is a set of mounds pocked by illegal shoveling. Potsherds litter the ground like the jagged remains of a jigsaw puzzle, a million pieces, and none of them match. In the last few years archaeologists have returned to Old Town, and their orange survey flags flap incongruously, attracting butterflies.

If we have friends or relatives visiting, we will drive to our main tourist attraction, the Gila Cliff Dwellings National Monument in the heart of the Gila National Forest and Gila Wilderness. As we walk up to the cliff dwelling, I watch for piñon pines. It's a good year; the trees are full of nuts. The forty-room ruin looks like a doll's house set cunningly against the bluff. My six-year-old son peers into tiny cubicles with stone bins of tiny corn cobs. Another larger room carries, faintly, the whiff of decay. In the late thirteenth century a small band of farmers built this high home and lived in it for a generation. Then they left, like so many Americans.

My son is not impressed. Often enough on these trips, he and his older sister are bored. They prefer the playground at McDonald's or the aisles of Wal-Mart. They are drawn to more modern artifacts: baseball cards, Barbie clothes, fluorescent colors, flashing lights, shrill sounds, a miniature green plastic garbage can stocked with inedible red candy—only fifty-nine cents! How can a corn cob compete?

Like most parents, we impose our passion.

We explore a nameless site in the Gila National Forest. The pottery sherd I find is small, an inch square, its white background crossed by impossibly thin black lines. This color scheme dates it to the Classic Period of the Mimbreno Indians, a time of cultural renaissance, when artists produced painted bowls that are world famous today. Mimbres designs are unique, startling, complex, humorous, mythic, bold, geometric, bawdy—a man with a penis that has a little face, a little face sticking out its tongue. This sherd may have once been such a pot, with its interior picture of a crane spearing fish or a creature half-bighorn, half-snake.

"Look," I tell my daughter. "The woman who made this lived right here. Maybe she had a little girl. They sat here together, making pots."

I motion to the surrounding scrub oak and juniper trees, the grass and dirt and rocks that would not have looked so different eight hundred years ago. Before I leave I will put this sherd back exactly in the place where I found it. To archaeologists, artifacts are mainly important in context. Taken from a site, they become casual souvenirs and lose much of their value. I doubt that this little bit of clay will ever really be of scientific interest. But there is a truth in the habit of returning it so carefully. It belongs here with the scrub oak and juniper, the grama grass and mule deer, in context. I will put it back, certainly, after I hold it a bit longer.

I am thrilled. I am thrilled nearly every time I see in the dirt the simplest piece of Mogollon plainware, the corrugated surface of a cooking bowl, the glamorous black on white of a Mimbres pot. This is the treasure seeker's glory. I found it. I found the Easter egg.

I do not know what links me to the person who shaped this clay. I cannot really imagine a specific woman; I tell that story only to my children. But I do feel a connection. This making of pots is part of what it means to be a human being. Perhaps it is the essence. Suddenly my own life seems like a dream. Wal-Mart, surely, is nothing but an amazing, amusing, fantastical dream. In the middle of that store, in a restaurant, at a street corner, I have often paused, confounded by an atavistic awe. Wow! I think, looking at a traffic light. Magic! Who did this? What happened to the world? Where are the trees? I am both appalled and appreciative.

Holding my sherd, I feel the substance of time, a place I can travel to while standing still. I heft its weight. This moment is a thousand years ago and a thousand years ago is this moment and we are both the same, that woman then and this woman now. Time folds in. I am at the center. It may be the closest I ever come to understanding quantum theory.

NOT LONG AGO

Barbara Kingsolver

Not long ago I went backpacking in the Eagle Tail Mountains.
This range is a trackless wilderness in western Arizona that
most people would call Godforsaken, taking for granted God's
preference for loamy topsoil and regular precipitation. Whoever created the Eagle Tails had dry heat on the agenda, and
a thing for volcanic rock. Also cactus, twisted mesquites, and
five-alarm sunsets. The hiker's program in a desert like this is
dire and blunt: carry in enough water to keep you alive till you
can find a water source; then fill your bottles and head for the
next one, or straight back out. Experts warn adventurers in this
region, without irony, to drink their water while they're still
alive, as it won't help later.

Several canyons looked promising for springs on our topo-
graphical map, but turned up dry. Finally, at the top of a narrow, overgrown gorge we found a blessed *tinaja*, a deep, shaded
hollow in the rock about the size of four or five claw-foot tubs,
holding water. After we drank our fill, my friends struck out
again, but I opted to stay and spend the day in the hospitable
place that had slaked our thirst. On either side of the natural
water tank, two shallow caves in the canyon wall faced each
other, only a few dozen steps apart. By crossing from one to
the other at noon, a person could spend the whole day here in
shady comfort—or in colder weather, follow the winter sun.
Anticipating a morning of reading, I pulled *Angle of Repose*
out of my pack and looked for a place to settle on the flat, dusty
floor of the west-facing shelter. Instead, my eyes were startled
by a smooth corn-grinding stone. It sat in the exact center of its
rock bowl, as if the Hohokam woman or man who used this
mortar and pestle had walked off and left them there an hour
ago. The Hohokam disappeared from the earth in AD 1450. It
was inconceivable to me that no one had been here since then,
but that may have been the case—that is the point of trackless

wilderness. I picked up the grinding stone. The size and weight and smooth, balanced perfection of it in my hand filled me at once with a longing to possess it. In its time, this excellent stone was the most treasured thing in a life, a family, maybe the whole neighborhood. To whom it still belonged. I replaced it in the rock depression, which also felt smooth to my touch. Because my eyes now understood how to look at it, the ground under my feet came alive with worked flint chips and pottery shards. I walked across to the other cave and found its floor just as lively with historic debris. Hidden under brittlebush and catclaw I found another grinding stone, this one some distance from the depression in the cave floor that once answered its pressure daily, for the grinding of corn or mesquite beans.

For a whole day I marveled at this place, running my fingers over the knife edges of dark flint chips, trying to fit together thick red pieces of shattered clay jars, biting my lower lip like a child concentrating on a puzzle. I tried to guess the size of whole pots from the curve of the broken pieces: some seemed as small as my two cupped hands, and some maybe as big as a bucket. The sun scorched my neck, reminding me to follow the shade across to the other shelter. Bees hummed at the edge of the water hole, nosing up to the water, their abdomens pulsing like tiny hydraulic pumps; by late afternoon they rimmed the pool completely, a collar of busy lace. Off and on, the lazy hand of a hot breeze shuffled the white leaves of the brittlebush. Once I looked up to see a screaming pair of red-tailed hawks mating in midair, and once a clatter of hooves warned me to hold still. A bighorn ram emerged through the brush, his head bent low under his hefty cornice, and ambled by me with nothing on his mind so much as a cool drink.

How long can a pestle stone lie still in the center of its mortar? That long ago—that recently—people lived here. *Here*, exactly, and not one valley over, or two, or twelve, because this place had all a person needs: shelter, food, and permanent water. They organized their lives around a catchment basin in a granite boulder, conforming their desires to the earth's charities; they never expected the opposite. The stories I grew up with lauded Moses for striking the rock and bringing forth the bubbling stream. But the stories of the Hohokam—oh, how they must have praised that good rock.

At dusk my friends returned with wonderful tales of the ground they had covered. We camped for the night, refilled our canteens, and hiked back to the land of plumbing and a fair guarantee of longevity. But I treasure my memory of the day I lingered near water and covered no ground. I can't think of a day in my life in which I've had such a clear fix on what it means to be human.

Want is a thing that unfurls unbidden like fungus, opening large upon itself, stopless, filling the sky. But *needs,* from one day to the next, are few enough to fit in a bucket, with room enough left to rattle like brittlebush in a dry wind.

HOW TO CLIMB

Lianne Elizabeth Mercer

Let the space breathe you;
feel it in your fingers,
in your spine. Taste it.
Hear breath sewing your soles
to your mother the earth.
Lose yourself
in the abundance of time.
Close your eyes and
see with your heart.
Let rhythm lead you
upward—foot in front of
foot, hand over hand—
let music climb you into sky.
Let your bones love rock.
Remember the animal you were
when you could go anywhere.

You still can.

ACKNOWLEDGMENTS

The editors wish to thank the Board of Directors of the Story Circle Network, whose unfailing encouragement made this book possible. Special thanks go to Peggy Moody, for her expert computer and Internet skills; to Theresa May, of the University of Texas Press, who believed in the book and its editors from start to finish; and to Connie Todd and Steve Davis of the Southwestern Writers Collection at Texas State University, for their many contributions of time and assistance as we began to plan for the conference and exhibit upon the book's publication.

ABOUT THE CONTRIBUTORS

DIANE ACKERMAN is the author of more than twenty books of poetry and nonfiction for adults and children. Her nature books include *The Moon by Whale Light* and *Cultivating Delight*. Her poetry has appeared in leading literary journals and in the books *Origami Bridges* and *I Praise My Destroyer*. She has received a Guggenheim Fellowship, the John Burroughs Nature Award, the Lavan Poetry Prize, and other honors.

PAULA GUNN ALLEN, professor of English at UCLA, is the author of *The Woman Who Owned the Shadow, The Sacred Hoop: Recovering the Feminine in American Indian Tradition,* and seven volumes of poetry. As well, she is the editor of numerous volumes of critical studies and writings by Native American women. Recently, she co-authored *As Long As the Rivers Shall Flow: 10 American Indian Biographies.*

GLORIA ANZALDÚA was a Chicana lesbian-feminist, poet, writer, and cultural theorist. She was born in Jesus Maria of the Valley, Texas, in a family of Mexican immigrants, was the only one of her neighborhood to graduate from college—and began her work teaching children from migrant families. Her first book, *Borderlands/La Frontera,* was named one of the Best Books of 1987 by the *Literary Journal.* Anzaldúa was awarded a National Endowment for the Arts Fiction Award, a Lesbian Rights Award, and a Sappho Award of Distinction. Her most recent book was the edited collection, *This Bridge We Call Home,* an anthology of feminist writings. She died in 2004.

REBECCA BALCÁRCEL earned an MFA degree from Bennington College in 2002, where she was awarded the Jane Kenyon Poetry Prize. Her work has appeared in more than twenty journals and magazines, including *North American Review, Concho River Review, Clockwatch Review,* and *South Dakota Review.*

CINDY BELLINGER earned a baccalaureate degree in creative writing and a master's in education, and taught junior high school. She has written a woman's guide to home improvement entitled *Someone Stole My Outhouse,* an essay in the anthology *Woven on the Wind,* and more than a thousand articles and columns in local, regional, and national publications. She lives in northern New Mexico.

JUDITH E. BOWEN'S work has been published in *The Mesquite Review,* a Rio Grande Valley arts magazine, and in *Occupational Practice,* an occupational therapy trade journal. She is an associate professor of occupational therapy at the University of Texas-Pan American in Edinburg, Texas, and also a certified Healing Touch practitioner. She lives in Edinburg.

JANICE EMILY BOWERS is a botanist with the U.S. Geological Survey. She conducts plant research (with a special interest in cacti) at the Desert Laboratory on Tumamoc Hill, Tucson. Her interest in cacti has led to investigations of their seed banks and floral biology. She has also compiled local floras and studied the history of the Desert Laboratory and its scientists. She is the author of several wildflower guides and four books of natural history essays, including *Fear Falls Away* and *A Full Life in a Small Place.*

SUEELLEN CAMPBELL is a professor of English at Colorado State University in Fort Collins. She is the author of *Even Mountains Vanish: Searching for Solace in an Age of Extinction* and *Bringing the Mountain Home.* She is an editor for the book series *Under the Sign of Nature,* published by the University of Virginia Press, and has written widely about American nature and the environment.

DENISE CHÁVEZ is an actress, teacher, and writer whose first novel, *The Last of the Menu Girls,* was awarded the Puerto del Sol Fiction Award. *Face of an Angel* received the American Book Award for 1995 and the Premio Axtlan award. Chávez, who calls herself a performance writer, has completed nearly two dozen plays, three novels, and a book for children, *The Woman Who Knew the Language of the Animals.*

ALISON HAWTHORNE DEMING is the author of *The Monarchs: A Poem Sequence* and *Science and Other Poems,* which received the 1993 Walt Whitman Award. Her three books of prose include *Temporary Homelands,* a collection of nature essays. She has received the Pushcart Prize for nonfiction and held the Wallace Stegner Fellowship at Stanford University and two National Endowment for the Arts fellowships. She lives in Tucson, where she teaches at the University of Arizona.

ROXANNE DUNBAR-ORTIZ, historian and college professor, is the author of an acclaimed three-volume memoir (*Red Dirt: Growing Up Okie, Outlaw Woman: A Memoir of the War Years, 1960–1975,* and *Blood on the Border: A Memoir of the Contra War*). Among her other books are *The Great Sioux Nation: An Oral History of the Sioux Nation and Its Struggle for Sovereignty* and *Roots of Resistance: A History of Land Tenure in New Mexico, 1680–1980.*

SYBIL PITTMAN ESTESS is a poet, essayist, and teacher who lives in Houston. Her books are *Seeing the Desert Green* (Poems), *Elizabeth Bishop and Her Art* (criticism) and *In a Field of Words* (creative writing textbook, co-authored with Janet McCann). Her poems have appeared in numerous journals.

CAROL FOX, a native Texan, lived in many places, including Peru, before returning to her home on the San Gabriel River. She teaches at Temple College in Taylor, Texas, and raises cattle.

JANIE FRIED grew up in Okarche, Oklahoma, and lives in Los Angeles. After attending Northwestern University in Evanston, Illinois, she worked as a reporter and editor for a variety of newspapers in New Jersey, Oklahoma, Texas, and California for more than twenty years.

JULIA GIBSON has been an animator and visual effects producer for movies. She lives in Los Angeles.

LAURA GIRARDEAU, a former Forest Service biologist, holds a master's degree in Environmental Studies from the University of Oregon. A poet and writer of short stories, she sees writing as a form of personal prayer. Her work has been nominated for the Pushcart Prize. Girardeau lives in a log home in Idaho.

SUSAN HANSON, author of *Icons of Loss and Grace: Moments from the Natural World,* teaches in the English Department at Texas State University in San Marcos. She has worked for twenty years as a newspaper journalist, winning more than thirty awards, and has served as lay chaplain for the Episcopal campus ministry at TSU since 1995.

JOY HARJO is the author of six books of poetry: *A Map to the Next World, The Woman Who Fell from the Sky, In Mad Love and War, Secrets from the Center of the World, She Had Some Horses,* and *What Moon Drove Me to This?* With Gloria Bird, she co-edited *Reinventing the Enemy's Language: Contemporary Native Women's Writings of North America.* She has received numerous awards and grants. She lives in Honolulu, Hawaii.

JOYCE SEQUICHIE HIFLER, a descendant of Cherokees who reached Oklahoma by way of the Trail of Tears, has written eight books, including the popular three-book series *The Cherokee Feast of Days,* and a syndicated newspaper column, "Think on These Things." She lives near Bartlesville, Oklahoma.

LINDA HOGAN, a Chickasaw writer, is the author of six volumes of poetry (beginning with *Calling Myself Home,* published in 1979), two short story collections, three novels (including the Pulitzer prize-nominated *Mean Spirit*), a collection of essays, a memoir, and several edited collections of women's writing and co-authored books. She received a master's degree from the University of Colorado and has held writing residencies with the states of Colorado and Oklahoma. She is associate professor of American Indian studies at the University of Minnesota.

JUDITH ANN ISAACS is director of a small rural library in Jemez Springs, New Mexico. She has been a teacher, journalist, and editor, as well as a writer. Isaacs is the author of *Jemez Valley Cookbook: The Food, The People, The Land.*

JOAN SHADDOX ISOM'S latest book is *Offerings in the Snow: A Christmas Story.* She is the author of *The First Starry Night* and co-editor of *The Leap Years: Women Reflect on Change, Loss and Love.* Isom's work has been anthologized widely, and her fiction and nonfiction work have appeared in such publications as *Nimrod, The Indian Historian, Negative Capability, Eclectica Magazine, storySouth,* and *Southern Scribe.*

TERESA JORDAN is the award-winning author of *Riding the White Horse Home, Cowgirls,* and *Field Notes from the Grand Canyon,* as well as the editor of two anthologies of western women's writing. She is a regular contributor to *The Savvy Traveler* and other public radio shows. She divides her time between a ranch in Nevada and Salt Lake City.

JOY KENNEDY is an English instructor at Brazosport College in Lake Jackson, Texas. She has been awarded a Writer's League of Texas Creative Nonfiction Fellowship. Her works have been published in such journals as *Organization and Environment, Petroglyph, Southwestern American Literature,* and *ISLE* (Interdisciplinary Studies for Literature and the Environment).

BARBARA KINGSOLVER was a journalist and science writer before the publication of her first novel, *The Bean Trees,* in 1988. Since then she has published four other novels, all of which have drawn critical praise: *Animal Dreams, Pigs in Heaven, The Poisonwood Bible,* and *Prodigal Summer.* Kingsolver has written numerous essays, poems, stories, and a nonfiction book, *Holding the Line: Women in the Great Arizona Mine Strike of 1983.* She lives in Arizona.

NANCY LINNON is Assistant Director of the Hassayama Institute for Creative Writing in Prescott, Arizona. Her work has appeared in *Creative Nonfiction, Yoga International, Brevity,* and *Mothering.* For her essay "Hair," she was a finalist in the National League of American Pen Women Contest in San Francisco.

SANDRA LYNN'S poetry has appeared in several journals and poetry collections, and her essays have been published in the *New York Times,* the *Albuquerque Journal,* and the *Dallas Morning News,* as well as in *Flower and Garden* and *New Mexico Magazine.* Her book, *Windows on the West: Historic Lodgings of New Mexico,* was the winner of several awards, including the 1999 Southwest Book Award.

NANCY MAIRS, poet and essayist, was awarded the 1984 Western States Book Award in poetry for *In All the Rooms of the Yellow House* and a National Endowment for the Arts Fellowship in 1991. She has written four collections of essays, including *Waist-High in the World: A Life Among the Nondisabled;* a memoir, *Remembering the Bone House;* and a spiritual autobiography, *Ordinary Time: Cycles in Marriage, Faith, and Renewal.* Mairs lives in Tucson, Arizona.

ELLEN MELOY is the author of *The Last Cheater's Waltz* and *Raven's Exile: A Season on the Green River,* which received the Spur Award for contemporary nonfiction. The Whiting Foundation honored her with a Writer's Award in 1997. Her environmental essays have been widely anthologized, and her work has been published in numerous journals. She died in 2004.

LIANNE ELIZABETH MERCER is a certified poetry therapist and nurse. Her fiction and poetry have appeared in various journals and anthologies. Her short story "For Sale" was nominated for a Pushcart Prize, and "Addie's War" won an award at the 1999 Judy and A. C. Greene Literary Festival in Salado, Texas.

DONNA MARIE MILLER teaches English and journalism at James A. Bowie High School in Austin, Texas. A veteran teacher of fifteen years, she also worked for eleven years as a reporter. Miller writes about issues faced daily by people living along the state's border with Mexico.

SUSAN CUMMINS MILLER holds degrees in history, anthropology, and geology from the University of California, Riverside. She has worked as a field geologist with the U.S. Geological Survey and has taught geology, oceanography, and creative writing. A Tucson resident, Miller is the author of two mystery novels, *Death Assemblage* and *Detachment Fault*. Her work has appeared in numerous publications, and she is the editor of the anthology *A Sweet, Separate Intimacy: Women Writers of the American Frontier, 1800–1922*.

PENELOPE MOFFET is the author of a book of poems titled *Keeping Still*. Her poems, stories, and articles have appeared in *Green Fuse, The Missouri Review, The Sun: A Magazine of Ideas*, the *Los Angeles Times, Publishers Weekly, The Devil's Millhopper*, and *Columbia*, among others. Moffet lives in southern California.

KATHLEEN DEAN MOORE is a professor of philosophy and the founding director of the Spring Creek Project for Ideas, Nature, and the Written Word at Oregon State University. She has published three books of essays: *The Pine Island Paradox, Holdfast: At Home in the Natural World*, and *Riverwalking: Reflections on Moving Water*. She is co-editor of a forthcoming collection of essays about Rachel Carson and is currently co-editing the papers of the late Viola Cordova.

PAT MORA, a native of El Paso, Texas, has written poetry, essays, and children's books. She is the recipient of a National Endowment for the Arts Creative Writing Fellowship in poetry and a Kellogg National Leadership Fellowship. *Agua Santa: Holy Water* is the most recent of her five poetry collections for adults. Among her twenty-five children's titles are *The Gift of the Poinsettia: El Regalo de la Flor de Nochebuena* and *Listen to the Desert: Oye al Desierto*.

LINDA JOY MYERS is the prize-winning author of *Don't Call Me Mother: Breaking the Chain of Mother-Daughter Abandonment* and *Becoming Whole: Writing Your Healing Story*. Linda is a therapist in Berkeley, California, and teaches memoir-as-healing workshops in the San Francisco Bay Area and nationally.

NANCY OWEN NELSON earned her master's and doctoral degrees in English from Auburn University. She has pursued the study of Western American literature with publications on Frederick Manfred and Wallace Stegner. She is the editor of *Private Voices, Public Lives: Women Speak on the Literary Life* and *The Lizard Speaks: Essays on the Writings of Frederick Manfred*. She lives in Prescott, Arizona, where she is assistant director of the Hassayampa Institute for Creative Writing.

NAOMI SHIHAB NYE is the author or editor of more than twenty volumes of poetry, fiction, essays, and children's literature, as well as eight prize-winning poetry anthologies for young readers. Her latest work of poetry is *You and Yours* and her latest work of fiction is a novel for teens, *Going Going,* both published in 2005. She has been a Lannan Fellow, a Guggenheim Fellow, and a Wittner Bynner Fellow of the Library of Congress, and is the recipient of numerous awards.

SANDRA RAMOS O'BRIANT'S work has appeared in *Whistling Shade, AIM Magazine, Ink Pot, NFG, La Herencia, The Copperfield Review,* and *Café Irreal*. In addition, her short stories have been anthologized in *Best Lesbian Love Stories of 2004, Life's Spices from Seasoned Sistahs,* and *Latinos Writing on Los Angeles*.

ERICA OLSEN lives in San Francisco. Her stories and essays have appeared in *High Country News, ZYZZYVA,* and other publications. She has held writing residencies at the Ucross Foundation and the Aspen Guard Station, San Juan National Forest, Colorado. She has been hiking southeastern Utah's canyon country since 1993.

PATRICIA NORDYKE PANDO, a Texas native, lives in Bainbridge, Georgia, where she writes a column on food and memories for the *Bainbridge Post Searchlight*.

BETH PAULSON lives in the San Juan Mountains near Ouray, Colorado, where she teaches poetry workshops and directs poetry events. Her work has been published in *Mountain Gazette, Writing on the Edge, The Kerf,* and *Blueline*. Paulson's first collection, *The Truth About Thunder,* was published in 2001. *By Stone, By Water,* a CD of her work, was produced in 2003.

LINDA ELIZABETH PETERSON'S essays about her relationship to her family's farm appear in her books *Heartlands* and *Black Earth and Ivory Tower: New American Essays from Farm and Classroom*. She divides her time between the farm in Michigan's Upper Peninsula and her home in Mt. Pleasant, where she teaches composition at Central Michigan University.

P. J. PIERCE is a freelance writer in Austin, Texas, and author of *"Let me tell you what I've learned": Texas Wisewomen Speak*. Her current project, *Liz: The Biography of Liz Carpenter,* is in press with the University of Texas Press. A long-distance bicyclist, Pierce also likes to scull on Town Lake in Austin and spend quiet time at Lost Pines.

LIZA PORTER is a poet and fiction writer whose work has appeared in *AGNI, Cimarron Review, Hotel Amerika, The Pedestal Magazine, Slipstream,* and other publications. She is director of the monthly Other Voices Women's Reading Series in Tucson.

CAROL COFFEE REPOSA'S poems have appeared in many literary magazines. She is the author of three books of poetry, *At the Border: Winter Lights, The Green Room,* and *Facts of Life.* Her work has twice been nominated for the Pushcart Prize. She has received two Fulbright/Hays Fellowships for study in Russia, Peru, and Ecuador. She teaches English at San Antonio College.

PATTIANN ROGERS is the author of ten books of poetry. Her first, *The Expectations of Light,* was published in 1981; her most recent is *Generations* (2004). Her collected poetry, *Song of the World Becoming,* was a finalist for the Los Angeles Times Book Award. She has received two National Endowment for the Arts grants, a Guggenheim Fellowship, and many awards. She has taught and held writing residencies at several universities. She lives in Colorado.

WENDY ROSE'S work as a Native American poet—her father was Hopi, her mother part Miwok—has been acclaimed for more than twenty years. Beginning with *Hopi Roadrunner Dancing* (1971) through *Itch Like Crazy* (2002), her poetry has been widely anthologized. She edited *American Indian Quarterly* and has worked with the Smithsonian Native Writers Series, the Women's Literature Project of Oxford University Press, and the Modern Language Association Commission on Languages and Literature of the Americas.

JAN JARBOE RUSSELL, journalist and biographer, is the author of *Lady Bird: A Biography of Mrs. Johnson.* Her syndicated opinion column has appeared in the *San Antonio Express-News,* the *Seattle Post-Intelligencer,* the *San Francisco Examiner,* and other newspapers. She has been a senior editor at *Texas Monthly* magazine and has written hundreds of stories for such publications as the *New York Times, George, Talk, Good Housekeeping, Working Woman,* and *Redbook.* Russell lives in San Antonio with her husband and two children.

SHARMAN APT RUSSELL, winner of the Mountain and Plains Booksellers Award for *Songs of the Fluteplayer,* has written six other books, including *An Obsession with Butterflies* and *When the Land was Young: Reflections on American Archaeology.* She teaches at Western New Mexico University.

JAN EPTON SEALE is the author of a collection of stories entitled *Airlift: Short Stories; Homeland,* a collection of essays; *The Nuts-&-Bolts Guide to Writing Your Life Story;* and five books of poetry, the latest of which are *Valley Ark* and *The Wonder Is.* She has received a National Endowment for the Arts fellowship. She lives in the Rio Grande Valley of Texas.

LISA SHIRAH-HIERS is a freelance writer and piano teacher in Austin, Texas. She has published articles, essays, book reviews, and poetry in the *Texas Episcopalian,* the *Hill Country Sun, austinwoman,* and *Austin Monthly.*

LESLIE MARMON SILKO, who grew up on Laguna Pueblo, near Albuquerque, is the author of three novels (*Ceremony, Almanac of the Dead,* and *Gardens in the Dunes*), as well as numerous short stories, essays, poetry, articles, and film scripts. Her work has won prizes, and she is the recipient of fellowships and grants from such sources as the MacArthur Foundation and the National Endowment for the Arts. She has taught at several southwestern universities and currently lives in Arizona.

JOANNE SMITH is a writer, naturalist, and hermit-in-residence at Paddock Place in the Prescott National Forest outside Prescott, Arizona. Her articles have appeared in the *Austin American-Statesman, austinwoman,* and other publications.

SANDRA S. SMITH is a photographer who lives in Tucson, Arizona, where she spends time in the desert writing and making art. Lately she has been creating Polaroid SX 70 images and compositing images using Adobe Photoshop. She likes to combine words and images. Her book, *Portraits of Clay: Potters of Mata Ortíz,* was published by the University of Arizona Press.

MARY SOJOURNER is a novelist, short story writer, and essayist. Her books include *Sisters of the Dream, Bonelight: Ruin and Grace in the New Southwest,* and *Delicate: Stories of Light and Desire.* Her essays appear in *High Country News'* syndicated column, "Writers on the Range," and she is a regular commentator for local and national NPR. She teaches writing workshops throughout the West.

CONNIE SPITTLER is a video producer, teacher, lecturer and writer of award-winning short stories, essays, and poetry. Her work has been published in multicultural anthologies. Spittler's *Wise Women* videos are archived in Harvard University's Arthur and Elizabeth Schlesinger Library on the History of Women in America.

MARY BRYAN STAFFORD is a fifth-generation Texan living near Liberty Hill, Texas, outside Austin. She is working on a memoir of her childhood on a South Texas ranch. Her poetry has appeared in *Slightly West.* Now retired from the teaching of English and Spanish, she writes, teaches aerobics, rides, and trains horses.

HALLIE CRAWFORD STILLWELL, author of *I'll Gather My Geese,* was born in Waco, Texas, in 1898 and moved to the Big Bend country with her parents in a covered wagon. She began operating her pioneer ranch in 1918, and began writing the "Ranch News" column for the *Alpine Avalanche* in 1930. During her long life (she died in 1997) she taught school, managed a restaurant, raised children, and served as a justice of the peace. She is a member of both the Texas Women's Hall of Fame and the National Cowgirl Hall of Fame.

JUDITH STRASSER is the author of a chapbook, *Sand Island Succession: Poems of the Apostles,* and a memoir, *Black Eye: Escaping a Marriage, Writing a Life.* Her poems have appeared in literary journals and anthologies. In 2000, Strasser held a three-month residency at the Helen Wurlitzer Foundation in Taos, New Mexico, where she worked on *The Reason/Unreason Project*—poems expressing the tension between science and spirituality. This collection won the 2005 Lewis-Clark Press Expedition Award.

LISA SWANSTROM earned a master's degree in creative writing from the Professional Writing Program at the University of Southern California, where she won an award for creative nonfiction. Her work has appeared in several magazines. Swanstrom also co-edits the online literary journal *Sunspinner.*

MARGO TAMEZ'S poetry, which is often anthologized, has appeared in the book *Naked Wanting* and the chapbook *Alleys & Allies.* Other poems and essays have appeared in numerous journals. She currently teaches at the University of Arizona and Pima Community College in Tucson, Arizona.

LUCI TAPAHONSO grew up on a farm in the Navajo Nation, Shiprock, New Mexico. She has taught at the University of New Mexico, the University of Kansas at Lawrence, and the University of Arizona at Tucson. She is the author of five books of poetry and two books for young readers.

NANCY ELLIS TAYLOR lives and writes in Los Angeles and gives readings locally several times a year. Her work has appeared in a variety of journals, including *Astropoetica, The Red River Review, Strange Horizons, Aldebaran,* and the anthology *There Is Something in the Autumn.*

PAT ELLIS TAYLOR, novelist, short story writer, and journalist, was born in Texas and spent her teenage years in Weisbaden, Germany. She received her baccalaureate in 1969 and her master's degree in 1976, both from the University of Texas at El Paso. Her first novel, *Border Healing Woman,* won a Southwest Book Award in 1981, and her third novel, *Afoot in a Field of Men and Other Stories from Dallas' East Side,* won a Texas Circuit Book Award. In 1991, under the name of Pat LittleDog, Taylor wrote *In Search of the Holy Mother of Jobs.*

CEIRIDWEN TERRILL is a writer and a teacher of science and memoir writing at the University of Nevada, Reno, and the University of California, Santa Barbara. She is completing a book about arid island plants and animals. Terrill is an avid backpacker and sea kayaker.

KELLY TIGHE, a freelance writer, has published two Arizona trail guides, including the first guide to the state's new border-to-border Arizona Trail. She is a frequent contributor to *Arizona Highways* magazine. Tighe enjoys exploring Arizona's mountains, deserts, and canyons.

ROSEMERRY WAHTOLA TROMMER received a master's degree in English language and linguistics from the University of Wisconsin, Madison. She directs the Telluride Writers Guild and leads poetry workshops across the West. Her books include *If You Listen: Poetry & Photographs of the San Juan Moun-*

tains, Charity: True Stories of Giving & Receiving, Celebration: The Christmas Candle Book with Poems of Light, and *Telluride's Victorian Vernacular: An Architectural Walking Tour.*

SUSAN J. TWEIT studied grizzly bear habitat, sagebrush, and wildfires before turning to writing. She is the author of numerous books, including *The San Luis Valley* and *Barren, Wild, and Worthless: Living in the Chihuahuan Desert,* as well as hundreds of articles, essays, radio commentaries, and newspaper columns. Tweit's work has appeared in many anthologies, most recently *Comeback Wolves* and *A Road of Her Own: Women's Journeys in the West.*

MARIE UNINI is a writer and massage therapist living near Pearblossom, California.

GLORIA VANDO'S first book of poems, *Promesas: Geography of the Impossible* (1995), won the Thorpe Menn Book Award. Her second, *Shadows & Supposes* (2002), won the Poetry Society of America's Alice Fay DiCastagnola Award and the Latino Literary Award. She has published poems in many journals, and her work is frequently anthologized. She is also the founder of Helicon Nine Editions, a literary press.

DAVI WALDERS grew up in the oilfields of Oklahoma and Texas. Her work has appeared in more than 150 publications, including *The American Scholar, Ms, Seneca Review,* and *Washington Woman.* Her most recent poetry collection, *Gifts,* was commissioned by the Milton Murray Foundation for Philanthropy and presented to the Carnegie Corporation's Medal of Philanthropy recipients. Walders developed and directs the Vital Signs Writing Project for patients and families at the National Institutes of Health in Bethesda, Maryland.

PATRICIA WELLINGHAM-JONES is a writer and editor and three-time Pushcart Prize nominee. Her work has been published in numerous anthologies, journals, and Internet magazines. She has edited two collections and is the author of *Don't Turn Away: Poems About Breast Cancer, Voices on the Land, A Gathering Glance,* and *Hormone Stew.*

KATHRYN WILDER is the editor of *Walking the Twilight: Women Writers of the Southwest* (volumes 1 and 2) and *Forbidden Talent.* She holds baccalaureate and master's degrees in creative writing and has taught writing privately and at Northern Arizona University and Coconino Community College. She lives in Flagstaff, Arizona.

TERRY TEMPEST WILLIAMS'S works include collections of essays on the nature and politics of place, edited anthologies of nature writing, two children's books, and an exploration of Hieronymus Bosch's painting. Her best-known work is the memoir *Refuge: An Unnatural History of Family and Place.* Her most recent is *Red: Patience and Passion in the Desert,* about the redrock wilderness of Southern Utah, where she lives.

DEBORAH K. WILSON'S ancestors were among the original settlers in Burnet County, Texas, where she grew up. She holds a degree in communications from the University of Texas at Austin, where she studied fine arts and film making, with particular interest in geographical documentary production. She composes and performs original music and collects oral histories of places.

ANN WOODIN is the author of three books: *Home Is the Desert* (1964), *In the Circle of the Sun* (1971, about a family journey through India), and *The Rule of Two: Observations on Close Relationships* (1985).

JACKIE WOOLLEY'S articles, fiction, and poetry have appeared in such publications as *Christian Science Monitor, Christian Herald, Sunday Digest, Lutheran Digest,* and *Sunshine* magazine. Her book, *All the Things You Aren't . . . Yet,* was published in 1980. Woolley was a semifinalist in the 2002 William Faulkner Writing Competition; the book, a historical novel titled *Windmills,* will be published in 2007.

PAULA STALLINGS YOST is a writer and editor whose work includes *Tales of a Scrapper, Profile of a Lone Star Legacy, A Country Cowboy, Cooking Up the Memories, Miracles on the Amazon,* and *Polishing the Pearl.* A personal historian and the founder of LifeSketches/Heirloom Memoirs Publishing, she leads memoir writing workshops across the country.

MARY E. YOUNG, a writer and editor since 1985, has taught creative writing and journalism in high school and college. She has published two books, *How To Make Your Airplane Last Forever* and *Desperate Measures.* Her work has appeared in writers' magazines and such publications as *America West Magazine, Arizona Business,* and *Capper's.*

ANN ZWINGER lives in Colorado Springs and teaches English and Southwest studies at Colorado College. Her latest book is *Shaped by Wind and Water: Reflections of a Naturalist.* She has written eighteen books since 1970, including the acclaimed *Run, River, Run, Wind in the Rock, Downcanyon,* and *The Near-Sighted Naturalist.*

SUSAN ZWINGER'S most recent book is *The Hanford Reach: A Land of Contrasts. Last Wild Edge* is an account of her kayak journey from the Arctic Circle to the Olympic Peninsula. She is also the author of *Stalking the Ice Dragon* and *Still Wild, Always Wild.* She and her mother, Ann Zwinger, are co-authors of *Women in Wilderness.* Zwinger's essays and poems have appeared in a wide variety of journals and anthologies.

ABOUT THE EDITORS

SUSAN WITTIG ALBERT

Susan Wittig Albert, PhD, is the best-selling author of three mystery series, numerous books for young adults, and several nonfiction books, including *Writing From Life: Telling Your Soul's Story,* a book for women memoirists. For fifteen years she taught college-level English and held administrative positions at the University of Texas at Austin, Newcomb College of Tulane University, and Texas State University. She is married to Bill Albert, with whom she co-authors a mystery series, and is the mother of three and grandmother of eight. She is the founder and past president of the Story Circle Network, and frequently leads memoir writing workshops. She is at work on a memoir, *Landscapes of Solitude,* forthcoming from the University of Texas Press.

SUSAN HANSON

Susan Hanson, author of *Icons of Loss and Grace: Moments from the Natural World,* teaches in the English Department at Texas State University in San Marcos, Texas. She has worked for twenty years as a newspaper journalist and has served as lay chaplain for the Episcopal campus ministry at TSU since 1995.

Susan's pastimes are native plant gardening, hiking, watching birds and other wildlife, traveling in the American West, and photographing plants and landscapes. She is a member of the Association for the Study of Literature and Environment and the Episcopal Society for Ministry in Higher Education. She is married and the mother of a grown daughter.

JAN EPTON SEALE

Jan Epton Seale is the author of *Airlift,* a group of short stories; *Homeland,* a collection of essays; and books of poetry, *Bonds* and *Sharing the House.* Her latest publications include a writing textbook, *The Nuts-&-Bolts Guide to Writing Your Life Story,* and *The Yin of It,* a collection of poems. Her stories and scripts have been performed in various theatrical settings and on National Public Radio. She was the recipient of a 1982 National Endowment for the Arts creative writing fellowship.

Jan and her husband, Carl, live in McAllen, on the Texas-Mexico border, where they raised three sons. Active in environmental causes to preserve the remaining natural habitat of the region, she edited *Creatures on the Edge: Wildlife along the Lower Rio Grande,* a book of color photographs and text featuring unique Valley flora and fauna.

PAULA STALLINGS YOST

Personal historian and founder of LifeSketches/Heirloom Memoirs Publishing in Yantis, Texas, Paula is a memoirist, editor, and publisher with a background in journalism and public relations. Her edited works include *Tales of a Scrapper, Profile of a Lone Star Legacy, A Country Cowboy, Cooking Up the Memories,* and *Miracles on the Amazon.* She is vice president of the Association of Personal Historians, served on the board of the Story Circle Network, and is editor of the Story Circle Network Book Review Web site. She also offers writing workshops across the country and online.

ABOUT THE STORY CIRCLE NETWORK

The Story Circle Network is a nonprofit membership organization that is dedicated to helping women tell their stories. It sponsors print and online publications, writing and reading circles, an Internet chapter, life-writing competitions, workshops, retreats, and conferences. On its extensive Web site (www.storycircle.org), SCN offers reviews of women's published memoirs; a speaker's bureau; a roster of SCN-member authors; a life-writers' market watch; and many tips and suggestions for writing personal narrative and creating women's life-writing and reading groups. Subscriptions to its monthly e-mail newsletters are free.

SCN's recent publications include *With Courage and Common Sense: Memoirs of the Older Women's Legacy Circles,* published by the University of Texas Press (2003), and *Discoveries,* a journaling book annotated with quotations from women's writing. The organization also publishes a quarterly journal, *The Story Circle Journal,* a book review Web site (http://www.storycircle.org/BookReviews/index.shtml), and an annual anthology of members' writing, *True Words by Real Women.*

Information about membership can be found on the SCN Web site (www.storycircle.org) or by writing to Story Circle Network, P.O. Box 500127, Austin, TX 78750-0127.

CREDITS

Diane Ackerman, "Working on the Tequesquite," from *Twilight of the Tenderfoot: A Western Memoir.* Copyright © 1980 by Diane Ackerman. Reprinted by permission of HarperCollins Publishers Inc.

Paula Gunn Allen, "The Trick Is Consciousness," from *Life Is a Fatal Disease: Collected Poems 1962–1995.* Copyright © 1997 by Paula Gunn Allen. Reprinted by permission of West End Press, Albuquerque, New Mexico.

Gloria Anzaldúa, "El Retorno," from *Borderlands/La Frontera: The New Mestiza.* Copyright © 1987 by Gloria Anzaldúa. Reprinted by permission of Spinsters Aunt Lute Books.

Rebecca Balcárcel, "Crepe Myrtles." Copyright © 2006 by Rebecca Balcárcel.

Cindy Bellinger, "This Land on My Face." Copyright © 2006 by Cindy Bellinger.

Judith E. Bowen, "Mowing." Copyright © 2006 by Judith E. Bowen.

Janice Emily Bowers, "A Full Life in a Small Place," from *A Full Life in a Small Place and Other Essays from a Desert Garden.* Copyright © 1993 by Janice Emily Bowers. Reprinted by permission of the University of Arizona Press.

SueEllen Campbell, "The World is a Nest," from *Even Mountains Vanish: Searching for Solace in an Age of Extinction.* Copyright © 2003 by SueEllen Campbell. Reprinted by permission of the University of Utah Press.

Denise Chávez, "Four Meditations on the Colorado River," excerpted from "Crossing Bitter Creek: Meditations on the Colorado River," in *Writing Down the River: Into the Heart of the Grand Canyon*, edited by Kathleen Jo Ryan for the Grand Canyon Association. Copyright © 1998 by Denise Chávez. Reprinted by permission of Denise Chávez.

Alison Hawthorne Deming, "Monarchs," from *Temporary Homelands: Essays on Nature, Spirit and Place.* Copyright © 1994 by Alison Hawthorne Deming. Reprinted by permission of Picador USA. "Sleep, Monarchs, rising and falling," from *The Monarchs: A Poem Sequence.*

LOCATION INDEX